D1100179

STARTING A BUSINESS IN IRELAND

A GUIDE & DIRECTORY

7TH EDITION

BRIAN O'KANE

www.oaktreepress.com

Oak Tree Press, Cork
www.oaktreepress.com / www.SuccessStore.com /
www.startingabusinessinireland.com

© 2018 Brian O'Kane

A catalogue record of this book is available from the British Library.

ISBN 978-1-78119-310-5 (Paperback)
ISBN 978-1-78119-311-2 (ePub)
ISBN 978-1-78119-312-9 (Kindle)
ISBN 978-1-78119-313-6 (PDF)

Cover image: zerbor / 123rf.com

First edition published 1993; Second edition 1995; Third edition 1998;
Fourth edition 2001; Fifth edition 2004; Sixth edition 2010.

CONTENTS

DEDICATION

This book is dedicated especially to my wife, Rita, without whose constant support and encouragement none of this would have been possible, and to our children – Niamh, Conall, Kevin and Deirdre – now all flourishing in their own careers and lives.

PREFACE

Writing the Preface of this 7th edition of *STARTING A BUSINESS IN IRELAND*, updated for 2019, I am struck by how much has changed since the first edition – most of all, public attitude towards enterprise, small business and start-ups. Where previously the 'proper job' – one with a pension after a lifetime of service – was the be-all-and-end-all, there's now a genuine interest across Irish society in entrepreneurship.

With all due modesty, *STARTING A BUSINESS IN IRELAND* can lay claim to credit for some of Ireland's entrepreneurial success and for the more positive view in Irish society towards enterprise. It struck a chord with the Irish public right from its launch in 1993. It sells consistently well, month in month out, mainly by word-of-mouth and recommendation – the most effective form of marketing! Of course, I cannot (and would not) claim all the credit – the many people whose job (in some cases, their mission) it is to assist start-ups and small businesses deserve their recognition, too.

But the real heroes in Irish enterprise are Irish entrepreneurs: the men and women who have taken the plunge and built successful businesses where none existed before. As I speak on courses, at conferences, or at exhibitions, I am always dumbstruck by the sheer inventiveness, innovation and enthusiasm of people whom I meet at these events, who have shared their dreams and ambitions with me, and who have done me the honour of asking for my advice or opinion. To them belongs the lion's share of the credit.

The Book

Starting a business in Ireland is frustrating, time-consuming and difficult. I know, because I have done it and have worked with thousands of people who have done it too – but it can also be highly satisfying and enjoyable.

The first edition of this book was born out of the frustration of dealing with the bureaucracy and information dead-ends that surrounded starting a business at that time – and, sadly, still do to some extent today. This 7th edition builds on earlier editions by:

- Taking you step-by-step through the stages in going into business for yourself.
- Helping you to identify, from the many organisations that provide assistance to entrepreneurs, those that are likely to be appropriate to your needs.

The chapters are arranged to take you through the stages:

- Deciding whether you have what it takes.
- Researching your idea.
- Writing a business plan.
- Raising money to set up your business.
- Getting help from State and other agencies.
- Getting your business up and running.

The ***Directory of Sources of Assistance*** provides information (including contact details) for many organisations that may be of use to you as you go through the stages of starting your own business. It will be kept up-to-date on **www.startingabusinessinireland.com**.

Thank You

A book such as this can never be the work of one person alone.

My idea lay fallow for several years, until David Givens (Oak Tree Press' first general manager, now managing director of his own business, The Liffey Press) pushed me to complete what I had begun – and so the first edition of *STARTING A BUSINESS IN IRELAND* was written. David's encouragement is appreciated more than he realises.

Ron Immink, who researched and co-wrote the first *STARTING YOUR OWN BUSINESS* workbook with me in 1997 for the then Department of Enterprise, Trade & Employment (it's now in its 4th edition – and still going strong too!), and also *TENBIZPLAN*, the *STEPS TO ENTREPRENEURSHIP* series and the *GROWING YOUR OWN BUSINESS* workbook, deserves special thanks for his constant encouragement and unstoppable flow of ideas.

I am also grateful to the staff of the many organisations listed in this book – not just for their helpfulness, patience and support in preparing this and previous editions and in recommending the book to so many people, but also for the trojan work that they do.

I am pleased and somewhat surprised to find *STARTING A BUSINESS IN IRELAND* now in its 7th edition and well into its third decade! The reaction to its publication has far exceeded all my expectations.

I have enjoyed writing and updating this book – in all its editions. I hope it is of help to you, the reader, as you take your first steps on your journey. May the road always rise to meet you!

Brian O'Kane
Cork
September 2018

1: GETTING STARTED

For some people, starting their own business is as obvious as the nose on their face. For others, it is a risk not to be contemplated.

For you, it is an idea in the back of your mind, one you cannot get rid of. You may already know what kind of business you want to be in. What you want from this book are a few short cuts to help you get there faster and with fewer problems.

On the other hand, you may simply be toying with the idea of starting a business of some kind, unsure of which direction to take. You are hoping that this book will present you with a ready-formed solution. The truth is that you must provide your own solution but this book can help by providing a structure for your thinking.

The Stages in a Start-up

The stages involved in starting a business include:

- Deciding whether you have the right temperament to start (and persevere with) your own business – a critical first step, often overlooked in the rush to get started.

- Finding an idea – it's worth taking time on this stage to explore all the options; sometimes your first idea is not always the best.

- Doing the market research – this involves finding out about your customers, your competition, how you will make your product or deliver your service, what price to charge, where your business will be located, how to market your product or service, what staff you require and with what skills, and so on.

- Writing a business plan – this draws together all the work you have done in the research stage and presents it in a form that is readily understandable.

- Finding the necessary money – since it's likely you won't have enough of your own capital to start, you'll have to raise money elsewhere.

- Identifying and accessing sources of assistance – as the *Directory* shows, there are hundreds of organisations dedicated to helping entrepreneurs to get started and small businesses to flourish.
- Implementing your plan – this is where you put your plan into action.

STAGES IN STARTING A BUSINESS

Self-assessment	Are you suited to be an entrepreneur?
Idea assessment	Will your idea for a product or service work in the market?
Market research	Who? What? When? Where? Why? How? The operational details of your business.
Business Plan	Document your research in a plan, with back-up evidence.
Finance	How much do you need? Where can you get it?
Assistance: State / Private	Where can you find help in starting your business? Who provides what assistance?
Implementation	Lights! Camera! Action! It's time for the show to begin!

Sometimes, in practice, these stages will not follow neatly in the order set out above; in other cases, you will have to double-back, perhaps even several times, to adjust the results of a particular stage because of new information you find out in a later stage.

For instance, your idea might be to sell locally a product that you make yourself. But as you do your market research, you find that there is a national demand for the product. To supply it, you need to plan on a larger scale and will need more money – so you revise your plans and finances accordingly.

Most of these stages in starting a business are covered in this book. Some are dealt with in greater detail in other books published by **Oak Tree Press** and available from our website at **www.SuccessStore.com**. Other stages, like finding an idea, lie with you alone.

Are You Suited to Life as an Entrepreneur?

Sadly, there is no fail-safe method of becoming a successful entrepreneur. Research, quoted in *YOU CAN DO IT* by Joyce O'Connor and Helen Ruddle (Gill & Macmillan, 1989), shows that successful entrepreneurs have:

- Strong needs for control and independence.
- Drive and energy.
- Self-confidence.
- A point of view of money as a measure of performance.
- A tolerance of ambiguity and uncertainty.
- A sense of social responsibility.

and that they are good at:

- Problem-solving.
- Setting (and achieving) goals and targets.
- Calculated risk-taking.
- Committing themselves for the long-term.
- Dealing with failure.
- Using feedback.
- Taking the initiative.
- Seeking personal responsibility.
- Tapping and using resources.
- Competing against self-imposed standards.

How do *you* measure on these criteria? Be honest with yourself.

Very few entrepreneurs can lay claim to all of these characteristics. Making the most of your best characteristics and using ingenuity (including the skills of others) to bridge the gaps is perhaps the most frequently encountered entrepreneurial characteristic of all!

However, despite the great variety of people who end up as business-owners, probably the most important personal characteristic for an entrepreneur is determination. It's easy to start a business; it's more difficult to keep it going. When you are faced with long hours, with working through nights and weekends, with extended periods away from your family, and with financial worries, the thought of a secure permanent pensionable job is tempting. Determination is what will see you through these lows until you break through to success!

You should also consider your general state of health. Both the physical and mental stresses of running your own business can be very great. If you are driven to a state of collapse by the experience, you may leave your family much more exposed financially than would be the case if you were in a secure job with benefits attached.

You should be aware of the part your family will play in achieving your ambition of becoming an entrepreneur. Are they as committed as you are? Are they as willing to accept the lows as the highs? Without their support, you will find it difficult to start and develop your business. If they are actively pulling against you, quit now!

Part of the experience of running your own business is learning to apply the appropriate personal resource at the right time. For example, deciding to become an exporter at a time when your resources – foreign language skills, contacts, finances – are not adequate is to misuse an opportunity that might lead to success in other circumstances. A touch of realism instead would have revealed the impracticality of your plan.

So the first thing you should do when thinking about starting a business is to conduct a rigorous self-assessment:

- What skills and experience do you have?
- What training do you need?
- What characteristics do you have that will help (or hinder) you?
- Why do you want to start a business?

Write down the answers – it's not as easy to fudge uncomfortable answers when you have to write them down.

Then write your own application for the position of managing director and general *factotum* of your proposed business. Give your application to a friend not noted for their tact and wait for the laughs. You need to be able to see yourself as others see you.

Are your keyboard and literary skills really up to sending out customer letters and writing marketing blurbs? Perhaps you excel in production and technical innovation? Maybe you need to acquire other skills? If so, can you get by with a little training for yourself or should you buy in these skills on a freelance basis as and when required? Will you need a management team, or are there family members who are sufficiently committed to help (and capable of doing so)? What will hiring all these people cost? You need to be realistic about how many people you need, and how many you can afford – and what you do about the difference.

In terms of your business skills, in addition to management experience, you should consider contacts and sales leads, as these are the concrete beginnings of your trading. If you plan to supply other retailers or manufacturers, you will be hoping to establish several guaranteed sales contracts before you finally start trading. But, if you are leaving employment to set up in business, check that your employment contract allows you to canvass business on your own account (and time) while still an employee.

You should read this chapter again in a year's time. Why? Because you will only begin to discover the extent of your personal resources as you go along. Starting your own business will not only lead you to find hidden resources within yourself, but will build up existing strengths. It may also, of course, identify unsuspected weaknesses, but recognising them is the first step towards correcting them.

Start Your Own Business Courses

This book is designed to help you through the early stages of starting a business. Together with other books and ebooks published by Oak Tree Press, it gives you an edge.

For further guidance, or for the comfort of meeting like-minded people who are about to embark on the same adventure as yourself, consider a Start Your Own Business course – perhaps one of those run regularly by the LOCAL ENTERPRISE OFFICES across the country (see the *Directory* under *Training & Mentoring*). These courses can be useful because they draw together all the aspects of running a business.

Another advantage of attending a course is that you get to know advisers who may be useful to contact later with queries. Many of the courses run by the LOCAL ENTERPRISE OFFICES or similar organisations are particularly useful for steering participants towards further support, when it is needed.

How Do You Choose the Right Course?

Before you book a place on a course, meet or talk to the organisers. Ask about the backgrounds of the presenters. Those who run their own business or who, like many accountants and other professionals, make their living from advising entrepreneurs are the best bet.

Ask about the success rate of the course in establishing new businesses. Ask about the success rate of those businesses after two or three years. Remember that the average failure rate of new businesses is very high – about 50 per cent of start-ups fail within the first three years. But this gloomy statistic need not apply to you, if you plan your start-up carefully.

Make an effort to find people who have completed any courses you are seriously considering, and talk to them. They are in the best position to know whether what they learnt on the course actually was of use in practice. Their answers will tell you whether you should take a place on the course.

If You Can't Attend a Course

If you cannot participate in a Start Your Own Business course, look online for elearning or attend seminars or workshops on specific aspects of small business development and small business management.

Otherwise, read as widely as you can in the area of business start-ups. There are plenty of good books, newspapers, magazines and websites that give useful advice (see the **Directory** under *Information*).

Incubators

Perhaps, instead of merely a training programme, what you need is a push-start. Here an 'incubator' may help.

An incubator is a training programme, usually focused on technology businesses, that encourages the faster development of a new business by providing a range of supports from training to workspace to finance to administrative assistance in order to free up the entrepreneur to concentrate on the business alone – for example, the NEW FRONTIERS programme, offered nation-wide by the INSTITUTES OF TECHNOLOGY and funded by ENTERPRISE IRELAND.

Note that 'accelerators' are different from incubators. Where an incubator aims to get you started, and accelerator (as its name suggests) aims to accelerate the development of a business. That means you need to be up and running – though not necessarily trading (you might still be in the thick of R&D) – to qualify for most accelerators.

Sometimes, the term 'incubator' is used loosely to cover provision of work space – if you're offered 'incubation workspace', check what is included.

Start Early – or Late!

You're never too young to start thinking about enterprise and running your own business. Even if you're still in school or at college, there are programmes designed to attract you towards the notion of self-employment and to help you begin to gain the necessary skills (see the *Directory* under *Young Enterprise*).

And you're never too old either! For example, SENIOR ENTERPRISE is an EU-funded programme for the over-50 entrepreneur – and Doris Drucker, the management guru Peter Drucker's wife, started a business at 82!

Start-up Alternatives

Of course, it's not always necessary to start a business from scratch. Brokers exist who will help you to identify and buy a suitable business, whose owner lacks the capital or enthusiasm to develop it further. Or you could consider buying a franchise (see the *Directory* under *Franchises*).

If you do go down either of these routes, make sure that you take professional advice before making any financial or legal commitment. And continue to read the rest of this book, since you will still need to plan for the development of your business.

2: RESEARCHING YOUR IDEA

After considering your own capacity to run a business, you need to ask yourself whether a market exists for your product or service. The market may be incredibly tough to break into but, as long as it exists, you can fight for your share of it. If there is no market at all for your product, it is clearly a non-starter.

You are not yet attempting to measure the size or location of the market, nor to distinguish its characteristics. What you want are the answers to the following questions:

- Do others already offer the same (or very similar) product / service that you intend to offer?
- Is your product / service an improvement on what already exists?
- What evidence is there that customers want to buy your improved product / service?

If your product / service is new to the market, you need to ask:

- What evidence is there that the market wants to buy it?
- What evidence is there that the market is aware of its need for your product / service?

You may be able to find answers to these questions quite easily. For example, the market for ready-mixed concrete is quite visible but is dominated by a few big companies. So the question here quickly changes from whether a market exists to whether it is feasible to enter that market when there are already strong competitors in place.

On the other hand, the inventor of a solar-powered bicycle might have more difficulty assessing the existence of a market. All the Irish cyclists he talks to may tell him that they only cycle for the exercise value, since they cannot depend on sufficient sun to make any difference to the energy they must expend in cycling. They might have no interest in any source of power beyond their own muscles. Yet, in environmentally conscious (and sunnier) countries that encourage the use of a bicycle and

/ or solar power, the product could be greeted with cries of delight and massive demand. However, if the inventor does not know where to look, he or she may never get their business off the ground.

This quick feasibility review will tell you whether it's worth progressing to more formal market research, or whether you should go back to the drawing board to think of a new product or service.

Market Research

Once you have provided yourself with proof – not just a gut feeling – of the existence of the market (see below, *Sources of Information*), you can move on to more detailed research. Analysing the nature of the market, customer base and competition will tell you whether your idea is feasible. The information you compile will allow you to develop your business plan in more detail.

Although a professional market research company (see the *Directory* under *Marketing*) will conduct research for you, at a price, you can often do your own research without too much difficulty, time or cost.

In collecting information during this research stage, remember that, as well as satisfying yourself, you may have to prove to outside investors that your figures and findings are valid. For this reason, independent proof is worth collecting wherever you can find it.

You need to sift carefully through the information you collect:

- To understand the business you are in.
- To work out the size and location of the market for your product / service.
- To build up a profile of your customers and their needs.
- To understand how competition operates in your market.
- To establish a reasonable price for your product / service – one at which your customers will buy.
- To forecast sales – both volume and value.
- To establish the cost of making your product or delivering your service – and how it will be done.
- To establish the investment needed to start your business.
- To decide what form your business must take.

MARKET RESEARCH

The business	What business are you in?
The market	Size? Location? Segmentation? Trends?
Your customers	Who are they? What and how much do they buy, at what price, when and why?
Your competition	Who are they? What and how much do they sell, at what price, and to whom?
Your price	What will your customers pay?
Your sales	Value and volume? When? How certain?
Your costs	What will your product/service cost you to make / deliver?
Your investment	How much money do you need to get started? For what? Where will you get it?
Your structure	Legal structure? Business functions? Internal organisation?

What Is Your Business?

This may seem an obvious question, one not worth asking, but setting it down in writing may provide a useful reference exercise.

For example, Waterford Crystal is not in the market of providing everyday glassware. Despite the fact that it produces glasses, bowls and vases, it does not compete with the producer of the everyday glass tumbler that you find in a supermarket or a department store. Rather, it is in the international market for luxury goods and special occasion gifts. It will look to growth trends in these luxury markets, mainly overseas, rather than to growth in glassware sales generally. In contrast, a contract carpet-cleaning business in Dublin is providing a very specific service in the city, or possibly even only in one area of the city.

Be aware that if you are a manufacturer, you are a manufacturer, not a retailer. You may sell your product to or through a retailer, but you are not a retailer, nor are you selling direct to the public. To try to be more than you are can spell doom for a small business, because your business may not have the resources and you may not have the necessary skills to take on your new ideas. More sales may be achieved by sticking firmly to your core activity of manufacturing, and developing a distribution network through dealers around the country.

In time, your business may have the resources to expand its operation and become something else, but, initially, if you try to start two businesses, you will have to generate the cash flow and return for both, which is (at least) twice as difficult as generating them for one.

Where Is Your Market?

Starting out, you are unlikely to be able to tackle the whole market for your product or service. Instead look for a suitable segment of that market, which might be defined geographically – Cork, the North West counties, even a particular housing estate. Alternatively, your segment might be defined as a product niche – for example, specialised stop-watches for use in sports, but not all sorts of watches or clocks.

However, even though you may decide only to tackle a small part of a market, you cannot afford to ignore what is happening in the whole market. For example, if you are opening the first small corner shop on a new housing estate, you should foresee that any one of several chains of supermarkets might open a shop nearby and become your main competition. Perhaps you could overcome this by becoming a franchisee of one of the chains yourself.

On the other hand, if your product will be manufactured and sold locally, for instance, in Dublin, but must compete against products from big international suppliers, you have to monitor what is going on in the international field as well as in the national market.

You need to look beyond your immediate market to see what the longer-term trends are:

- Is the size of your market growing or declining?
- Is it characterised by rapid innovation or evolution of products?
- Is it expanding geographically (as might be the case with an innovative product / service)?
- Is the number of competitors expanding or declining?
- Are prices rising or falling?

You need to end up with figures that show the size and growth potential of the total market – but these must be made relevant to your business proposal, in terms of the part of the market (the market segment) that you are targeting.

These concepts will help you to define your market:

- Wholesale or retail?
- One product or a range of products?
- A service?
- The luxury market?
- Necessities?

And don't forget that, through the power of the Internet, the market for your product or service could be global. Some products / services lend themselves better to online supply – for example, intangible products that can be downloaded know few geographic restrictions – but the point stands that your customers now potentially can be worldwide.

If your idea is very innovative and no market yet exists for it, it may be difficult to define what your market is likely to be. Obtaining hard information about the size and value of your market may be daunting. However, you must be able to provide this information in your business plan because it is a key element in establishing both the market share and the cost structure that your business must attain in order to be competitive.

If you get this information wrong, other assumptions are likely to be invalid and your project may fail, perhaps at considerable loss to yourself. Equally, if bankers and investors cannot find independent verification for the figures in your proposal, they will have doubts regarding its overall viability, and are likely to refuse to finance you.

Who Are Your Customers?

You must build as accurate a profile of your customers as you can. This depends on the type of business that you plan to start.

For a corner shop, the customers will be diverse in age, gender and requirements: everyone from children wanting sweets for a few cents to adults wanting newspapers, grocery items and perhaps small gift items. On the other hand, an information technology company producing a single product, say an automated accounting package for bookmakers, has a very narrowly defined customer base.

Some useful questions to ask about your customers are:

- General public or business, or both?
- Public sector or private?
- Where do they live / operate?
- What and how much do they buy, at what price, when and why?
- What age are they?
- What gender?
- Are they spending for a necessity or a luxury; in other words, do they buy out of surplus income?
- Are they rich or poor?

For your product / service, are there criteria that define your customers, such as:

- A particular interest (for example, travel or sport)?
- Need for a particular service (for example, training to use accounting software)?

In terms of business customers, there may be other criteria to consider:

- Size of customer – will you supply only customers taking more than (or less than) a certain volume?
- Quality levels for the product (these may be imposed by certain wholesale purchasers, department / chain stores, etc.).
- Type of packaging preferred.

- How easy will it be to deal with them? Larger organisations have more decision-makers than small ones, and so it may take longer to negotiate contracts and persuade them to take your product – although the resulting orders are likely to be bigger. To deal with the public sector, it is necessary to understand how it is structured, how decisions are made and who makes them.

- Will your business deal only with one segment of the market, such as the public sector, or will you be tackling several segments? How much experience do you have in dealing with each segment? Do you have the resources to service more than one segment? Will you deal with them on the same terms? And, if not, how will you prevent sales 'leaking' from the segment that gets the most favourable terms?

Who Is Your Competition?

Look hard at your own product / service. How does it differ from competing products / services? Very few businesses are genuinely innovative; most compete with existing businesses.

Why should a customer prefer your product / service:

- Better quality?
- Lower price?
- Higher profile?

What do your sales depend on:

- Price?
- Design?
- Advertising?
- Quality?
- Volume?
- After-sales service?
- Speed of delivery?
- Accessibility?

An important question is whether the differentiating feature of your product / service's is the one that makes the customer prefer it. Take the example of a Hermès scarf or a Rolls Royce car. It would be pointless to sell cheaper versions of either, since buyers value the image that the high price gives. Exclusive products are characterised by low-volume / high-margin sales. Their success depends on high marketing expenditure and careful selection and monitoring of distribution.

If, on the other hand, your product / service's sale is characterised by high volumes and low margins, such as margarine or flour or fast food, your business needs to be structured very differently, with more emphasis on volume production, warehousing, constancy of supply and a good distribution network.

When looking at your competition, you may need to consider products / services that compete indirectly with yours, as well as those that compete directly. For example, if you produce frozen hamburgers, you compete not only against other frozen hamburger manufacturers, but against a variety of other cheap frozen food products, including fish fingers, vegetable burgers, pies and so on.

You need to find out:

- How many other companies supply products / services similar to yours?
- How will they react to your entry to the market place?
- Are all the companies in the market place the same size?
- Are they very much bigger than you?
- Have you the resources to equal their power in the market?
- Do new entrants normally start small and grow, or will you have to make a major commitment from the start?

Price

The next piece of market information that you should research is the price that customers will pay for your product / service. Generally, you will be constrained by the market. You cannot charge more for your product / service than the going price for similar products / services unless it has something special to recommend it. Even then, a large number of customers may still choose the lower-priced option.

Forecasting Sales

If you thought the earlier elements of your market research were hard, forecasting sales makes them look like child's play.

You need to have a good idea of likely sales (with some evidence to underpin your figures) in order to:

- Build your financial projections.
- Estimate the production capacity you require.
- Arrange for supply of materials.
- Hire staff.

Your requirements in each of these areas will vary depending on the sales volumes and values that you expect.

One way to do this is to start with a clean sheet of paper. Draw columns for each month and rows for each product or service (or variant thereof) that you expect to sell. Within each row, list the promotional and other activity that you plan to use to generate sales. (If you haven't planned any yet, it's time to start – products don't just sell on their own, they usually have to be sold).

Then, make some estimates month by month of the sales that will result from this promotional activity. You may find it easier to forecast unit sales first and then to estimate sales value.

For example, if you intend to design and sell St Patrick's Day greetings cards direct to the public, it's likely that most of your sales will happen in February and March – with perhaps a few early orders in January – but none after that, until the next year. If, instead, you sell to wholesalers / retailers, your sales will happen earlier. In either case, your sales forecast exercise will quickly show that sales of St Patrick's Day cards spike for a short while and then disappear until next year, which then should lead you into new product development – Easter cards, or cards for Mother's Day or Halloween and so on – to create a more even spread of sales revenues across the year.

It's important to break down sales to the lowest level of product / service that you can manage without overwhelming yourself in detail. For example, if you were designing and selling greeting cards, it would be easy to overlook the potential for niche opportunities during the year, unless you specifically identified St Patrick's Day cards or the like.

Where you can, get forward orders or 'letters of comfort' from customers. These are better evidence in support of your forecasts than any market research – although your market research is still essential.

Calculating Costs and Profit Margins

As part of writing your business plan (see **Chapter 3**), you will have to prepare financial projections for inclusion in your business plan.

However, even at this early stage, it is a good idea to estimate the minimum size or capacity at which you will make a profit – the break-even point – as well as the maximum operating capacity that you can afford to establish. To do this, you will need to work out what your costs of production will be – you already know the price the market will pay for your product, and how many units you expect to be able to sell.

You also need to identify the current market profit margins – how much your competitors are making. You may be prepared to accept a slimmer margin, but this may reduce your flexibility to deal with unexpected demands. It may also shorten the length of time your business can afford to wait to reach the break-even point. If you look for larger than average profit margins, without either reducing costs or convincing customers that your product is worth paying more for, you will quickly find yourself in difficulty.

Will your entry to the market place reduce profit margins generally? If you increase the total supply of product available, it may have the effect of reducing the price for which it sells. It may even trigger a price war, as existing suppliers try to kill off your business before it gets going by cutting their prices below the price you must get to stay in business. You will most likely get only a part of the market, not the whole. Yet, if you cannot meet the average costs achieved by your direct competitors, you may fail, even though your product / service may be better.

The income generated by sales must provide sufficient cash flow to enable your business to cover all costs. If money comes in too slowly, your business may choke to death while demand booms. Cash flow – collecting money from customers as quickly as possible and getting the longest possible credit period from your suppliers – is often more important in the short term for a small business than profit. But, overall, you must make a profit to stay in business.

Estimating Your Initial Investment

At this stage, you should draw up a list of what premises and equipment you absolutely must have (not what it would be nice to have).

You need to answer these questions:

- Will it be possible to keep overheads low by working from your garage or a spare room initially?
- Do you need retail premises in a good location?

- What about warehouse space?
- Do you need specialised equipment? How big is it?
- Will you have to make a large capital investment in equipment? Can you lease equipment instead? Can you buy it second-hand?

From this information, and your other market research, you will be able to estimate your initial investment – what you need to get started.

Finding the Best Business Structure

Lastly, you need to decide what form your business organisation should take. When starting in business, you have a choice of five main types of business entity through which to conduct your enterprise:

- Sole trader.
- Partnership (and limited liability partnership in Northern Ireland).
- Unlimited company.
- Limited liability company.
- Co-operative.

Four things will decide which structure you choose:

- The kind of business you are starting: Some professional firms, for instance, can only be formed as sole traders or partnerships.
- The expectations of those with whom you plan to do business: Many business people expect to deal with limited companies and are wary of other forms of business entities as trading partners.
- Your attitude to risk – in particular, to risking those of your assets that you are not planning to commit to the business: A limited liability company limits the risk of losing your non-business assets if your enterprise is not successful.
- How you wish to organise your tax affairs: Certain kinds of favourable tax treatment are only available to limited companies.

You are taking a risk in starting an enterprise. You are risking your money, time and reputation. You are entitled to protect those of your assets that you do not wish to commit to your enterprise. For this reason, and for your family's sake, you are strongly advised to form a limited liability company. Nonetheless, you should take professional advice for your accountant or solicitor in making your decision. If you do not yet have an accountant or solicitor, read the appropriate sections in **Chapter 9** and see the *Accounting & Business Planning* and *IP & Legal* categories in the **Directory**.

Next, consider how your business will be organised. The main functional areas in any business are:

- Sales.
- Marketing.
- Production.
- Distribution.
- Administration.

What should be the balance between these functions within your company? Among the questions you need to ask yourself are:

- How will you get your product / service to the purchaser?
- Will you need large amounts of warehouse or office space?
- What are your costs of production?
- What are the overheads involved?

Sources of Information

There is no shortage of information available to help you in your market research – most entrepreneurs find that their main problem is too much information!

Yourself

Most people have started to research their idea long before they come to the formal planning stage. Often, the idea has grown out of a long period of personal interest and the 'research' is based on:

- Personal experience.
- Talking to friends.
- Talking to suppliers.

If you have an idea for a new type of light fitting, it is probably because over the years you have been driven mad by the failings of the many light fittings that you have used. So, immediately, you know what advantage your potential product offers above others in the market.

You may have to find out about the costs of making it, how it is distributed and who your competitors will be before you can make an estimate of the size of the market and, most importantly, whether it is financially feasible to be a small manufacturer of light fittings only.

Professional Advisers

Bank managers and accountants often have a good idea of how different types of businesses are faring, and what differentiates the successes from those that cannot pay the bills. Also, talking to your bank manager like this is a gentle introduction for him / her to your idea of starting your own business.

Banks and investment businesses often have specialists in a variety of industry sectors, who can be useful sources of market information and statistics. Approach the small business lending unit of your bank as a first step. They may be able to find the information for you, or direct you to the appropriate person / section in the bank.

Trade and Professional Associations

If a trade or professional association exists for the market sector in which you are interested, it may be an excellent source of information about the total size and value of your market. It may even have statistics broken down by region.

Some associations may only make this information available to members – and, if you are not yet in business, you may find it difficult to gain access. Other associations make the information publicly available, though there is usually a charge involved as the organisation tries to recover some of its own costs.

Many associations have links to sister bodies internationally and thus can be a source of international statistics and information also.

Most of these organisations provide training, networking and other services to their members so, if an association is relevant to your business, it's worth considering joining at the earliest possible opportunity.

Libraries

Often overlooked, local libraries have a wealth of information available – either on the spot or available through inter-library loans. Make a friend of your local librarian – he or she has valuable research skills that you will spend a great deal of time to acquire yourself. And, increasingly, libraries provide access to the Internet (see below) for a modest charge.

Other People in the Business

Talk to people already involved in the industry. Make use of their experience. Find them online. Trade and professional associations may be able to put you in contact with some of their members who may be willing to share their experience and expertise.

If yours is (or will be) a technology business, identify a 'Centre of Excellence' in your field. The INSTITUTES OF TECHNOLOGY and UNIVERSITIES have a wealth of information and experience at their disposal, much of which is available – though, usually, for a fee. Start by contacting the Technology Transfer Office or Industrial Liaison Office.

Support Agencies

There is a vast range of support available to entrepreneurs thinking of starting a business – much expanded since the first edition of this book. Much of it is provided by State or State-funded agencies; some of it is provided by the private sector.

The **Directory** lists the many organisations mentioned throughout this book – first by category and then alphabetically (with contact details) – and **www.startingabusinessinireland.com** will keep this information up-to-date, as well as providing additional information.

Professional Researchers

If the market for your product is geographically extensive, or highly competitive, you might consider getting professional market researchers to prepare a report for you (look under *Marketing* in the **Directory**).

The Internet

Another source of information – particularly on international trends – is the Internet. If you are not already connected to the Internet, ask a friend to show you or visit your local library or a 'cybercafé', where you can rent access by the hour.

Use search engines – Google, Yahoo or Bing, etc. – to help narrow your enquiries. Contact the companies whose websites you visit for more information.

Interpreting Research Results

Researching your proposed business is not just a matter of asking the right questions. Interpreting the results is equally important. You may be too close to your idea to see problems (or, less often, to see opportunities). Bringing in outsiders may be helpful. Consider friends whose business skills you respect. Ask your accountant or other professional adviser – even if you have to pay for their opinion. It is important to arrive at an independently objective point of view, and it will be worth paying for if it saves you from disaster.

In addition to giving an independent view of your plans, a good accountant can help you draw up financial projections. In any case, you will probably need an accountant once you have begun trading. An accountant who is introduced at the planning stage will have a greater insight into the objectives of the business as well as the systems by which it functions. Your planning will benefit from the experience of your accountant, who, in turn, will be better placed to give you good service in future years.

The Final Question

Now you are in a position to answer the question at the start of this chapter: Does a market for your product or service exist? Your answer will tell you whether to proceed to the next stage.

If not, don't despair. It's better to have found out that your idea won't work before you have invested too much time, effort and money into it – and, if you're serious about starting your own business, there'll be plenty of other opportunities.

3: WRITING YOUR BUSINESS PLAN

Once you have thoroughly done the necessary market research for your project and decided to go ahead and start your own business, your next step is to write a business plan that summarises the following points about your business:

- Where it has come from.
- Where it is now.
- Where it is going in the future.
- How it intends to get there.
- How much money it needs to fulfil its plans.
- What makes it likely to succeed.
- What threats or disadvantages must be overcome on the way.

The document can range in length from a few typed sheets of paper to several hundred pages. However, since professional readers of business plans – bankers, investors and support agency staff – are offered more business plans than they can intelligently digest, the more concise your business plan, the more likely it is to be read.

The Purpose of a Business Plan

A business plan can have several purposes. The main ones usually are:

- To establish the fundamental viability of your project.
- To document your plan for the business.
- To act as a yardstick for measuring progress against plans.
- To communicate your plans for your business to outsiders, particularly those you want to invest in your business.

Although the business plan is most often used as a marketing document for raising finance, even if you do not need to raise finance you should still prepare one since it will:

- Focus your thoughts.
- Check your numbers.
- Provide a basis for monitoring results.
- Enable communication of your ideas.

Each of these purposes places its own demands on the format and contents of the business plan. The focus of your business plan will vary, depending on the relative priorities that you assign to these purposes.

Establishing the Viability of Your Project

There are many ways of researching whether your project will succeed. All, however, finally require an act of faith from the entrepreneur when the time comes to commit to the business. Before this point is reached, a great deal of planning and careful thought should have been completed.

A well-prepared business plan will assist immeasurably with that process, simply through the discipline it imposes. Often, entrepreneurs are carried away with their own enthusiasm. They neglect the most cursory checks on the viability of their brainchild. Broad, and sometimes rash, assumptions are made about the market for the product, its cost of manufacture, distribution channels, acceptability to customers, etc. But when a reasoned, written case must be made – even if only to oneself – it is less easy to overlook the unpalatable. At least, it is difficult to do so without being aware of it.

Documenting the Plan

"The plan doesn't matter, it's the planning that counts", said former US President Eisenhower. He was right. The quality of the planning you do for your business is critical to its success; how you document that planning process is less so. Nonetheless, a good business plan document actively aids the planning process by providing a structure. It forces you:

- To cover ground that you might otherwise, in your enthusiasm, skip over.
- To clarify your thinking – it is almost impossible to get your plan onto paper until you have formulated it clearly.
- To justify your arguments, since they will be written down for others to see.

- To focus on the risks and potential for loss in your plans as well as on the potential for profit and success.

Avoid unnecessary pessimism. Be realistic, but don't carry caution to extremes. If your proposal is realistic, have confidence in it.

A Yardstick for Measuring Progress

Preparing any plan demands an objective. An objective assumes that you are going to make some effort to achieve it. Some objectives are quantifiable: if your aim is to sell 500 gadgets, sales of 480 is below target, while 510 units sold gives you reason to feel pleased with your performance. Other objectives cannot be quantified; all the more reason then to document them so that you can clearly establish whether you have achieved them.

Your business plan should contain the objectives, quantifiable and otherwise, that you have set for your business. Reading through your plan at regular intervals and comparing your performance to date with the objectives you set yourself one month, six months or two years earlier can help to focus your attention on the important things that need to be done if targets are to be achieved.

Communicating Plans to Third Parties

Though they would readily acknowledge the importance of good planning, many businesspeople would not prepare a formal business plan document if it were not for the need to present their plans for the business to outsiders – usually to raise finance. But, if you wish to raise finance for your business to develop, you will have to prepare a plan.

Financiers, whether bankers, investors or support agency staff, need:

- A document they can study in their own time, and which makes its case independently of the promoters of the business.
- Evidence that the future of the business has been properly thought through and that all risks have been taken into account.
- Information about the business.

In addition, others may have reason to read your business plan – key employees or suppliers, for example. So it must communicate your message clearly.

No matter how good a writer you consider yourself to be, if you can't put your business proposition clearly and persuasively in writing, it suggests that you have more thinking to do. It doesn't mean that your project won't work. On the contrary, your business may be a resounding success – but you still need to be able to communicate it!

Who Should Write Your Business Plan?

Very simply, *you*. No one else. You may receive offers from consultants, many of them highly reputable and professional in their work, to write your business plan for you. They will quote their extensive experience of business, of raising finance for start-up businesses, of presenting financial information – all valid points and, in many cases, true.

However, whatever experience consultants may have of business in general, and of drafting business plans in particular, they lack one essential ingredient: your intimate relationship with your business. You are the one who has spent your waking hours – and many of your sleeping ones, too, probably – dreaming, planning and guiding your frail creation to this point. You know what makes you tick; what makes your team tick; what will and will not work for you. Only you can assemble these thoughts.

Therefore, the first draft of the business plan is your responsibility. Do it yourself. Refine and redraft it – again, and again, if necessary – until it's finished.

Then, and only then, should you entrust it to someone who can put the right gloss on it. But let them do only that. Don't let them put *their* words on your pages.

How Long Should Your Business Plan Be?

How long is a piece of string? Your business plan should be as long as it needs to be – no longer and no shorter.

How long is that? No one can decide that except yourself. It depends on the purpose for which you are preparing the plan, the level of knowledge that likely readers will have of your business, and the complexity of your business.

Few businesses can be done justice to in less than, say, 10 A4 pages; equally, it will be a dedicated reader (or one who has spotted an outstandingly good business proposition) who will continue past the first 100 pages or so!

If a reader wants more information, they will ask for it. But make sure that they don't have to ask for information they should have had from the start – or, worse still (and sometimes fatal to your hopes of raising finance), that the absence of the information doesn't lead them to discard your plan altogether.

Figures

Too many figures and your plan may become off-putting, but too few and your plans will simply be treated as ambitions without any underlying substance. Quantify as much as you can. Your plan is likely to be read by people whose currency is numbers. You help your cause by talking their language.

Make sure figures add up correctly. Nothing is more worrying to a reader of your business plan than the suspicion that:

- You can't handle figures.
- There's a figure wrong or missing – or worse still, hidden.

You need to be able to show the existence of a market for your product, and some indication of its size, in a way that can be verified independently. You will also have to prove to the satisfaction of lenders or investors that adequate margins can be achieved to cover cash flow needs and meet repayment of debt or growth objectives.

Don't clog up the body of the business plan with detailed statistical analysis, although it must contain all the information a reader needs. For example, quote the proposed sales target, but show how you will achieve it at the back in an Appendix, and explain the underlying assumptions there also. The same applies to the CVs of key employees – mention crucial information where appropriate in the plan, but place the details in an Appendix.

Business Models and Projected Figures

A financial model of the business is effectively a set of accounts, represented on computer spreadsheets or in a dedicated modelling package for ease of manipulation – for example, LIVEPLAN.com.

While a financial model is useful for businesses of all sizes, for a business of any complexity it is essential. Your model should enable you to change certain variables, such as the number of units of product sold, or the price at which you sell them, or the cost of supplies, and discover what the effect will be on the business.

Your financial model should provide – for three years at least:

- Profit and loss account.
- Cash flow statement.
- Balance sheet.

You may also create some management accounts that look in more detail at production and overhead costs and allow you to manipulate certain of those variables.

It is crucial that the figures you use in your model are as close to reality as can be. Your model must show what your breakeven point is likely to be in different circumstances, and allow you to estimate how long it will take to reach it. This calculation is important when it comes to raising finance. If you will be able to repay borrowings in three to six months, you (and your lender) may be willing to risk a bigger initial loan than if your earliest estimated repayment date is several years away.

The rule is to be cautious and prudent, but realistic. If your figures are too optimistic, you could find that you cannot meet your repayment schedule, and the additional cost of borrowing over a longer time frame damages your business' growth prospects, if not its viability – and your credibility with your bank manager. Equally, if you are unnecessarily pessimistic about the length of time it will take to repay the loan, your calculations may indicate that the entire project should be dropped – which is exactly what your bank manager will do!

If you have no experience of business planning or financial modelling, you should seek help from your bank, LOCAL ENTERPRISE OFFICE, your accountant or one of the other organisations listed in the *Accounting & Business Planning* section of the **Directory** where their alphabetical entry shows they provide such support.

Again, the details of the assumptions on which the model is based should go into an Appendix to the business plan, as should any detailed statistical analysis. Quote the important final figures in the body of the plan.

A Standard Business Plan Format

Each business plan is unique. However, those whom you seek to convince to invest in your project have come to expect certain information in a broadly standard format that presents information in an easily-digested logical sequence.

For a very small or simple business, the following intuitive format (adapted from *APPLYING THE RULES OF BUSINESS*, one of the *Steps to Entrepreneurship* series, Ron Immink & Brian O'Kane, Oak Tree Press) may be sufficient.

It sets out 10 key questions, the answers to which:

- Cover all the information that a reader is likely to want to know in order to come to a decision on your business plan.
- Ensure that you have fully thought through all aspects of your business.

For larger businesses, the second format shown later in this chapter, adapted from *PLANNING FOR SUCCESS* (another in the *Steps to Entrepreneurship* series, Ron Immink & Brian O'Kane, Oak Tree Press) may be more appropriate.

Sometimes the Summary / Overview is preceded by an Executive Summary, a concise one- or two-page summary of the entire plan.

This Executive Summary is the last thing to be written, and the first to be read. It must persuade the reader that the idea is good, otherwise he or she may not read on. It summarises the company, its objectives, why it will be successful. It describes the products, the market, critical financial information and, finally, outlines what form of finance is required, how much, and when. It assumes that its reader is not expert in your industry and knows nothing about your business. And it does all this in as few words as possible!

You should avoid giving detailed personal reasons for wanting to be your own boss. It is very easy to confuse your personal ambitions with your objectives for the business. Bankers and investors are primarily considering your prospects for success (getting them a good return), not your prospects for personal satisfaction. It is quite important to keep your focus, like theirs, on the business. Nonetheless, your character and skills will be of importance to them; these are the things to mention.

SIMPLE BUSINESS PLAN OUTLINE

I am ...	Explain who you are, your education / work experience etc, especially insofar as it applies to your proposed business.
My product is ...	Explain your product: What it is, what is does, how it works, how it is made, what makes it different / unique, etc.
My customers are ...	Explain who your customers will be and what evidence you have to support this.
My customers will buy my product because ...	Explain why your customers will buy your product and what evidence you have to support this.
My customers will pay ...	Explain how much your customers will pay for each unit of your product and what evidence you have to support this.
At this price, my customers will buy ...	Explain how many units of your product your customers will buy at the price set and what evidence you have to support this.
I can make ...	Explain how many units of your product you can make in a given time period and what evidence you have to support this.
To make each unit of product costs ...	Explain how much each unit of product costs you to make and what evidence you have to support this.
The start-up investment I require is ...	Explain the start-up investment you need, what it will be used for and what evidence you have to support this.
I have a viable business because ...	Explain why you believe you have a viable business and what evidence you have to support this.
In summary ...	On a single page, list the main points of your plan, in bullet point form. This is the part of the business plan that will make the biggest impression on your reader – make sure it's easy to read and understand. Then put it at the front of your plan, where it will be seen!

PLANNING FOR SUCCESS BUSINESS PLAN OUTLINE

1: Summary / Overview

- Founder(s).
- Business name.
- **Contact details:** Address, telephone / fax, e-mail, website.
- **Status:** Sole trader, partnership or limited company.
- **Registered for:** VAT, PAYE, Corporation Tax.
- **Formed as:** Purchase of existing business / purchase of franchise / start-up / other.
- Business objective.
- **External accountant:** Address, telephone / fax number, e-mail, contact name.
- **Product / service range:** Include descriptions and prices.
- **Staff:** Numbers (to be) employed in production, sales / promotion, administration, other duties.
- **Competitors:** Include estimates of competitors' turnover.
- **Investment and financing:** Details of fixed assets, personal assets, current assets, long-term / medium-term assets, liquid assets, short-term finance, start-up costs, subsidies / grants, allowance for contingencies, total investment, total available finance.
- **Budgets:** Forecasts for turnover, gross profit, gross profit percentage, net profit, cash flow and personal expenses over first three years.
- Other information.

2: The Entrepreneur

(If there is more than one founder, each must complete this section.)

- **Personal details:** Name, contact details, date of birth, etc.
- **Income:** Details of present income, source of income, benefits, income of spouse / partner, etc.
- **Education:** Details of post-primary education, including any courses that you are currently attending.
- **Practical experience:** Details of your working history and experience and any other significant experience that could be useful for your business.
- **Motivation, objectives and goals:** Why do you want to start a business? What do you want to achieve with your business?

- **Personal qualities**: What special qualities of yours are important for your business? List both your strong and your weak points. What are you going to do about your weak points?

3: Formal Requirements

- **Overall description:** Give a general description of your proposed business.
- **Research:** List the organisations you have contacted to discuss your plans and summarise the outcome of these discussions.
- **Legal status:** What legal status will your business take? What considerations led you to this choice?
- **Name and location:** What is the name of the business? Have you checked that this name is available? Describe your location. How can customers reach your location? Is access for supply and removal of goods available? Is there enough parking for your customers' cars and for your own cars? How big are your office premises? Are there expansion possibilities at these premises? Are the premises leased or purchased? Give details of cost of lease / mortgage. Have the premises been professionally valued? Has a lease or purchase contract been prepared by a solicitor? (If so, give the name of the solicitor.) Is there any pollution in the ground at your premises?
- **Licences:** Do you fulfil all of the licensing and permit requirements for the field you will be working in? If so, which and on what grounds? If not, why not and what are you doing about it? Is your business registered at the Companies Registration Office? What other licences do you need? Are there any other legal applications required (for example, environmental concerns)? If so, which?
- **Employer and employees:** Initially, how will your staffing be organised? Have you drawn up clear job descriptions for your future employees? Do you plan to expand your employee numbers quickly? Who will replace you during any required absences?
- **Administration:** Who will do your accounting? Who will do your bookkeeping? Give names, addresses and contact numbers.
- **Insurance:** Are you insured against the normal risks? If so, what is insured and for how much?
- **Terms of trade:** How is responsibility for product delivery arranged? Are product deliveries insured? If so, for how much? Summarise your terms of trade.
- **VAT:** Is your business registered for VAT? What is your VAT number? What rates of VAT apply to your business?

- **Start date:** When do you want to start the business, or when did you start?

4: Marketing

- **Market:** Who are your target groups? What do you have to offer? What is your business objective in seven words?
- **Market research:** Describe your market, future developments and your potential customers (local, county, national, and international). Describe the level of competition you face. What are the leading indicators in your market sector? Estimate the size of the Irish market for your product. What part of this market do you intend to service? Have you contacted future customers? What was their reaction? Have you obtained any forward orders? What comments did you receive with these orders?
- **Image:** What image will your business present? Set out your marketing plan based on your target groups, product assortment, price level, etc.
- **Product (range):** Describe briefly the product(s) you want to launch. Describe the primary and secondary functions of your product(s). What choices do you offer your customers? What extras do you offer compared to the competition?
- **Price**: What are customers prepared to pay? What are customers accustomed to paying? What are your competitors' prices? What is your price? How is your price made up? Will you offer discounts? If so, what will they be? Will you give special offers? If so, what will they be? Will cost calculations be monitored during operation? If so, how?
- **Place:** Explain your choice of location. Are there future developments that will change the attractiveness of your location? How did you allocate space for the various necessary functions?
- **Personnel:** Profile yourself as a business person. How many people will be involved in production, sales / promotion, administration, other duties? How are you going to make sure that your staff uphold the image of your business?
- **Presentation:** How are you going to present your business (layout, colours, music, atmosphere, correspondence, brochures, business cards, van signs)?
- **Promotion:** Rate those areas your customers are most interested in, and your relative strengths in those areas. How are you going to approach your customers and what buying motives are you going to emphasise? What marketing and promotion resources will you emphasise? Explain your promotion methods (how, where, frequency, etc.)
- **Competitors:** List your main competitors. Assess their strengths compared to your own. In what ways do your products / services differ from those of your

competitors? Can you estimate the total turnover of your competitors? What are your strong points compared to those of your direct competitors? What are your weak points compared to those of your direct competitors?

- **Purchasing:** Have you contacted your future suppliers? If so, what are their terms of trade? Are there alternative suppliers? What advantages do these alternative suppliers offer you?

- **Production process:** Are you involved with (or will you be using) new techniques or new products in your production processes? If so, are you receiving assistance from experts? If so, who are they and how are they involved? Describe your production process. What experience do you have with this process? What equipment do you use in the production process? List the equipment you intend to lease, buy new, or buy used. What guarantees / back-up do you have for this equipment in case of malfunction? Have you enough capacity to achieve the revenue for which you have budgeted? Have you checked your products and production processes for environmental considerations? If so, are there any environmental objections? If so, what are you planning to do about them?

5: Investment and Financing

- **Investment**: Describe the investment you will have to make to start your business, and to run it over the first three years (amounts exclusive of VAT).

- **Personal assets**: What assets can you (and your business partner(s)) put up yourselves? How did you value your personal assets?

- **Other (bank) finance**: Details of long-term / medium-term finance, short-term finance, subsidies / grants; shortfall, surplus, etc.

- **Credit assessment**: Can you support the required investment in fixed assets with quotations from suppliers? If not, how did you calculate your investment? Is your investment cost-effective? In your estimates, did you take seasonal business influences into account, and calculate based on your maximum requirements? How did you estimate your stock and work-in-progress levels? How did you estimate the value of your debtors? Do you have sufficient liquid assets to cope with disappointments and unexpected expenses? Did you approach a bank(s) about the financing of your plans? If yes, which bank(s), and who was your contact person? Did those contacts lead to any agreements? Did you approach other finance companies about your plans? If yes, with whom did you speak? Were any decisions reached, or arrangements made?

6: The Operating Budget

- **Turnover forecast:** List your revenue sources, and project the amounts you expect from each in the first three years.

- **Costs:** Give details of costs for staff, production, premises, transport, sales and promotion, general expenses, finance and depreciation in each of the first three years.

- **Profits and cash flow:** Give detailed cash flow projections for the first three years.

- **Comments on the budget:** Describe how you calculated and estimated your revenue (number of customers, average order per customer, turnaround). What expansion do you expect over the next few years? How did you calculate your purchase costs? How did you estimate salaries? What effect will any shortfall in turnover have on your business and how do you plan to handle it? What is your minimum required turnover?

7: Personal Expenses

- **Personal expenses:** Fixed expenses; rent / interest and repayment gas, water, electricity; taxes / charges; insurance; study expenses; membership expenses / contributions; TV licence; private use of car; repayments (enclose loan details); household expenses, etc.

- **Home equity:** Do you own your own home? If so, have you had it valued? What is its market value? How much equity do you have in your house?

- **Additional debts:** What other debts do you have (personal / private loan or credit, car financing, study costs, etc.)?

- **Minimum required turnover:** What is the minimum required turnover for your business, including your personal expenses?

8: Cash Flow

- Detailed cash flow projections for each month / quarter, outlining all income and expenditure, together with the opening and closing bank balances each quarter over the first three years.

How a Financier Reads a Business Plan

How a financier reads a business plan depends on what kind of financier he, or increasingly she, is. There are two types of financier – the lender and the investor. The lender is typically your bank manager. Lenders will invest money in your business, if they think it worth doing so by their criteria, in return for interest on the capital. The professional investor, on the other hand, will invest equity in your business and share in your risk as owner of the business. Professional investors will postpone their return for a period – typically, three to five years – but will look for an above-average return for the risk involved in doing so.

The Lender

The average bank manager will be looking to see how you have handled, or propose to handle, the risks, particularly the financial risks, that your business is likely to encounter. Bank managers are concerned about the security of the bank's money – or more properly, the depositors' money – which you are seeking and for which they are responsible.

That is not to say that a bank manager will not back you. Most bank managers have discretion in the amounts they lend to businesses and will sometimes back their own hunches or gut feelings against the apparent odds. But do not bet on it. Turn the odds in your favour by writing your business plan and framing your funding request in the best possible light.

Arnold S. Goldstein, American author of *STARTING ON A SHOESTRING* (John Wiley & Sons), suggests the following likely line of questioning from a bank manager:

- Why do you need the amount requested?
- What will you do with it?
- How do you know it's enough?
- How much less can you live with?
- Who else will you borrow from?
- How do you propose to repay it?
- How can you prove that you can?
- What collateral can you offer?

Unless you can answer these questions to your bank manager's satisfaction (especially the last two), it is unlikely that you will get the money you are looking for.

And don't wait for the interview with the manager for an opportunity to think about the answers to these questions – that is far too late. The bank manager's mind will already be made up, more or less, before your meeting. Your plan will have been read thoroughly. The interview is intended to firm up the manager's decision. If you have not answered the relevant questions in the plan, you are not likely to have much chance to do so later.

You don't need to write your business plan in a style that asks the questions in the form above and then gives the answers. What you need to do is to ensure that the information that answers the questions is:

- Contained within the plan.
- Visible within the plan.
- Capable of being extracted by a reader from the plan.

Putting all this in another way, a bank manager will look for three things: character, collateral and cash flow.

Character means you. A bank manager who has any reason to distrust or disbelieve you – from previous dealings or because of your reputation or because of errors or inconsistencies in your business plan – will not invest money with you.

Collateral means the backing that you can give as security for the loan. In some cases, collateral is not needed. But to the banker, who is responsible to the bank's depositors for their money, security is all. If you can offer collateral, it will certainly help your case.

Cash flow means your ability to repay the loan on time, out of the proceeds of the investment. The bank manager will prefer to see the loan repaid at regular monthly or quarterly intervals with interest paid on the due dates – anything else upsets the bank's system. Unless you can show that the business will generate enough cash to make the payments the bank manager requires – or you have explained clearly in your business plan why this will not be possible for an initial period – you will not get the money that you ask for.

Professional Investors

Professional investors have a different viewpoint. They accept risk, though, like any prudent person, they will avoid undue risk and seek to limit their exposure to unavoidable risk. David Silver, another American venture capitalist and author on enterprise, suggests that their questions will be along the lines of:

- How much can I make?
- How much can I lose?
- How do I get my money out?
- Who says this is any good?
- Who else is in it?

How much can I make? decides whether the project fits the profile of 30 to 50 per cent annual compound growth (well in excess of bank interest) usually required by investors.

How much can I lose? identifies the downside risk. Although investors are used to investing in several projects that fail for every one that succeeds, they cannot invest in projects that would jeopardise their own business of investment in the event of their failure.

How do I get my money out? is important since few investors invest for the long term. Most are happy to turn over their investments every three to five years. None will invest in a project unless they can see clearly an exit mechanism. There is no point in holding a 25 per cent share in a company valued at several millions if you cannot realise the shareholding when you want to.

Who says this is any good? Professional investors maintain networks of advisers, often on an informal basis. They will check out all that you say or include in your business plan. This is part of the 'due diligence' process. If you can supply an investor with evidence that people who ought to know support your plans, you will strengthen your case.

Who else is in this? panders to investors' residual need for security. Although investors know that they are going to take a risk, by placing their faith and money in your hands, they like to know that others have come to the same conclusion. There is nothing like unanimity to convince people that they are right. Don't mock – particularly if you're trying to persuade someone to invest. Some investors have such a reputation for being right, for picking winners, that others try to follow their lead whenever they can.

Above all, in assessing the project itself, a professional investor will look at three key areas:

- The market: Is it large and growing rapidly?

- The product: Does it solve an important problem in the market, one that customers are prepared to pay for?
- Management: Are all the key functional areas on board and up to strength?

Writing the Business Plan

There are three stages in writing a business plan:

- Thinking.
- Writing.
- Editing.

Each is important but the most important is the first – thinking. Be prepared to spend at least 75 per cent of the time you have allocated to preparing your business plan in thinking (and researching). Time spent here will not be wasted. Use this time to talk through your business with anyone who will listen; read widely, especially about others in your area of business; and avoid finding reasons why things cannot be done.

Writing can be done fastest of all. Use a word-processor to give yourself the flexibility you will need to edit the document later.

If you find it difficult to start writing on a blank page or computer screen, talk instead. Buy, or borrow, a hand-held dictating machine. Talk to yourself about your business. Explain it as if to someone who knows nothing about it. Get the tape transcribed and your business plan will be on the way.

Editing is the last task. Editing is an art. Some people are better at it than others, but everyone can learn the basics. Essentially, it's about clear communication. Read through your draft business plan – aloud, if you find that helps. Does what you have written say what you want? Start deleting. You will find that quite a lot of text can come out without doing any damage to the reader's understanding of what you are trying to communicate. When you are happy with your draft, put it aside for a day or two. Come back to it fresh and see whether it still makes sense. Edit again where it does not. And when it is right, leave it alone!

4: FINANCING YOUR START-UP

The 'Golden Rule' for financing a new business is: as little as possible, as cheaply as possible. Do not put money into the unnecessary. It is better to start off running your business from the attic without a loan than in a glossy, but unnecessary, high-street office with heavy bank borrowings.

On the other hand, do adopt a realistic position on the amount of money that you need to get going. Your financing must be sufficient to carry the business until it reaches the point where money coming in equals (or exceeds) money going out. In addition to capital investment in plant, equipment and premises, your financing may have to supply most of the working capital until sales begin to generate sufficient income to give you an adequate cash flow.

You have two options in raising finance:

- Equity: Capital invested in the business, usually not repayable.
- Debt: Capital lent to the business, usually repayable at a specified date.

Equity

For equity, the alternatives are:

- Your own equity – which leads to two questions: How much do you have? How much do you need?
- Other people's equity – which also leads to two questions: Are you prepared to allow other people to own part of your business? Can your business offer the sort of return that will attract outside investors?

Because equity means giving away part of your business, it's in your interest to minimise the amount held by outside investors. However, be sensible – it's better to own 70% (or even 30%) of a thriving and profitable business than 100% of a business going nowhere because it's starved for funds.

Owners' Equity

In terms of the equity that you are able to put into the business, you must establish what assets you must retain as a fall-back position, and remove them from the equation. For example, you may not want to mortgage your house to raise finance for your business. Then consider what assets remain in the following terms:

- How easily can they be sold and how much will their sale raise?
- Are they mortgageable assets?
- Will they be acceptable as collateral?

Typical assets include: cash; shares; car; land; house; and boats, second or holiday homes, antiques, jewellery, paintings.

If you are considering mortgaging your family home for the sake of the business, you should be aware that this is a very serious step and professional advice should be obtained before you do so. The issues to be considered include:

- Ownership of the property.
- What would happen to the family home and your family if the business fails.
- The approach that the banks and the courts take in such circumstances.

Note that if you mortgage your home, or borrow personally, in order to invest equity into your business and the business fails, you still remain liable to repay the loan. There's a big difference between this and the situation where the bank lends directly to the business.

Other Equity

For many small businesses, the option of raising equity capital is not a reality. Either the sums they need are too small to interest an investor, or the level of return, while adequate to pay a standard bank loan, is not sufficient to tempt the investor who is exposed to a greater risk. Most equity investors look to invest at least €500,000 in a company, arguing that amounts below this do not justify the amount of checking they need to do before making an investment. Thus, perversely perhaps, it is easier to raise €5,000,000 than it is to raise €50,000.

Fuelled by the 'Celtic Tiger' economy, the recent spectacular successes of some Irish technology companies and a growing awareness of the importance of private equity for business development, the number of venture capital funds in Ireland has increased significantly in the past few years. Some of these will consider investing seed capital (less than €250,000), although most prefer to invest venture (€250,000 to €1 million, for businesses at an early stage of development) or development (€1 million+) capital. Note that these amounts are arbitrary; some funds will invest in more than one category.

In most cases – certainly where you require seed capital – you can approach the fund manager directly. A check on the fund's website to make sure that you meet the fund's criteria, a phone call to check the name of the person to whom you should send your business plan – then go for it! Larger, technology-based projects requiring greater and more complex financing can choose whether to go directly to an appropriate fund or to work through a corporate finance house, which has specialist skills in fund-raising.

Whatever your route, remember that it's not just about money, as the growth of incubators shows. Depending on the strengths of your new business, early-stage supports may be as important as cash.

Family equity

But, despite all the new funds, the best source of small-scale seed capital for most start-ups continues to be family or friends. If you do decide to involve family and friends as investors in your business, make sure both sides know – and agree on – the ground rules:

- Their investment is 'risk capital' – it may be lost and is not repayable (unless you agree otherwise).
- Equity investment does not automatically give a right to management involvement – even if it's clear that you can't cope.
- Their investment may be diluted by other later investors, whose money is needed to continue the development of the business.

Put everything in writing – in a formal shareholders' agreement, if appropriate, or a simple letter of understanding signed by all parties.

Business Angels

'Business Angels', a term adapted from the world of theatre where private investors ('angels') are often the source of finance for a new show on New York's Broadway or in London's West End, are private investors who take (usually) a minority stake in a business – sometimes with an active management role, too. They're hard to find and, since they're usually experienced businesspeople, often hard to convince.

Tax and equity

While the REVENUE COMMISSIONERS will not invest directly in your business, they offer a tax break on equity capital introduced by an entrepreneur into their own company (subject to conditions) through the START UP REFUNDS FOR ENTREPRENEURS scheme.

Note also, when raising equity from external investors, that under the Employment & Investment Incentive scheme the Revenue offers tax relief to investors who invest in 'qualifying' companies under certain conditions. This makes equity investment in start-ups more attractive to investors – and so makes it easier for start-ups to raise equity funding.

Crowdfunding

Although primarily seen as a form of non-equity, non-debt finance (see later in this chapter), equity crowdfunding websites are beginning to emerge.

Debt

When considering financing your business with debt, consider:
- Fixed or floating.
- Long-term or short-term.

Fixed debt is a loan that is secured on a specific asset, for example, on premises. Floating debt is secured on assets that change regularly, for example, debtors. 'Secured' means that, if the loan is not repaid, the lender can appoint a receiver to sell the asset on which the loan is secured in order to recover the amount due. Thus, giving security for a loan is not something to be done lightly. Long-term for most lenders means five to seven years; short-term means one year or less.

Because you have to pay interest on debt, you should try to manage with as little as possible. However, few businesses get off the ground without putting some debt on the balance sheet. The issues are usually:

- What is the cheapest form of debt?
- What is the correct balance between debt and equity?
- How can you sensibly reduce the borrowing you require?
- To what extent must borrowing be backed by personal assets?

Matching Loans and Assets

It is a good idea to try to match the term of the loan to the type of asset that you are acquiring:

- To avoid constant renewing or restructuring problems.
- To ensure that each loan is covered by the break-up value of the assets in case of disaster.

For example, a loan to buy premises should be a long-term loan, unless you can see clearly that you will have enough money within a short period to repay the loan. Taking out a short-term loan or overdraft to buy premises is a recipe for disaster. You may have to renegotiate it time and again – and, if your business runs into temporary difficulties, you run the risk of losing everything.

Short-term loans, or even overdrafts, are more suited to funding stock or debtors because you should be able to repay the loan once you have sold the goods or got the money in.

Short-term finance is also used to fund other forms of working capital and cash flow. It should always be repaid within the year – even if at the end of the period you still need to borrow more to fund future cash flow. In other words, your overdraft or short-term loan should be periodically cleared (or substantially reduced) by money coming in before you need to increase it again. If you have to borrow the same sum of money against the same asset for longer than a year at a time, you should be considering longer-term finance.

If disaster strikes and you have to repay the loan suddenly, it will be much easier to do so if the value of the assets is roughly equivalent to the outstanding value of the loan. Thus, for instance, you will hope to sell your premises for at least as much as you borrowed to buy them. Machinery may be more difficult, as the resale price is rarely comparable with the purchase price. For this reason, you may consider purchasing second-hand equipment for your start-up.

If you can, you should arrange your loans so that unrealisable assets are purchased out of your own equity, using borrowing only for realisable assets. If an asset is easily realisable, the bank is much more likely to accept it as security.

Although the main sources of loan finance (overdrafts, term loans and commercial mortgages) for start-ups are the banks, don't look only to banks for debt. Credit unions (see the IRISH LEAGUE OF CREDIT UNIONS' website for a list) may consider a small loan to get your business off the ground, particularly if you have been a regular saver.

As well as dealing with banks, you may also find yourself dealing with finance companies, which sometimes may be more willing to lend than a bank, though they are usually more expensive. Some finance companies specialise in certain types of finance, or special industry sectors. Because of their greater expertise and knowledge, they may be able to give you a better deal than the main retail banks because they understand your situation better.

When looking for finance, beware of 'specialists' who claim that they can find you money at favourable rates of interest if you pay an up-front fee. Don't pay anything until you have the money.

Consider also peer-to-peer borrowing. Although largely aimed at established businesses, some peer-to-peer lending networks may consider start-ups.

If you are having trouble getting finance, it may be an indication that you should reappraise the project. Talk to those who have refused you finance about their reasons before proceeding to other financiers. You may end up increasing your chances of success, both in raising finance second time around and in the business itself.

Expanding Your Credit Line

When (or, preferably, before) you have exhausted the borrowing facilities that your bank is prepared to provide (your credit line), you should consider two other forms of financing: leasing and factoring.

Leasing is particularly attractive as a way of acquiring the use of fixed assets – for example, plant and machinery, cars, office equipment – with the minimum up-front cost. Instead, you pay a regular monthly or quarterly payment, which is usually allowable for tax purposes. At the end of the lease, depending on the terms of the particular lease, you may have the option to continue using the asset for a modest continuing payment or to buy it outright from the lessor. Most of the major banks provide leasing facilities.

Factoring, or invoice discounting, is a means of raising working capital, by 'selling' your debtors. The factoring company (usually a division or subsidiary of a bank) will pay you, say, 80 per cent of the face value of an invoice when it is issued. The balance, less charges, will be paid to you when the debt is settled. This form of financing, though expensive, is especially useful for the company that is rapidly expanding and in danger of being choked for lack of cash flow.

Who to Approach?

Who you approach for funds will depend on:

- How much finance you need.
- What you need finance for.
- Your company's risk profile.

Often, if you only need a small amount of money, the best way to raise it is still to approach a bank or credit union with which you have already built up some relationship, whether on a personal basis or in a business capacity. The larger borrower may feel it worthwhile to seek professional help to put together a more sophisticated finance package. Your accountant is the best person to give you advice in this area and may have contacts that will ease your path.

Dealing with Banks

Whatever the means of finance you adopt, you will almost certainly have to deal with a bank for your daily needs, if not for your whole financial package. Banks are conservative institutions with fixed procedures. You will hopefully have laid a good foundation for your business relationship with the bank by the way in which you have handled your personal finances. In smaller towns, you may already be well-known to the bank manager.

However, the relationship that your business will have with the bank is likely to be different from any personal relationship that you had with them before. While you were employed by someone else, you probably had a regular, guaranteed income going into your personal account. You may have had an overdraft, a mortgage, or perhaps a personal loan, but unless you were careless with your finances, the risk of getting into serious financial difficulty was limited. But, in dealing with you now as a business, some of the personal element disappears from the relationship and is replaced by an 'unknown risk' factor, which stems from the following facts:

- The business is (usually) a separate legal entity from yourself and has no previous relationship with the bank.
- The business has no guaranteed income (to the extent that your previous employment was secure, your personal income was 'guaranteed' – it no longer is, and don't be surprised if that changes your bank manager's attitude towards your personal account, too).
- A high proportion of new businesses fail or experience financial difficulty for a variety of reasons that are difficult to predict.
- The amount you have borrowed from the bank – for which the bank manager is responsible to shareholders – is likely to be much larger than any personal loan you have had in the past.

The more of the unknown risk that you are able to eliminate for the bank manager, the more he or she will be able to do for you, both in terms of providing the money you want and, in many cases, by giving you the benefit of their experience in commenting on your plans.

The sort of information you can supply includes:

- A business plan, and updates when necessary.
- Regular reports on the financial state of your business.
- Information on a timely basis about any emerging problems that are going to result in late repayments, choked cash flow or a need for additional funding. A problem many bankers mention is that clients do not tell the bank what is wrong until the situation has grown so terrible that it is too late to correct it.
- Encouraging your banker to visit on-site to see for themselves.

It is also true that too many bankers put a lot of effort into the initial analysis of a start-up loan, but fail to keep a close enough eye on their investment thereafter – hence, at least some of the losses on their small business lending the banks have experienced in recent years.

You can gain the maximum amount of assistance from your bank, not only by keeping the manager informed, but by asking occasionally for an opinion of the financial outcome of a certain course of action. You should certainly have a face-to-face chat with your banker at least twice a year, if you can arrange it.

Other Points

If your business plan is approved and you are awarded your loan:

- Don't be afraid to negotiate for the best possible terms. Most entrepreneurs will haggle over the price of a computer but will accept a bank's terms like lambs.

- It may be a good idea to have an accountant or solicitor look at any loan agreement before you sign it. They may spot gaps, or unnecessary clauses, and their professional backing will give you added confidence in arguing your case.

- Make all payments on time and in the agreed manner. If, for some reason, you will be late with a repayment, at least warn the bank in advance and, if possible, discuss the reasons with your bank manager.

Security

Providing security – pledging assets against a loan in case you are unable to repay it – is an ongoing issue (and a most vexatious one) between the small business community and the banks. Small business owners often feel it unjust that a large corporation can borrow a huge amount of money often without providing security, while they have to produce security for small loans.

Ideally, bankers will look for security in the business itself – premises, equipment or stock – but often small businesses rent their premises, lease their equipment and hold limited quantities of stock. Business machinery is not always suitable as security because it may have a low resale value, or may be built into the building where it is housed, making it difficult for the bank to sell it, if necessary, without incurring substantial additional costs. For this reason, the bank will often seek personal guarantees, that is, the pledge of personal assets against business loans.

Beware of personal guarantees. The bank may ask for them, although the major banks have repeatedly told the SMALL FIRMS ASSOCIATION and the IRISH SMALL & MEDIUM ENTERPRISES ASSOCIATION that they do not ask for guarantees 'as a matter of course'. A personal guarantee is exactly that. You are guaranteeing that, if the company cannot pay back the loan to the bank, you will do so. *How?* Think about it before you sign. Try to avoid giving a personal guarantee. It is probably better to borrow less, or pay a higher rate of interest, or use leasing as a means of financing specific fixed assets, than to be saddled with a personal guarantee.

As a condition of a loan, you may be asked by the bank not to pay any dividends or repay any other loans (especially ones you have made personally to the company) until the bank has been repaid. Though this is less onerous than a personal guarantee, only agree if these conditions are reasonable.

Check that whatever legal document you sign agrees with what you agreed with your bank manager. And, if the condition is for a limited period of time or until the loan is repaid, don't be shy about asking to be released from it when you have done your part and repaid the bank.

Non-equity, Non-debt Finance

Although equity and debt represent the classic forms of financing, consider other sources – for example:

- The START UP REFUNDS FOR ENTREPRENEURS scheme operated by the REVENUE COMMISSIONERS, which can give you back some of your previous years' PAYE if you leave employment to start a new business.
- Enterprise competition prizes, for example, the ENTERPRISE IRELAND Student Enterprise Awards or the Seedcorn Business Plan Competition run by INTERTRADE IRELAND.
- Grants from support agencies, such as the LOCAL ENTERPRISE OFFICES or LEADER organisations.

Sources of Finance

Sources of finance are shown in the *Directory* under *Funding*, covering equity, debt, grants and alternative financing.

5: STATE SUPPORT FOR START-UPS

There is no shortage of State support in Ireland for start-ups and small businesses. Instead, the number of agencies, nationally and locally, that co-exist (and, on occasion, appear to compete for the entrepreneur pool) can give rise to confusion. The starting point, however, for most entrepreneurs is their LOCAL ENTERPRISE OFFICE, which should be able to signpost appropriate sources of assistance if they cannot help directly themselves.

But, first, a note about the focus of State support. When *STARTING A BUSINESS IN IRELAND* was first published, the expressed priority of Irish enterprise support agencies was the creation of sustainable jobs. "How many jobs?" was the benchmark used to assess projects. To be sure, other criteria were used too, but jobs over-rode everything else. That remains the case today – which is often challenging for 'next-generation' businesses that operate with few tangible resources and fewer staff, relying instead on the Internet, branding and outsourcing to achieve their objectives.

Key State / Semi-State Agencies

Overall responsibility for enterprise lies with the DEPARTMENT OF BUSINESS, ENTERPRISE & INNOVATION, which is responsible for promoting competitiveness in the economy and for creating a favourable climate for the creation of self-sustaining employment. It works to monitor and improve the environment for business by ensuring that the framework of law, regulation and Government policy promotes effective company performance and both public and business confidence.

The next layer consists of IDA IRELAND and ENTERPRISE IRELAND. IDA Ireland focuses on inwards investment – bringing foreign multinationals into Ireland – while Enterprise Ireland is tasked with supporting indigenous (local) businesses. In Gaeltacht (native Irish-speaking) areas, ÚDARÁS NA GAELTACHTA replaces Enterprise Ireland.

Then, there is a range of specialist agencies, tasked with the development of a particular industry sector – FÁILTE IRELAND, in relation to tourism – or specialist area – SOLAS, in relation to employment and training. Some agencies have a regulatory role or monitoring role – the ENVIRONMENTAL PROTECTION AGENCY or the FOOD SAFETY AUTHORITY. Not all the agencies report to the Department for Business, Enterprise & Innovation, but instead to the Government Department most closely associated with their work – so BORD BIA reports to the DEPARTMENT OF AGRICULTURE, FOOD & THE MARINE.

The various State agencies all operate at a national level, although many have regional or local offices. But, to ensure that local needs are met at local level, LOCAL ENTERPRISE OFFICES operate in every county and city, as well as:

- Area Partnerships.
- Community Groups.
- IRD (Integrated Rural Development) Companies.
- LEADER groups.

Most of these groups are State-funded, through the Social Inclusion & Community Activation Programme or LEADER / Rural Development Programme – though they may have other income streams too.

So, where should the potential entrepreneur begin to look for help? Indeed, what sort of help is available, and from whom? Your starting point, as mentioned above, should be your LOCAL ENTERPRISE OFFICE – if you prefer to start online, try SUPPORTINGSMES.ie.

If you can show that you are likely to employ more than 10 people within three years of start-up (and meet some other criteria, including showing export potential), Enterprise Ireland (or Údarás na Gaeltachta, as appropriate, depending on your location) may classify your business as a 'high potential start-up' (HPSU) and take you under its wing.

Local Enterprise Offices

LOCAL ENTERPRISE OFFICES (LEOs) are arguably the most important source of assistance for a start-up business.

LEO funding includes:

- Priming grants – for business less than 18 months old.
- Business Expansion grants – for businesses more than 18 months old.
- Feasibility / Innovation grants.

The LEOs do not fund projects that are contrary to public policy, nor do they duplicate support for projects that would be eligible for assistance from any existing sectoral or grant structure, or which involve primary agricultural production.

Assistance is not confined to grants, since the LEOs have authority to provide loans and loan guarantees and to take equity stakes in businesses. In addition, they act as a primary source of advice and information. Many also provide training and mentoring services.

Since the activities of each LEO is tailored to the needs of its local community, you should check with your local LEO for the full range of assistance available.

Enterprise Ireland

The best source for information on ENTERPRISE IRELAND and how it helps small businesses is its own website, **www.enterprise-ireland.com**.

Enterprise Ireland helps manufacturing and internationally-traded services businesses that employ more than 10 people to grow internationally. The agency is primarily focused on providing advice and support to companies in three areas: technology innovation, business development and internationalisation. Its aim is to work in partnership with these businesses to develop a sustainable competitive advantage that leads to a significant increase in profitable sales, exports and employment.

Accordingly, a strong, well-thought-through business plan is essential for any application for Enterprise Ireland support, which is usually a mix of non-repayable grants and equity investment (in the form of preference and ordinary shares).

Údarás na Gaeltachta

As noted earlier, in the Gaeltacht areas, ÚDARÁS NA GAELTACHTA carries out the functions handled by Enterprise Ireland elsewhere. In addition to its enterprise development role, Údarás has a mission to preserve and promote the Irish language. Its remit spreads across a wide geographical area – from Macroom in Co. Cork through Connemara and into Donegal – which adds to the complexity of its task.

Other Local Support Agencies

The 38 Area Partnerships were originally set up under the Programme for Economic & Social Progress (PESP) in 1993. Most now operate under the Social Inclusion & Community Activation Programme or the Rural Development Programme / LEADER, with funding co-ordinated by POBAL.

Each Partnership is autonomous and works on an Area Action Plan for its own region. Practical measures are taken to discriminate in favour of the long-term unemployed and those who are socially excluded. There is variety in what each Partnership offers – some have no direct involvement in enterprise support – so entrepreneurs should contact the Partnership in their area for further details.

Another strand of local enterprise support are the Community Groups, established by Pobal. Their remit is more broadly focused on community development, although some have direct enterprise development activity. As each Community Group identifies and responds to needs within its own communities, its activities are unique to its own situation. Entrepreneurs seeking assistance should make contact with their local Community Group to see whether and what help is available.

Many of the Partnerships and Community Groups are members of the IRISH LOCAL DEVELOPMENT NETWORK.

IRD Companies were another strand of local and community development. Three remain: IRD DUHALLOW in Co. Cork, and IRD KILTIMAGH and MOY VALLEY RESOURCES IRD in Co. Mayo.

LEADER is an EU initiative for rural development (part-funded by the Irish Government) and is administered by Local Action Groups (LAGs). These are partnerships of both public and private entities from a defined geographical area that are responsible for selecting and approving projects in their respective areas in accordance with local development strategies developed specifically for their area under the following themes:

- Economic development, enterprise development and job creation.

- Social inclusion.
- Rural environment.

A list of LEADER LAGs appears in the *Directory*, under LEADER, with separate entries for each LAG.

Again, as each LEADER Group identifies and responds to needs within its own communities, its activities are unique to its own situation. Because of this, entrepreneurs seeking assistance should make contact with their local LEADER Group to see whether and what help is available.

Note that, as they have evolved from their beginnings in the 1990s, there has been some overlap between Area Partnerships, Community Groups, IRD Companies and LEADER organisations, with some organisations combining two or more roles.

Other State and Semi-State Agencies

As mentioned earlier, there are a wide range of these agencies, covering a variety of roles and responsibilities and reporting to appropriate Government Departments.

Regional, industry or sector-related bodies include:

o   ARTS COUNCIL.
o   BORD BIA.
o   BORD IASCAIGH MHARA.
o   DESIGN & CRAFTS COUNCIL OF IRELAND.
o   EASTERN & MIDLAND REGIONAL ASSEMBLY.
o   FÁILTE IRELAND.
o   MARINE INSTITUTE.
o   NORTHERN & WESTERN REGIONAL ASSEMBLY.
o   SEA-FISHERIES PROTECTION AGENCY.
o   SOUTHERN REGIONAL ASSEMBLY.
o   SUSTAINABLE ENERGY AUTHORITY OF IRELAND.
o   TEAGASC.
o   WESTERN DEVELOPMENT COMMISSION.

Bodies that collect and disseminate information include:

o   CENTRAL STATISTCIS OFFICE.
o   COMPANIES REGISTRATION OFFICE.
o   PATENTS OFFICE.

Bodies with a regulatory or monitoring role include:
o   COMPETITION & CONSUMER PROTECTION COMMISSION.
o   CREDIT REVIEW OFFICE.
o   DATA PROTECTION COMMISSION.
o   ENVIRONMENTAL PROTECTION AGENCY.
o   FOOD SAFETY AUTHORITY OF IRELAND
o   HEALTH & SAFETY AUTHORITY.
o   NATIONAL STANARDS AUTHORITY OF IRELAND.
o   OFFICE OF THE DIRECTOR OF CORPORATE ENFORCEMENT.
o   REVENUE COMMISSIONERS.

Details of all these bodies and their activities are included in the *Directory*.

Government Departments

Not all the State agencies that have a role in enterprise development or support report to the DEPARTMENT OF BUSINESS, ENTERPRISE & INNOVATION. Other Departments that support start-ups include:
o   DEPARTMENT OF AGRICULTURE, FOOD & THE MARINE.
o   DEPARTMENT OF EMPLOYMENT AFFAIRS & SOCIAL PROTECTION.
o   DEPARTMENT OF HOUSING, PLANNING & LOCAL GIOVERNMENT.
o   DEPARTMENT OF JUSTICE & EQUALITY.
o   DEPARTMENT OF RURAL & COMMUNITY DEVELOPMENT.

A useful website for information on Government Departments and their activities is **www.gov.ie**.

Universities & Institutes of Technology

A final source of State support for enterprise are the UNIVERSITIES and INSTITUTES OF TECHNOLOGY. All have Industrial Liaison Officers, or Heads of External Services or Development, whose task it is to build links between the college and the business world. In many cases, this results in the college carrying out technical research for a local business or commercialising through a local business the fruits of their own research. More important, all have incubation facilities, offering work space as well as often training, mentoring and other supports.

Support by Category

To make it easy to find the appropriate source of State (or State-funded) assistance, this section lists State organisations by the type of support they offer. See the *Directory* (*By Category* section) for explanations of the categories.

Accounting & Business Planning

o   MOY VALLEY RESOURCES IRD.

Community & Rural Development

o   AVONDHU BLACKWATER PARTNERSHIP CLG.
o   BALLYFERMOT CHAPELIZOD PARTNERSHIP COMPANY LTD.
o   BALLYHOURA DEVELOPMENT CLG.
o   BRAY AREA PARTNERSHIP.
o   BREFFNI INTEGRATED CLG.
o   CARLOW COUNTY DEVELOPMENT PARTNERSHIP.
o   CLARE LOCAL DEVELOPMENT COMPANY LTD.
o   COMHAR NA NOILEÁN CTR.
o   CORK CITY PARTNERSHIP CLG.
o   COUNTY KILDARE LEADER PARTNERSHIP.
o   COUNTY SLIGO LEADER PARTNERSHIP COMPANY LTD.
o   COUNTY WICKLOW PARTNERSHIP.
o   DEPARTMENT OF RURAL & COMMUNITY DEVELOPMENT.
o   DONEGAL LOCAL DEVELOPMENT COMPANY CLG.
o   DUBLIN NORTH WEST AREA PARTNERSHIP.
o   DUBLIN SOUTH CITY PARTNERSHIP.
o   EMPOWER.
o   FÁILTE IRELAND.
o   FINGAL LEADER PARTNERSHIP.
o   FORUM CONNEMARA CLG.
o   GALWAY CITY PARTNERSHIP.
o   GALWAY RURAL DEVELOPMENT COMPANY.
o   INISHOWEN DEVELOPMENT PARTNERSHIP.
o   INSTITUTE FOR MINORITY ENTREPRENEURSHIP.
o   IRD DUHALLOW LTD.
o   IRD KILTIMAGH.
o   KILKENNY LEADER PARTNERSHIP LTD.

- LAOIS PARTNERSHIP COMPANY.
- LEADER.
- LEITRIM INTEGRATED DEVELOPMENT COMPANY LTD.
- LIMERICK ENTERPRISE DEVELOPMENT PARTNERSHIP.
- LONGFORD COMMUNITY RESOURCES LTD.
- LOUTH LEADER PARTNERSHIP.
- MAYO NORTH EAST LEADER PARTNERSHIP.
- MEATH PARTNERSHIP.
- MONAGHAN INTEGRATED DEVELOPMENT LTD.
- MOY VALLEY RESOURCES IRD.
- NORTH TIPPERARY LEADER PARTNERSHIP.
- NORTH, EAST & WEST KERRY DEVLOPMENT.
- NORTHSIDE PARTNERSHIP.
- OFFALY INTEGRATED LOCAL DEVELOPMENT CLG.
- PAUL PARTNERSHIP LIMERICK.
- ROSCOMMON LEADER PARTNERSHIP.
- SOUTH & EAST CORK AREA DEVELOPMENT LTD.
- SOUTH DUBLIN COUNTY PARTNERSHIP.
- SOUTH KERRY DEVELOPMENT PARTNERSHIP.
- SOUTH TIPPERARY DEVELOPMENT CLG.
- SOUTH WEST MAYO DEVELOPMENT COMPANY CLG.
- SOUTHSIDE PARTNERSHIP DLR LTD.
- ÚDARÁS NA GAELTACHTA.
- WATERFORD AREA PARTNERSHIP.
- WATERFORD LEADER PARTNERSHIP CLG.
- WEST LIMERICK RESOURCES LTD.
- WESTERN DEVELOPMENT COMMISSION.
- WESTMEATH COMMUNITY DEVELOPMENT LTD.
- WEXFORD LOCAL DEVELOPMENT.

Consulting

- CENTRE FOR CO-OPERATIVE STUDIES.
- FOOD PRODUCT DEVELOPMENT CENTRE.
- TEAGASC.

Enterprise Support

- CORK INSTITUTE OF TECHNOLOGY.
- DUBLIN CITY UNIVERSITY.

- o DUBLIN INSTITUTE OF TECHNOLOGY.
- o ENTERPRISE & RESEARCH INCUBATION CAMPUS.
- o INSTITUTE OF TECHNOLOGY BLANCHARDSTOWN.
- o INSTITUTE OF TECHNOLOGY CARLOW.
- o KILKENNY LEADER PARTNERSHIP LTD.
- o MIDLANDS INNOVATION & RESEARCH CENTRE.
- o NATIONAL UNIVERSITY OF IRELAND GALWAY.
- o NATIONAL UNIVERSITY OF IRELAND MAYNOOTH.
- o POBAL.
- o RUBICON CENTRE.
- o THE LINC.
- o TRINITY COLLEGE DUBLIN.
- o UNIVERSITY COLLEGE CORK.
- o UNIVERSITY COLLEGE DUBLIN.
- o UNIVERSITY OF LIMERICK.

Franchises

- o NATIONAL FRANCHISE CENTRE.

Funding

- o ARTS COUNCIL.
- o AVONDHU BLACKWATER PARTNERSHIP CLG.
- o BALLYHOURA DEVELOPMENT CLG.
- o BORD BIA.
- o BORD IASCAIGH MHARA.
- o BREFFNI INTEGRATED CLG.
- o CARLOW COUNTY DEVELOPMENT PARTNERSHIP CLG.
- o CAVAN COUNTY ENTERPRISE FUND.
- o CLARE LOCAL DEVELOPMENT COMPANY LTD.
- o COMHAR NA NOILEÁN CTR.
- o COUNTY KILDARE LEADER PARTNERSHIP.
- o COUNTY SLIGO LEADER PARTNERSHIP COMPANY LTD.
- o COUNTY WICKLOW PARTNERSHIP.
- o CREDIT REVIEW OFFICE.
- o DCU RYAN ACADEMY.
- o DEPARTMENT OF EMPLOYMENT AFFAIRS & SOCIAL PROTECTION.
- o DONEGAL LOCAL DEVELOPMENT COMPANY CLG.
- o DONEGAL LOCAL ENTERPRISE OFFICE.

o DUBLIN SOUTH LOCAL ENTERPRISE OFFICE.
o ENTERPRISE IRELAND.
o FINGAL LEADER PARTNERSHIP.
o FORUM CONNEMARA CLG.
o GALWAY RURAL DEVELOPMENT COMPANY.
o INISHOWEN DEVELOPMENT PARTNERSHIP.
o IRD DUHALLOW LTD.
o KERRY LOCAL ENTERPRISE OFFICE.
o KILKENNY LEADER PARTNERSHIP LTD.
o LAOIS PARTNERSHIP COMPANY.
o LEADER.
o LEITRIM INTEGRATED DEVELOPMENT COMPANY LTD.
o LEITRIM LOCAL ENTERPRISE OFFICE.
o LOCAL ENTERPRISE OFFICE CARLOW.
o LOCAL ENTERPRISE OFFICE CAVAN.
o LOCAL ENTERPRISE OFFICE CLARE.
o LOCAL ENTERPRISE OFFICE CORK CITY.
o LOCAL ENTERPRISE OFFICE CORK NORTH & WEST.
o LOCAL ENTERPRISE OFFICE DUBLIN CITY.
o LOCAL ENTERPRISE OFFICE DUN LAOGHAIRE-RATHDOWN.
o LOCAL ENTERPRISE OFFICE FINGAL.
o LOCAL ENTERPRISE OFFICE GALWAY.
o LOCAL ENTERPRISE OFFICE KILDARE.
o LOCAL ENTERPRISE OFFICE KILKENNY.
o LOCAL ENTERPRISE OFFICE LAOIS.
o LOCAL ENTERPRISE OFFICE LIMERICK.
o LOCAL ENTERPRISE OFFICE LOUTH.
o LOCAL ENTERPRISE OFFICE MAYO.
o LOCAL ENTERPRISE OFFICE MONAGHAN.
o LOCAL ENTERPRISE OFFICE OFFALY.
o LOCAL ENTERPRISE OFFICE ROSCOMMON.
o LOCAL ENTERPRISE OFFICE SLIGO.
o LOCAL ENTERPRISE OFFICE SOUTH CORK.
o LOCAL ENTERPRISE OFFICE WESTMEATH.
o LOCAL ENTERPRISE OFFICE WICKLOW.
o LOCAL ENTERPRISE OFFIFES.
o LONGFORD COMMUNITY RESOURCES LTD.
o LONGFORD LOCAL ENTERPRISE OFFICE.

o   LOUTH LEADER PARTNERSHIP.
o   MAYO NORTH EAST LEADER PARTNERSHIP.
o   MEATH LOCAL ENTERPRISE OFFICE.
o   MEATH PARTNERSHIP.
o   MONAGHAN INTEGRATED DEVELOPMENT LTD.
o   MOY VALLEY RESOURCES IRD.
o   NEW FRONTIERS.
o   NORTH TIPPERARY LEADER PARTNERSHIP.
o   NORTH, EAST & WEST KERRY DEVLOPMENT.
o   OFFALY INTEGRATED LOCAL DEVELOPMENT CLG.
o   ROSCOMMON LEADER PARTNERSHIP.
o   SOCIAL INNOVATION FUND IRELAND.
o   SOUTH & EAST CORK AREA DEVELOPMENT LTD.
o   SOUTH KERRY DEVELOPMENT PARTNERSHIP.
o   SOUTH TIPPERARY DEVELOPMENT CLG.
o   SOUTH WEST MAYO DEVELOPMENT COMPANY CLG.
o   START UP REFUNDS FOR ENTREPRENEURS.
o   STRATEGIC BANKING CORPORATION OF IRELAND.
o   TIPPERARY LOCAL ENTERPRISE OFFICE.
o   ÚDARÁS NA GAELTACHTA.
o   WATERFORD LEADER PARTNERSHIP CLG.
o   WATERFORD LOCAL ENTERPRISE OFFICE.
o   WEST LIMERICK RESOURCES LTD.
o   WESTERN DEVELOPMENT COMMISSION.
o   WESTMEATH COMMUNITY DEVELOPMENT LTD.
o   WEXFORD LOCAL DEVELOPMENT.
o   WEXFORD LOCAL ENTERPRISE OFFICE.

Incubation & Work space

o   ARCLABS.
o   ATHLONE INSTITUTE OF TECHNOLOGY.
o   BALLYHOURA DEVELOPMENT CLG.
o   BUSINESS INCUBATION CENTRE.
o   BUSINESS INNOVATION CENTRE NUI GALWAY.
o   CAVAN COUNTY ENTERPRISE FUND.
o   CAVAN INNOVATION & TECHNOLOGY CENTRE.
o   COLAB LYIT.
o   CORK INCUBATOR KITCHEN.

- o   CORK INSTITUTE OF TECHNOLOGY.
- o   CROOM COMMUNITY ENTERPRISE CENTRE.
- o   DCU ALPHA INNOVATION CAMPUS.
- o   DCU INVENT.
- o   DIGITAL HUB DEVELOPMENT AGENCY.
- o   DIT HOTHOUSE.
- o   DUBLIN CITY UNIVERSITY.
- o   DUBLIN INSTITUTE OF TECHNOLOGY.
- o   DUNDALK INSTITUTE OF TECHNOLOGY.
- o   ENTERPRISE & RESEARCH INNOVATION CAMPUS.
- o   ENTERPRISING MONAGHAN.
- o   GALWAY-MAYO INSTITUTE OF TECHNOLOGY.
- o   GATEWAY UCC.
- o   GMIT INNOVATION HUBS.
- o   HARTNETT ENTERPRISE ACCELERATOR CENTRE.
- o   IADT MEDIA CUBE.
- o   INNOVATION CENTRE.
- o   INSTITUTE OF ART, DESIGN & TECHNOLOGY.
- o   INSTITUTE OF TECHNOLOGY BLANCHARDSTOWN.
- o   INSTITUTE OF TECHNOLOGY CARLOW.
- o   INSTITUTE OF TECHNOLOGY SLIGO.
- o   INSTITUTE OF TECHNOLOGY TRALEE.
- o   IRD KILTIMAGH.
- o   ITT DUBLIN.
- o   LETTERKENNY INSTITUTE OF TECHNOLOGY.
- o   LIMERICK ENTERPRISE DEVELOPMENT PARTNERSHIP.
- o   LIMERICK INSTITUTE OF TECHNOLOGY.
- o   MAYNOOTHWORKS.
- o   MIDLANDS INNOVATION & RESEARCH CENTRE.
- o   MOY VALLEY RESOURCES IRD.
- o   NATIONAL COLLEGE OF IRELAND.
- o   NATIONAL FRANCHISE CENTRE.
- o   NATIONAL UNIVERSITY OF IRELAND GALWAY.
- o   NATIONAL UNIVERSITY OF IRELAND MAYNOOTH.
- o   NEXUS INNOVATION CENTRE.
- o   NOVAUCD
- o   ORIGIN8.
- o   QUESTUM ACCLERATOR CENTRE.

- REGIONAL DEVELOPMENT CENTRE.
- RUBICON CENTRE.
- SHANNON COMMERCIAL PROPERTIES.
- SHANNON GROUP.
- SLIGO ENTERPRISE & TECHNOLOGY CENTRE.
- SYNERGY CENTRE.
- SYNERGY GLOBAL.
- THE LINC.
- TOM CREAN BUSINESS CENTRE.
- TRINITY COLLEGE DUBLIN.
- TRINITY TECHNOLOGY & ENTERPRISE CAMPUS.
- ÚDARÁS NA GAELTACHTA.
- UNIVERSITY COLLEGE CORK.
- UNIVERSITY COLLEGE DUBLIN.
- UNIVERSITY OF LIMERICK.
- WATERFORD INSTITUTE OF TECHNOLOGY.
- WESTMEATH COMMUNITY DEVELOPMENT LTD.

Information

- ;OCAL ENTERPRISE OFFICES.
- BeSMART.ie.
- BORD BIA.
- BORDBIAVANTAGE.
- BUSINESS INFORMATION CENTRE.
- BUSINESSREGULATION.ie.
- CENTRAL STATISTICS OFFICE.
- COMPANIES REGISTRATION OFFICE.
- DCCOIENTERPRISE.ie.
- DEPARTMENT OF EMPLOYMENT AFFAIRS & SOCIAL PROTECTION.
- DONEGAL LOCAL ENTERPRISE OFFICE.
- DUBLIN SOUTH LOCAL ENTERPRISE OFFICE.
- ENTERPRISE IRELAND.
- ENVIRONMENTAL PROTECTION AGENCY.
- FÁILTE IRELAND.
- FOOD SAFETY AUTHORITY OF IRELAND.
- GOV.ie.
- GOVERNMENT PUBLICATIONS OFFICE.
- HEALTH & SAFETY AUTHORITY.

- IRISH SINGLE POINT OF CONTACT.
- KERRY LOCAL ENTERPRISE OFFICE.
- KNOWLEDGE TRANSFER IRELAND.
- LEITRIM LOCAL ENTERPRISE OFFICE.
- LOCAL ENTERPRISE OFFICE CARLOW.
- LOCAL ENTERPRISE OFFICE CAVAN.
- LOCAL ENTERPRISE OFFICE CLARE.
- LOCAL ENTERPRISE OFFICE CORK CITY.
- LOCAL ENTERPRISE OFFICE CORK NORTH & WEST.
- LOCAL ENTERPRISE OFFICE DUBLIN CITY.
- LOCAL ENTERPRISE OFFICE DUN LAOGHAIRE-RATHDOWN.
- LOCAL ENTERPRISE OFFICE FINGAL.
- LOCAL ENTERPRISE OFFICE GALWAY.
- LOCAL ENTERPRISE OFFICE KILDARE.
- LOCAL ENTERPRISE OFFICE KILKENNY.
- LOCAL ENTERPRISE OFFICE LAOIS.
- LOCAL ENTERPRISE OFFICE LIMERICK.
- LOCAL ENTERPRISE OFFICE LOUTH.
- LOCAL ENTERPRISE OFFICE MAYO.
- LOCAL ENTERPRISE OFFICE MONAGHAN.
- LOCAL ENTERPRISE OFFICE OFFALY.
- LOCAL ENTERPRISE OFFICE ROSCOMMON.
- LOCAL ENTERPRISE OFFICE SLIGO.
- LOCAL ENTERPRISE OFFICE SOUTH CORK.
- LOCAL ENTERPRISE OFFICE WESTMEATH.
- LOCAL ENTERPRISE OFFICE WICKLOW.
- LONGFORD LOCAL ENTERPRISE OFFICE.
- MEATH LOCAL ENTERPRISE OFFICE.
- NATIONAL STANDARDS AUTHORITY OF IRELAND.
- OFFICE OF THE DIRECTOR OF CORPORATE ENFORCEMENT.
- PATENTS OFFICE.
- REVENUE COMMISSIONERS
- SUPPORTINGSMES.ie.
- TIPPERARY LOCAL ENTERPRISE OFFICE.
- WATERFORD LOCAL ENTERPRISE OFFICE.
- WEXFORD LOCAL ENTERPRISE OFFICE.
- WORKPLACERELATIONS.ie.

Innovation & R&D

o   ARCLABS.
o   ATHLONE INSTITUTE OF TECHNOLOGY.
o   BALLYHOURA DEVELOPMENT CLG.
o   COLAB LYIT.
o   DCU INVENT.
o   DIT HOTHOUSE.
o   DUBLIN INSTITUTE OF TECHNOLOGY.
o   EDEN CENTRE FOR DESIGN, ENTREPRENEURSHIP & INNOVATION.
o   FOOD PRODUCT DEVELOPMENT CENTRE.
o   GALWAY-MAYO INSTITUTE OF TECHNOLOGY.
o   GATEWAY UCC.
o   GMIT INNOVATION HUBS.
o   INNOVATION CENTRE.
o   INSTITUTE OF TECHNOLOGY BLANCHARDSTOWN.
o   INSTITUTE OF TECHNOLOGY CARLOW.
o   INSTITUTE OF TECHNOLOGY SLIGO.
o   INSTITUTE OF TECHNOLOGY TRALEE.
o   ITT DUBLIN.
o   KILKENNY RESEARCH & INNOVATION CENTRE.
o   LETTERKENNY INSTITUTE OF TECHNOLOGY.
o   LIMERICK INSTITUTE OF TECHNOLOGY.
o   MARINE INSTITUTE.
o   NATIONAL UNIVERSITY OF IRELAND GALWAY.
o   NATIONAL UNIVERSITY OF IRELAND MAYNOOTH.
o   NOVAUCD.
o   ORIGIN8.
o   TEAGASC.
o   TRINITY COLLEGE DUBLIN.
o   TYNDALL NATIONAL INSTITUTE.
o   UNIVERSITY COLLEGE CORK.
o   UNIVERSITY COLLEGE DUBLIN.
o   UNIVERSITY OF LIMERICK.
o   WATERFORD INSTITUTE OF TECHNOLOGY.
o   WORKPLACE INNOVATION TOOLKIT.

Intellectual Property & Legal

o   OFFICE OF THE DIRECTOR OF CORPORATE ENFORCEMENT.

o PATENTS OFFICE.
o WORKPLACERELATIONS.ie.

Inwards Investment

o IDA IRELAND.
o IRISH NATURALISATION & IMMIGRATION SERVICE.

Marketing

o BORD BIA.
o BORD IASCAIGH MHARA.
o DESIGN & CRAFTS COUNCIL OF IRELAND.
o DUBLIN FOOD CHAIN.
o FÁILTE IRELAND.

Networking

o COLAB LYIT.
o DUBLIN FOOD CHAIN.
o INNOVATION CENTRE.
o MAYNOOTHWORKS.

Policy

o DEPARTMENT OF AGRICULTURE, FOOD & THE MARINE.
o DEPARTMENT OF BUSINESS, ENTERPRISE & INNOVATION.
o DEPARTMENT OF EMPLOYMENT AFFAIRS & SOCIAL PROTECTION.
o DEPARTMENT OF HOUSING, PLANNING & LOCAL GOVERNMENT.
o DEPARTMENT OF JUSTICE & EQUALITY.
o DEPARTMENT OF RURAL & COMMUNITY DEVELOPMENT.
o EASTERN & MIDLAND REGIONAL ASSEMBLY.
o MARINE INSTITUTE.
o NORTHERN & WESTERN REGIONAL ASSEMBLY.
o SOUTHERN REGIONAL ASSEMBLY.
o WESTERN DEVELOPMENT COMMISSION.

Regulation & Standards

o BORD BIA.
o BORD IASCAIGH MHARA.
o BUSINESSREGULATION.ie.
o COMPANIES REGISTRATION OFFICE.

- o   COMPETITION & CONSUMER PROTECTION COMMISSION.
- o   CREDIT REVIEW OFFICE.
- o   DATA PROTECTION COMMISSION.
- o   DEPARTMENT OF AGRICULTURE, FOOD & THE MARINE.
- o   DEPARTMENT OF BUSINESS, ENTERPRISE & INNOVATION.
- o   DEPARTMENT OF EMPLOYMENT AFFAIRS & SOCIAL PROTECTION.
- o   DEPARTMENT OF HOUSING, PLANNING & LOCAL GOVERNMENT.
- o   DEPARTMENT OF JUSTICE & EQUALITY.
- o   DEPARTMENT OF RURAL & COMMUNITY DEVELOPMENT.
- o   ENVIRONMENTAL PROTECTION AGENCY.
- o   FOOD SAFETY AUTHORITY OF IRELAND.
- o   HEALTH & SAFETY AUTHORITY.
- o   IRISH NATURALISATION & IMMIGRATION SERVICE.
- o   LICENCES.ie.
- o   NATIONAL STANDARDS AUTHORITY OF IRELAND.
- o   OFFICE OF THE DIRECTOR OF CORPORATE ENFORCEMENT.
- o   PATENTS OFFICE.
- o   REVENUE COMMISSIONERS.
- o   SEA-FISHERIES PROTECTION AGENCY.

Social Enterprise

- o   CENTRE FOR CO-OPERATIVE STUDIES.
- o   DONEGAL LOCAL DEVELOPMENT COMPANY CLG.
- o   FORUM CONNEMARA CLG.
- o   GALWAY CITY PARTNERSHIP.
- o   MOY VALLEY RESOURCES IRD.
- o   NORTHSIDE PARTNERSHIP.
- o   PAUL PARTNERSHIP LIMERICK.
- o   SOCIAL INNOVATION FUND IRELAND.
- o   SOUTH DUBLIN COUNTY PARTNERSHIP.
- o   SOUTHSIDE PARTNERSHIP DLR LTD.

Training & Mentoring

- o   ARCLABS.
- o   ATHLONE INSTITUTE OF TECHNOLOGY.
- o   BALLYFERMOT CHAPELIZOD PARTNERSHIP COMPANY LIMITED.
- o   BORD BIA.
- o   BORD IASCAIGH MHARA.

- o BORDBIAVANTAGE.
- o BRAY AREA PARTNERSHIP.
- o BREFFNI INTEGRATED CLG.
- o BUSINESS INCUBATION CENTRE.
- o BUSINESS INNOVATION CENTRE NUI GALWAY.
- o CARLOW COUNTY DEVELOPMENT PARTNERSHIP CLG.
- o CAVAN INNOVATION & TECHNOLOGY CENTRE.
- o CENTRE FOR CO-OPERATIVE STUDIES.
- o CLARE LOCAL DEVELOPMENT COMPANY LTD.
- o COLAB LYIT.
- o CORK CITY PARTNERSHIP CLG.
- o CORK INSTITUTE OF TECHNOLOGY.
- o COUNTY SLIGO LEADER PARTNERSHIP COMPANY LTD.
- o COUNTY WICKLOW PARTNERSHIP.
- o DCCOIENTERPRISE.ie.
- o DCU INVENT.
- o DCU RYAN ACADEMY.
- o DESIGN & CRAFTS COUNCIL OF IRELAND.
- o DIT HOTHOUSE.
- o DONEGAL LOCAL DEVELOPMENT COMPANY CLG.
- o DONEGAL LOCAL ENTERPRISE OFFICE.
- o DUBLIN CITY UNIVERSITY.
- o DUBLIN FOOD CHAIN.
- o DUBLIN INSTITUTE OF TECHNOLOGY.
- o DUBLIN NORTH WEST AREA PARTNERSHIP.
- o DUBLIN SOUTH CITY PARTNERSHIP.
- o DUBLIN SOUTH LOCAL ENTERPRISE OFFICE.
- o DUNDALK INSTITUTE OF TECHNOLOGY.
- o EDEN CENTRE FOR DESIGN, ENTREPRENEURSHIP & INNOVATION.
- o EMPOWER.
- o ENTERPRISE & RESEARCH INNOVATION CAMPUS.
- o ENTERPRISE IRELAND.
- o FÁILTE IRELAND.
- o FINGAL LEADER PARTNERSHIP.
- o FOOD ACADEMY.
- o FOOD PRODUCT DEVELOPMENT CENTRE.
- o FOOD SAFETY AUTHORITY OF IRELAND.
- o FOODWORKS.

- o GALWAY CITY PARTNERSHIP.
- o GALWAY RURAL DEVELOPMENT COMPANY.
- o GALWAY-MAYO INSTITUTE OF TECHNOLOGY.
- o GATEWAY UCC.
- o GMIT INNOVATION HUBS.
- o HARTNETT ENTERPRISE ACCELERATION CENTRE.
- o HEALTH & SAFETY AUTHORITY.
- o HSALEARNING.ie.
- o IADT MEDIA CUBE.
- o INISHOWEN DEVELOPMENT PARTNERSHIP.
- o INNOVATION CENTRE.
- o INSTITUTE FOR MINORITY ENTREPRENEURSHIP.
- o INSTITUTE OF ART, DESIGN & TECHNOLOGY.
- o INSTITUTE OF TECHNOLOGY BLANCHARDSTOWN.
- o INSTITUTE OF TECHNOLOGY CARLOW.
- o INSTITUTE OF TECHNOLOGY SLIGO.
- o INSTITUTE OF TECHNOLOGY TRALEE.
- o IRD DUHALLOW LTD.
- o IRD KILTIMAGH.
- o ITT DUBLIN.
- o KERRY LOCAL ENTERPRISE OFFICE.
- o LEITRIM INTEGRATED DEVELOPMENT COMPANY LTD.
- o LEITRIM LOCAL ENTERPRISE OFFICE.
- o LETTERKENNY INSTITUTE OF TECHNOLOGY.
- o LIMERICK INSTITUTE OF TECHNOLOGY.
- o LOCAL ENTERPRISE OFFICE CARLOW.
- o LOCAL ENTERPRISE OFFICE CAVAN.
- o LOCAL ENTERPRISE OFFICE CLARE.
- o LOCAL ENTERPRISE OFFICE CORK CITY.
- o LOCAL ENTERPRISE OFFICE CORK NORTH & WEST.
- o LOCAL ENTERPRISE OFFICE DUBLIN CITY.
- o LOCAL ENTERPRISE OFFICE DUN LAOGHAIRE-RATHDOWN.
- o LOCAL ENTERPRISE OFFICE FINGAL.
- o LOCAL ENTERPRISE OFFICE GALWAY.
- o LOCAL ENTERPRISE OFFICE KILDARE.
- o LOCAL ENTERPRISE OFFICE KILKENNY.
- o LOCAL ENTERPRISE OFFICE LAOIS.
- o LOCAL ENTERPRISE OFFICE LIMERICK.

- LOCAL ENTERPRISE OFFICE LOUTH.
- LOCAL ENTERPRISE OFFICE MAYO.
- LOCAL ENTERPRISE OFFICE MONAGHAN.
- LOCAL ENTERPRISE OFFICE OFFALY.
- LOCAL ENTERPRISE OFFICE ROSCOMMON.
- LOCAL ENTERPRISE OFFICE SLIGO.
- LOCAL ENTERPRISE OFFICE SOUTH CORK.
- LOCAL ENTERPRISE OFFICE WESTMEATH.
- LOCAL ENTERPRISE OFFICE WICKLOW.
- LOCAL ENTERPRISE OFFICES.
- LONGFORD LOCAL ENTERPRISE OFFICE.
- MAYNOOTHWORKS.
- MAYO NORTH EAST LEADER PARTNERSHIP.
- MEATH LOCAL ENTERPRISE OFFICE.
- MEATH PARTNERSHIP.
- MIDLANDS INNOVATION & RESEARCH CENTRE.
- MOY VALLEY RESOURCES IRD.
- NATIONAL COLLEGE OF IRELAND.
- NATIONAL FRANCHISE CENTRE.
- NATIONAL UNIVERSITY OF IRELAND GALWAY.
- NATIONAL UNIVERSITY OF IRELAND MAYNOOTH.
- NEW FRONTIERS.
- NEXUS INNOVATION CENTRE.
- NORTH TIPPERARY LEADER PARTNERSHIP.
- NORTH, EAST & WEST KERRY DEVELOPMENT.
- NORTHSIDE PARTNERSHIP.
- OFFALY INTEGRATED LOCAL DEVELOPMENT CLG.
- PAUL PARTNERSHIP LIMERICK.
- REGIONAL DEVELOPMENT CENTRE.
- ROSCOMMON LEADER PARTNERSHIP.
- RUBICON CENTRE.
- SOLAS.
- SOUTH & EAST CORK AREA DEVELOPMENT LTD.
- SOUTHSIDE PARTNERSHIP DLR LTD.
- SUSTAINABLE ENERGY AUTHORITY OF IRELAND.
- SYNERGY CENTRE.
- TEAGASC.
- THE LINC.

- o TIPPERARY LOCAL ENTERPRISE OFFICE.
- o TOM CREAN BUSINESS CENTRE.
- o TRINITY COLLEGE DUBLIN.
- o UNIVERSITY COLLEGE CORK.
- o UNIVERSITY COLLEGE DUBLIN.
- o UNIVERSITY OF LIMERICK.
- o WATERFORD INSTITUTE OF TECHNOLOGY.
- o WATERFORD LOCAL ENTERPRISE OFFICE.
- o WESTMEATH COMMUNITY DEVELOPMENT LTD.
- o WEXFORD LOCAL DEVELOPMENT.
- o WEXFORD LOCAL ENTERPRISE OFFICE.

Young Enterprise

- o DONEGAL LOCAL ENTERPRISE OFFICE.
- o DUBLIN SOUTH LOCAL ENTERPRISE OFFICE.
- o ENTERPRISE IRELAND.
- o KERRY LOCAL ENTERPRISE OFFICE.
- o LEITRIM LOCAL ENTERPRISE OFFICE.
- o LOCAL ENTEPRRISE OFFICES.
- o LOCAL ENTERPRISE OFFICE CARLOW.
- o LOCAL ENTERPRISE OFFICE CAVAN.
- o LOCAL ENTERPRISE OFFICE CLARE.
- o LOCAL ENTERPRISE OFFICE CORK CITY.
- o LOCAL ENTERPRISE OFFICE CORK NORTH & WEST.
- o LOCAL ENTERPRISE OFFICE DUBLIN CITY.
- o LOCAL ENTERPRISE OFFICE DUN LAOGHAIRE-RATHDOWN.
- o LOCAL ENTERPRISE OFFICE FINGAL.
- o LOCAL ENTERPRISE OFFICE GALWAY.
- o LOCAL ENTERPRISE OFFICE KILDARE.
- o LOCAL ENTERPRISE OFFICE KILKENNY.
- o LOCAL ENTERPRISE OFFICE LAOIS.
- o LOCAL ENTERPRISE OFFICE LIMERICK.
- o LOCAL ENTERPRISE OFFICE LOUTH.
- o LOCAL ENTERPRISE OFFICE MAYO.
- o LOCAL ENTERPRISE OFFICE MONAGHAN.
- o LOCAL ENTERPRISE OFFICE OFFALY.
- o LOCAL ENTERPRISE OFFICE ROSCOMMON.
- o LOCAL ENTERPRISE OFFICE SLIGO.

- ○ LOCAL ENTERPRISE OFFICE SOUTH CORK.
- ○ LOCAL ENTERPRISE OFFICE WESTMEATH.
- ○ LOCAL ENTERPRISE OFFICE WICKLOW.
- ○ LONGFORD LOCAL ENTERPRISE OFFICE.
- ○ MEATH LOCAL ENTERPRISE OFFICE.
- ○ TIPPERARY LOCAL ENTERPRISE OFFICE.
- ○ WATERFORD LOCAL ENTERPRISE OFFICE.
- ○ WEXFORD LOCAL ENTERPRISE OFFICE.

6: PRIVATE SECTOR SUPPORT FOR START-UPS

If confusion exists in the State sector due to the number of organisations that provide support for enterprise, it's nothing compared to the private sector, where the range of organisations – and the breadth of their activities – is even greater and lacks any form of co-ordination.

Support by Category

The simplest way through this maze is to identify the main private sector enterprise support organisations by the type of support they provide (clearly, some fit into more than one category). Check the *Directory* for information on the various categories.

Accounting & Business Planning

o   ACCA EUROPE.
o   AISLING SOFTWARE.
o   BIG RED BOOK.
o   BULLET.
o   BYRNE & MCCALL.
o   CHARTERED ACCOUNTANTS IRELAND.
o   CHARTERED INSTITUTE OF MANAGEMENT ACCOUNTANTS.
o   INSTITUTE OF CERTIFIED PUBLIC ACCOUNTANTS IN IRELAND.
o   INVEST-TECH.
o   LIFFEY TRUST.
o   LIVEPLAN.com.
o   SAGE IRELAND.

Community & Rural Development

o   ACE ENTERPRISE PARK.
o   ALLENWOOD COMMUNITY DEVELOPMENT ASSOCIATION LTD.
o   ARDEE COMMUNITY DEVELOPMENT COMPANY LTD.
o   CLANN CREDO.

- CONNEMARA WEST.
- DUBLIN CITY COMMUNITY CO-OP.
- IRISH LOCAL DEVELOPMENT NETWORK.
- IRISH RURAL LINK.
- MOUNTMELLICK DEVELOPMENT ASSOCIATION.
- NATIONAL RURAL NETWORK.
- PARTAS.
- PREMIER SERVICES.
- SCHOOL OF FOOD.
- TALLOW ENTERPRISE CENTRE.
- TERENURE ENTERPRISE CENTRE.
- WEST CORK DEVELOPMENT PARTNERSHIP LTD.

Consulting

- AMÁRACH CONSULTING.
- ENERGY CO-OPERATIVES IRELAND.
- INSTITUTE OF MANAGEMENT CONSULTANTS & ADVISERS.
- KILLARNEY TECHNOLOGY INNOVATION LTD.
- LIFFEY TRUST.
- OPTIMUM RESULTS.

Enterprise Support

- BOLTON TRUST.

Franchises

- FRANCHISEDIRECT.
- IRISH FRANCHISE ASSOCIATION.
- ULSTER BANK.

Funding

- 4TH LEVEL VENTURES LTD.
- ACT VENTURE CAPITAL LTD.
- AIB BANK.
- ATLANTIC BRIDGE.
- BANK OF IRELAND.
- BROADLAKE.
- BUSINESS VENTURE PARTNERS.
- CLANCY BUSINESS FINANCE LTD.

- CLANN CREDO.
- COMMUNITY FINANCE (IRELAND).
- DELTA PARTNERS.
- DRAPER ESPRIT.
- ENTERPRISE EQUITY.
- FINISTERE VENTURES.
- FOCUS CAPITAL PARTNERS.
- FOUNTAIN HEALTHCARE PARTNERS.
- FRONTLINE VENTURES.
- FUNDIT.
- GUINNESS WORKERS' EMPLOYMENT FUND.
- HALO BUSINESS ANGEL NETWORK.
- INNER CITY ENTERPRISE.
- IRISH LEAGUE OF CREDIT UNIONS.
- IRISH VENTURE CAPITAL ASSOCIATION.
- KERNEL CAPITAL PARTNERS.
- KICKSTARTER.
- LINKEDFINANCE.
- LOMBARD.
- LOUGH SHORE INVESTMENTS.
- LOUTH CRAFTMARK.
- MICROFINANCE IRELAND.
- MML GROWTH CAPITAL PARTNERS.
- NDRC.
- OYSTER CAPITAL PARTNERS.
- PERMANENT TSB.
- POLARIS PARTNERS.
- POWERSCOURT CAPITAL PARTNERS.
- SCREEN IRELAND.
- SEEDUPS.ie.
- SEROBA LIFE SCIENCES LTD.
- SOCIAL ENTREPRENEURS IRELAND.
- SOS VENTURES.
- SPARK CROWDFUNDING.
- SUIR VALLEY VENTURES.
- ULSTER BANK.
- WHITEROCK CAPITAL PARTNERS.

Incubation & Work space

o   ACE ENTERPRISE PARK.
o   ALLENWOOD COMMUNITY DEVELOPMENT ASSOCIATION LTD.
o   ARDEE COMMUNITY DEVELOPMENT COMPANY LTD.
o   ARKLOW BUSINESS ENTERPRISE CENTRE.
o   ATHY COMMUNITY ENTERPRISE COMPANY LTD.
o   BAILIEBOROUGH BUSINESS CENTRE.
o   BALBRIGGAN ENTERPRISE & TRAINING CENTRE.
o   BALBRIGGAN ENTERPRISE DEVELOPMENT GROUP.
o   BALLINAMORE ENTERPRISE CENTRE.
o   BALLINASLOE AREA COMMUNITY DEVELOPMENT LTD.
o   BALLYHAUNIS ENTERPRISE CENTRE.
o   BANK OF IRELAND WORKBENCH.
o   BASE ENTERPRISE CENTRE CLG.
o   BNEST.
o   BOLTON TRUST.
o   BOYLE ENTERPRISE & MORE.
o   CARLOW COMMUNITY ENTERPRISE CENTRES LTD.
o   CARRICK BUSINESS CENTRE.
o   CASTLEBLAYNEY ENTERPRISE CENTRE.
o   CASTLECOMER ENTERPRISE GROUP LTD.
o   CLANE PROJECT CENTRE.
o   CONVOY ENTERPRISE CENTRE.
o   COOLOCK DEVELOPMENT COUNCIL.
o   COWORKING IN IRELAND.
o   CREATIVE SPARK CLG.
o   DOGPATCH LABS.
o   DRINAN ENTERPRISE CENTRE.
o   DRUMSHANBO ENTERPRISE CENTRE.
o   DÚN LAOIRE ENTERPRISE CENTRE.
o   DUNGARVAN ENTERPRISE CENTRE.
o   DUNHILL ECOPARK.
o   ENNISCORTHY INCUBATION & TECHNOLOGY CENTRE.
o   ENNISTYMON ENTERPRISE CENTRE LTD.
o   ENTERPRISE YOUGHAL.
o   FERBANE BUSINESS & TECHNOLOGY PARK.
o   FERBANE FOOD CAMPUS.

o FIONTARLANN TEO.

o FOOD HUB.

o FUMBALLY EXCHANGE.

o GALWAY TECHNOLOGY CENTRE.

o GUINNESS ENTERPRISE CENTRE.

o HOUR KITCHEN.

o JOE GILMORE ENTERPRISE CENTRE.

o KELLS ENTERPRISE & TECHNOLOGY CENTRE.

o KILLARNEY TECHNOLOGY INNOVATION LTD.

o LIFFEY TRUST.

o LUDGATE HUB.

o MACROOM E BUSINESS CENTRE.

o MEATH ENTERPRISE.

o MOHILL ENTERPRISE CENTRE.

o MOUNTMELLICK DEVELOPMENT ASSOCIATION.

o MULLINGAR EMPLOYMENT ACTION GROUP.

o NATIONAL ASSOCIATION OF COMMUNITY ENTERPRISE CENTRES.

o NEWMARKET KITCHEN.

o NORTH TIPPERARY FOODWORKS.

o NORTHSIDE ENTERPRISE CENTRE.

o NSC CAMPUS.

o NUTGROVE ENTERPRISE PARK.

o PARTAS.

o PILTOWN COMMUNITY ENTERPRISE.

o PLUS 10.

o PORTARLINGTON ENTERPRISE CENTRE.

o PORTLAOISE ENTERPRISE CENTRE.

o PREMIER BUSINESS CENTRES.

o REPUBLIC OF WORK.

o SCCUL ENTERPRISE CENTRE.

o SCHOOL OF FOOD.

o SPADE ENTERPRISE CENTRE.

o TALENT GARDEN DUBLIN.

o TALLOW ENTERPRISE CENTRE.

o TERENURE ENTERPRISE CENTRE.

o THE BASE ENTERPRISE CENTRE.

o THE HIVE.

o WEXFORD ENTERPRISE CENTRE.

o WICKLOW ENTERPRISE CENTRE.

Information
o AIB BANK.
o BUSINESS PLUS.
o BUSINESS POST.
o BUSINESSACHIEVERS.com.
o CREATIVEIRELAND.com.
o ENERGY CO-OPERATIVES IRELAND.
o FOUNTAIN RESOURCE GROUP.
o FRANCHISEDIRECT.
o INSTITUTE OF MANAGEMENT CONSULTANTS & ADVISERS.
o INSTITUTE OF PUBLIC ADMINISTRATION.
o OAK TREE PRESS.
o SILICONREPUBLIC.com.
o STARTUPS.ie.
o TERENURE ENTERPRISE CENTRE
o THINKBUSINESS.ie.
o WOMENMEANBUSINESS.ie.

Innovation & R&D
o FOOD HUB.
o MEATH ENTERPRISE.
o TECHNOLOGY IRELAND.
o TECHNOLOGY IRELAND INNOVATION FORUM.
o YOUNG SOCIAL INNOVATORS.

IP & Legal
o ANNE RYAN & CO.
o CHARTERED INSTITUTE FOR PERSONNEL & DEVELOPMENT.
o COMPANY FORMATIONS INTERNATIONAL LTD.
o COMPANY SETUP.
o CRUICKSHANK & CO.
o DEFINITION IP.
o FF GORMAN & CO.
o FR KELLY & CO.
o HANNA MOORE & CURLEY.
o ISLAND PATENTS.

- o LAW SOCIETY OF IRELAND.
- o MacLACHLAN & DONALDSON.
- o MURGITROYD.
- o O'BRIEN (JOHN A.) & ASSOCIATES.
- o O'CONNOR IP.
- o PURDYLUCEY.
- o RDJSTARTUPS.ie.
- o SMALL FIRMS ASSOCIATION.
- o TOMKINS.
- o WELDON (MICHAEL) & CO.

Inwards Investment

- o BYRNE & McCALL.

Marketing

- o AMÁRACH CONSULTING.
- o ASPIRE! MARKETING CONSULTANTS.
- o EXCELLENCE IRELAND QUALITY ASSOCIATION.
- o GUARANTEED IRISH.
- o LIFFEY TRUST.
- o LOUTH CRAFTMARK.
- o MARKETING INSTITUTE OF IRELAND.
- o PUBLIC RELATIONS CONSULTANTS ASSOCIATION OF IRELAND.
- o PUBLIC RELATIONS INSTITUTE OF IRELAND.
- o SALES INSTITUTE OF IRELAND.

Networking

- o BANK OF IRELAND WORKBENCH.
- o BUSINESSACHIEVERS.com.
- o CHAMBERS IRELAND.
- o CREATIVEIRELAND.com.
- o ENTREPRENEURS ANONYMOUS.
- o INSTITUTE OF DIRECTORS IN IRELAND.
- o IRISH COUNTRYWOMEN'S ASSOCIATION.
- o IRISH EXPORTERS ASSOCIATION.
- o IRISH INSTITUTE FOR TRAINING & DEVELOPMENT.
- o IRISH INTERNET ASSOCIATION.
- o IRISH MANAGEMENT INSTITUTE.

- o   IRISH SMALL & MEDIUM ENTERPRISES ASSOCIATION.
- o   LOUTH CRAFTMARK.
- o   LUDGATE HUB.
- o   NATIONAL GUILD OF CRAFTSMEN.
- o   NETWORK IRELAND.
- o   REPUBLIC OF WORK.
- o   SALES INSTITUTE OF IRELAND.
- o   SMALL FIRMS ASSOCIATION.
- o   TALENT GARDEN DUBLIN.
- o   TECHNOLOGY IRELAND INNOVATION FORUM.
- o   TECHNOLOGY IRELAND.
- o   WOMENMEANBUSINESS.com.

Policy

- o   IBEC.
- o   IRISH SMALL & MEDIUM ENTERPRISES ASSOCIATION.
- o   SMALL FIRMS ASSOCIATION.

Regulation & Standards

- o   EXCELLENCE IRELAND QUALITY ASSOCIATION.
- o   IE DOMAIN REGISTRY LTD.
- o   IRISH ORGANIC ASSOCIATION.
- o   NATIONAL GUILD OF MASTER CRAFTSMEN.

Social Enterprise

- o   BNEST.
- o   CLANE PROJECT CENTRE.
- o   CLANN CREDO.
- o   CO-OPERATIVE HOUSING IRELAND.
- o   COMMUNITY FINANCE (IRELAND).
- o   DUBLIN CITY COMMUNITY CO-OP.
- o   DUNHILL ECOPARK.
- o   ENACTUS IRELAND.
- o   ENERGY CO-OPERATIVES IRELAND.
- o   INNER CITY ENTERPRISE.
- o   IRISH CO-OPERATIVE SOCIETY LTD.
- o   IRISH LEAGUE OF CREDIT UNIONS.
- o   IRISH SOCIAL ENTERPRISE NETWORK.

- o   PARTAS.
- o   SOCIAL ENTERPRISE DEVELOPMENT COMPANY LTD.
- o   SOCIAL ENTREPRENEURS IRELAND.
- o   WEXFORD ENTERPRISE CENTRE.
- o   YOUNG SOCIAL INNOVATORS.

Training & Mentoring

- o   ACE ENTERPRISE PARK.
- o   ALLENWOOD COMMUNITY DEVELOPMENT ASSOCIATION LTD.
- o   ARDEE COMMUNITY DEVELOPMENT COMPANY LTD.
- o   ARKLOW BUSINESS ENTERPRISE CENTRE.
- o   ASPIRE! MARKETING CONSULTANTS.
- o   BALBRIGGAN ENTERPRISE & TRAINING CENTRE.
- o   BALBRIGGAN ENTERPRISE DEVELOPMENT GROUP.
- o   BIZMENTORS.ie.
- o   BLACKSTONE LAUNCHPAD.
- o   BNEST.
- o   CASTLEBLAYNEY ENTERPRISE CENTRE.
- o   CHARTERED INSTITUTE OF PERSONNEL & DEVELOPMENT.
- o   DRUMSHANBO ENTERPRISE CENTRE.
- o   DUNGARVAN ENTERPRISE CENTRE.
- o   DUNHILL ECOPARK.
- o   ENNISCORTHY ENTERPRISE CENTRE LTD.
- o   ENNISTYON ENTERPRISE CENTRE LTD.
- o   FOOD ACADEMY.
- o   FOOD HUB.
- o   FOUNTAIN RESOURCE GROUP.
- o   GOOGLE.
- o   INSTITUTE OF DIRECTORS IN IRELAND.
- o   IRISH COUNTRYWOMEN'S ASSOCIATION.
- o   IRISH EXPORTERS ASSOCIATION.
- o   IRISH INSTITUTE OF TRAINING & DEVELOPMENT.
- o   IRISH MANAGEMENT INSTITUTE.
- o   IRISH SMALL & MEDIUM ENTERPRISES ASSOCIATION.
- o   KELLS ENTERPRISE & TECHNOLOGY CENTRE.
- o   LARKIN UNEMPLOYED CENTRE.
- o   LIFFEY TRUST.
- o   MACROOM E BUSINESS CENTRE.

- MARKETING INSTITUTE OF IRELAND.
- MEATH ENTERPRISE.
- MICROFINANCE IRELAND.
- MOHILL ENTERPRISE CENTRE.
- MULLINGAR ENTERPRISE ACTION GROUP.
- NDRC.
- NETWORK IRELAND.
- NEWMARKET KITCHEN.
- OAK TREE PRESS.
- OPTIMUM RESULTS LTD.
- ORGANIC COLLEGE.
- PARTAS.
- PLATO DUBLIN.
- PORTARLINGTON ENTERPRISE CENTRE.
- SCHOOL OF FOOD.
- SMALL BUSINESS ADVICE.
- SMALL FIRMS ASSOCIATION.
- SMILE.
- TALENT GARDEN DUBLIN.
- TALLOW ENTERPRISE CENTRE.
- TERENURE ENTERPRISE CENTRE LTD.
- WESTERN MANAGEMENT CENTRE.
- WICKLOW ENTERPRISE CENTRE.
- YOUNG SOCIAL INNOVATORS.

Young Enterprise

- YOUNG SOCIAL INNOVATORS.

7: EU SUPPORT FOR START-UPS

Some EU institutions provide assistance direct to Irish start-up entrepreneurs – mainly in the form of information or policy, though sometimes through funding also. However, most EU support for start-ups is delivered indirectly – for example:

- The Global Loan Facility for SMEs from the European Investment Bank, which cannot be accessed by businesses directly but is made available through the major banks.
- The European Investment Fund, which has invested in a number of Irish venture capital funds.
- EU Structural Funds, which support Government spending.
- BUSINESS INNOVATION CENTRES.
- LEADER.
- CO-INNOVATE PROGRAMME, funded by INTERREG and delivered by InterTradeIreland.

Business Innovation Centres

The five Business Innovation Centres in Ireland (a list appears in the *Directory*) are part of an EU-funded, EU-wide network, primarily targeted at technology-based businesses. They encourage and foster innovation in new or existing businesses, through services directed at the development of new ideas and their conversion into real business projects. As BIC support services may vary between centres, entrepreneurs seeking assistance should make contact with their local BIC to see whether and what help is available.

LEADER

LEADER (*Liaison Entre Actions pour le Development de l'Économie Rurale*) is an EU initiative for rural development (part-funded by the Irish Government) and is administered by Local Action Groups (LAGs). These are partnerships of both public and private entities from a defined geographical area. They are responsible for selecting and approving projects in their areas in accordance with local development strategies developed specifically for their area under the following themes:

- Economic development, enterprise development and job creation.
- Social inclusion.
- Rural environment.

A list of LEADER LAGs appears in the *Directory*, with separate entries for each LAG. Check the *Directory* for information on the various categories.

Full information on the European Union and its support for enterprise is available on the **Europa** website.

Support by Category

Accounting & Business Planning
- ○ MOY VALLEY RESOURCES IRD.
- ○ WESTBIC.

Community & Rural Development
- ○ ARDS & NORTH DOWN RURAL AREA PARTNERSHIP.
- ○ AVONDHU BLACKWATER PARTNERSHIP.
- ○ BALLYHOURA DEVELOPMENT CLG.
- ○ BREFFNI INTEGRATED CLG.
- ○ CARLOW COUNTY DEVELOPMENT PARTNERSHIP CLG.
- ○ CAUSEWAY COAST & GLENS LOCAL ACTION GROUP.
- ○ CLARE LOCAL DEVELOPMENT COMPANY.
- ○ COMHAR NA NOILEÁN CTR.
- ○ COUNTY KILDARE LEADER PARTNERSHIP.
- ○ COUNTY SLIGO LEADER PARTNERSHIP COMPANY.
- ○ COUNTY WICKLOW PARTNERSHIP.
- ○ DERRY & STRABANE RURAL PARTNERSHIP.
- ○ DONEGAL LOCAL DEVELOPMENT COMPANY.
- ○ FERMANAGH & OMAGH LOCAL ACTION GROUP.
- ○ FINGAL LEADER PARTNERSHIP.
- ○ FORUM CONNEMARA CLG.

o   GALWAY RURAL DEVELOPMENT COMPANY.
o   GROW SOUTH ANTRIM.
o   INISHOWEN DEVELOPMENT PARTNERSHIP.
o   IRD DUHALLOW LTD.
o   KILKENNY LEADER PARTNERSHIP LTD.
o   LAGAN RURAL PARTNERSHIP.
o   LAOIS PARTNERSHIP COMPANY.
o   LEITRIM INTEGRATED DEVELOPMENT COMPANY LTD.
o   LONGFORD COMMUNITY RESOURCES LTD.
o   LOUTH LEADER PARTNERSHIP.
o   MAYO NORTH EAST LEADER PARTNERSHIP.
o   MEATH PARTNERSHIP.
o   MID & EAST ANTRIM LOCAL ACTION GROUP.
o   MID ULSTER RURAL DEVELOPMENT PARTNERSHIP.
o   MONAGHAN INTEGRATED DEVELOPMENT LTD.
o   MOURNE, GULLION & LECALE RURAL DEVELOPMENT PARTNERSHIP.
o   MOY VALLEY RESOURCES.
o   NORTH TIPPERARY LEADER PARTNERSHIP.
o   NORTH, EAST & WEST KERRY DEVLOPMENT.
o   OFFALY INTEGRATED LOCAL DEVELOPMENT CLG.
o   ROSCOMMON LEADER PARTNERSHIP.
o   SOAR (ABC).
o   SOUTH & EAST CORK AREA DEVELOPMENT LTD.
o   SOUTH KERRY DEVELOPMENT PARTNERSHIP.
o   SOUTH TIPPERARY DEVELOPMENT CLG.
o   SOUTH WEST MAYO DEVELOPMENT COMPANY CLG.
o   ÚDARÁS NA GAELTACHTA.
o   WATERFORD LEADER PARTNERSHIP CLG.
o   WEST LIMERICK RESOURCES LTD.
o   WESTMEATH COMMUNITY DEVELOPMENT LTD.
o   WEXFORD LOCAL DEVELOPMENT.

Consulting

o   CORK BUSINESS INNOVATION CENTRE.
o   SOUTH EAST BUSINESS INNOVATION CENTRE.

Cross-Border

o CO-INNOVATE PROGRAMME.

Enterprise Support

o COSME.
o KILKENNY LEADER PARTNERSHIP LTD.

Funding

o ARDS & NORTH DOWN RURAL AREA PARTNERSHIP
o AVONDHU BLACKWATER PARTNERSHIP.
o BALLYHOURA DEVELOPMENT CLG.
o BREFFNI INTEGRATED CLG.
o CARLOW COUNTY DEVELOPMENT PARTNERSHIP CLG.
o CAUSEWAY COAST & GLENS LOCAL ACTION GROUP.
o CLARE LOCAL DEVELOPMENT COMPANY.
o COMHAR NA NOILEÁN TEO.
o COSME.
o COUNTY KILDARE LEADER PARTNERSHIP.
o COUNTY SLIGO LEADER PARTNERSHIP COMPANY.
o COUNTY WICKLOW PARTNERSHIP.
o CRUCIAL CROWDFUNDING.
o DERRY & STRABANE RURAL PARTNERSHIP.
o DONEGAL LOCAL DEVELOPMENT COMPANY.
o DUBLIN BUSINESS INNOVATION CENTRE.
o EUROPEAN INVESTMENT PORTAL.
o EUROPEAN SPACE AGENCY.
o EXECUTIVE AGENCY FOR SMES.
o FERMANAGH & OMAGH LOCAL ACTION GROUP.
o FINGAL LEADER PARTNERSHIP.
o FORUM CONNEMARA CLG.
o GALWAY RURAL DEVELOPMENT COMPANY.
o GROW SOUTH ANTRIM.
o HORIZON 2020.
o INISHOWEN DEVELOPMENT PARTNERSHIP.
o INNOVATE-NI.
o IRD DUHALLOW LTD.
o KILKENNY LEADER PARTNERSHIP LTD.
o LAGAN RURAL PARTNERSHIP.

- o   LAOIS PARTNERSHIP COMPANY.
- o   LEITRIM INTEGRATED DEVELOPMENT COMPANY LTD.
- o   LONGFORD COMMUNITY RESOURCES LTD.
- o   LOUTH LEADER PARTNERSHIP.
- o   MAYO NORTH EAST LEADER PARTNERSHIP.
- o   MEATH PARTNERSHIP.
- o   MID & EAST ANTRIM LOCAL ACTION GROUP.
- o   MID ULSTER RURAL DEVELOPMENT PARTNERSHIP.
- o   MONAGHAN INTEGRATED DEVELOPMENT LTD.
- o   MOURNE, GULLION & LECALE RURAL DEVELOPMENT PARTNERSHIP.
- o   MOY VALLEY RESOURCES.
- o   NORTH TIPPERARY LEADER PARTNERSHIP.
- o   NORTH, EAST & WEST KERRY DEVLOPMENT.
- o   OFFALY INTEGRATED LOCAL DEVELOPMENT CLG.
- o   ROSCOMMON LEADER PARTNERSHIP.
- o   SOAR (ABC).
- o   SOUTH & EAST CORK AREA DEVELOPMENT LTD.
- o   SOUTH KERRY DEVELOPMENT PARTNERSHIP.
- o   SOUTH TIPPERARY DEVELOPMENT CLG.
- o   SOUTH WEST MAYO DEVELOPMENT COMPANY CLG.
- o   ÚDARÁS NA GAELTACHTA.
- o   WATERFORD LEADER PARTNERSHIP CLG.
- o   WEST LIMERICK RESOURCES LTD.
- o   WESTMEATH COMMUNITY DEVELOPMENT LTD.
- o   WEXFORD LOCAL DEVELOPMENT.

Information

- o   CRUCIAL CROWDFUNDING.
- o   ENTERPRISE EUROPE NETWORK.
- o   EUROPA.
- o   EUROPEDIRECT.ie.
- o   SENIOR ENTERPRISE.
- o   START UP EUROPE CLUB.
- o   YOUR EUROPE.

Incubation & Work space

- o   BALLYHOURA DEVELOPMENT CLG.

o BUSINESS INNOVATION CENTRES.
o CORK BUSINESS INNOVATION CENTRE.
o DUBLIN BUSINESS INNOVATION CENTRE.
o INNOVATE-NI.
o MOY VALLEY RESOURCES IRD.
o SOUTH EAST BUSINESS INNOVATION CENTRE.
o WESTBIC.
o WESTMEATH COMMUNITY DEVELOPMENT LTD.

Innovation & R&D

o BALLYHOURA DEVELOPMENT CLG.
o CO-INNOVATE PROGRAMME.
o EUROPEAN SPACE AGENCY.
o HORIZON 2020.

IP & Legal

o EUROPEAN IPR HELP DESK.

Marketing

o WESTBIC.

Networking

o DUBLIN BUSINESS INNOVATION CENTRE.
o START UP EUROPE CLUB.
o WESTBIC.

Training & Mentoring

o BUSINESS INNOVATION CENTRES.
o CARLOW COUNTY DEVELOPMENT PARTNERSHIP CLG.
o CORK BUSINESS INNOVATION CENTRE.
o COUNTY SLIGO LEADER PARTNERSHIP COMPANY LTD.
o COUNTY WICKLOW PARTNERSHIP.
o DONEGAL LOCAL DEVELOPMENT COMPANY CLG.
o DUBLIN BUSINESS INNOVATION CENTRE.
o FINGAL LEADER PARTNERSHIP.
o GALWAY RURAL DEVELOPMENT COMPANY.
o INNOVATE-NI.
o IRD DUHALLOW LTD.

- o   ISIHOWEN DEVELOPMENT PARTNERSHIP.
- o   LEITRIM INTEGRATED DEVELOPMENT COMPANY LTD.
- o   MAYO NORTH EAST LEADER PARTNERSHIP.
- o   MEATH PARTNERSHIP.
- o   MOY VALLEY RESOURCES IRD.
- o   NORTH TIPPERARY LEADER PARTNERSHIP.
- o   NORTH, EAST & WEST KERRY DEVELOPMENT.
- o   OFFALY INTEGRATED LOCAL DEVELOPMENT CLG.
- o   ROSCOMMON LEADER PARTNERSHIP.
- o   SOUTH & EAST CORK AREA DEVELOPMENT LTD.
- o   SOUTH EAST BUSINESS INNOVATION CENTRE.
- o   WESTBIC.
- o   WESTMEATH COMMUNITY DEVELOPMENT LTD.
- o   WEXFORD LOCAL DEVELOPMENT.

Social Enterprise

- o   DONEGAL LOCAL DEVELOPMENT COMPANY CLG.
- o   MOY VALLEY RESOURCES IRD.

8: SUPPORT FOR START-UPS IN NORTHERN IRELAND

This chapter identifies the organisations and agencies involved in supporting start-ups and small businesses in Northern Ireland. Check the *Directory* for information on the various categories.

Government Support

The Government Department responsible for enterprise in Northern Ireland is the DEPARTMENT FOR THE ECONOMY. As with the DEPARTMENT OF BUSINESS, ENTERPRISE & INNOVATION in the Republic, much of the Department's work is in creating an environment in which enterprise can flourish. Implementation is handled primarily by INVESTNI.

Support by Category

Accounting & Business Planning
- ADVANTAGE.
- ENTERPRISE NORTHWEST.

Community & Rural Development
- ARDS & NORTH DOWN RURAL AREA PARTNERSHIP.
- CAUSEWAY COAST & GLENS LOCAL ACTION GROUP.
- COLLEGE FOR AGRICULTURE, FOOD & RURAL ENTERPRISE.
- CREGGAN ENTERPRISES LTD.
- DEPARTMENT OF AGRICULTURE, ENVIRONMENT & RURAL AFFAIRS.
- DERRY & STRABANE RURAL PARTNERSHIP.
- FERMANAGH & OMAGH LOCAL ACTION GROUP.
- FLAX TRUST.
- GROW SOUTH ANTRIM.
- LAGAN RURAL PARTNERSHIP.
- LEADER NORTHERN IRELAND.

- o LOCAL ENTERPRISE DEVELOPMENT COMPANY LTD.
- o MICHELIN DEVELOPMENT.
- o MID & EAST ANTRIM LOCAL ACTION GROUP.
- o MID ULSTER RURAL DEVELOPMENT PARTNERSHIP.
- o MOURNE, GULLION & LECALE RURAL DEVELOPMENT PARTNERSHIP.
- o RURAL COMMUNITY NETWORK.
- o RURAL DEVELOPMENT COUNCIL.
- o RURAL NETWORK NI.
- o RURAL PARTNERS ARDS & NORTH DOWN.
- o RURAL SUPPORT.
- o SOAR (ABC).
- o TOURISM NORTHERN IRELAND.
- o ULSTER COMMUNITY INVESTMENT TRUST.
- o WORKSPACE ENTERPRISES LTD.

Consulting
- o LOCAL ENTERPRISE DEVELOPMENT COMPANY LTD.

Cross-Border
- o CENTRE FOR CROSS-BORDER STUDIES.
- o CO-INNOVATE PROGRAMME.
- o INTERTRADEIRELAND
- o LEGAL-ISLAND.
- o ULSTER COMMUNITY INVESTMENT TRUST.

Enterprise Support
- o ERNE ENTERPRISE DEVELOPMENT COMPANY LTD.

Franchises
- o ULSTER BANK.

Funding
- o ANTRIM ENTERPRISE AGENCY LTD.
- o ARDS & NORTH DOWN RURAL ENTERPRISE.
- o ARDS BUSINESS CENTRE LTD.
- o ARMAGH BUSINESS CENTRE LTD.
- o ARTS COUNCIL OF NORTHERN IRELAND.

- o BALLYMENA BUSINESS CENTRE LTD.
- o BANBRIDGE DISTRICT ENTERPRISES LTD.
- o BANK OF IRELAND NORTHERN IRELAND.
- o CARRICKFERGUS ENTERPRISE AGENCY LTD.
- o CATALYST INC.
- o CAUSEWAY COAST & GLENS LOCAL ACTION GROUP.
- o CAUSEWAY ENTERPRISE AGENCY.
- o CLARENDON FUND MANAGERS.
- o CO-INNOVATE PROGRAMME.
- o CRAIGAVON INDUSTRIAL DEVELOPMENT ORGANISATION LTD.
- o CRESCENT CAPITAL.
- o CROWDCUBE.
- o DANSKE BANK UK.
- o DEPARTMENT FOR THE ECONOMY.
- o DEPARTMENT OF AGRICULTURE, ENVIRONMENT & RURAL AFFAIRS.
- o DERRY & STRABANE RURAL PARTNERSHIP.
- o DOWN BUSINESS CENTRE.
- o DUNGANNON ENTERPRISE CENTRE LTD.
- o EAST BELFAST ENTERPRISE.
- o ENTERPRISE NORTHERN IRELAND.
- o FERMANAGH & OMAGH LOCAL ACTION GROUP.
- o FERMANAGH ENTERPRISE LTD.
- o FIRST TRUST BANK.
- o FUNDING COMMONS NI.
- o GROW SOUTH ANTRIM.
- o INNOVATE UK.
- o INNOVATE-NI.
- o INNOVATION ULSTER LTD.
- o INSPIRE BUSINESS CENTRE.
- o INTERTRADEIRELAND.
- o INVESTNI.
- o LAGAN RURAL PARTNERSHIP.
- o LEADER NORTHERN IRELAND.
- o LISBURN ENTERPRISE ORGANISATION LTD.
- o LOCAL ENTERPRISE DEVELOPMENT COMPANY LTD.
- o MALLUSK ENTERPRISE PARK.
- o MICHELIN DEVELOPMENT.
- o MID & EAST ANTRIM LOCAL ACTION GROUP.

- o   MID ULSTER RURAL DEVELOPMENT PARTNERSHIP.
- o   MOURNE, GULLION & LECALE RURAL DEVELOPMENT PARTNERSHIP.
- o   NEWRY & MOURNE ENTERPRISE AGENCY.
- o   NORTH CITY BUSINESS CENTRE LTD.
- o   NORTH DOWN DEVELOPMENT ORGANISATION LTD.
- o   NORTHERN IRELAND SCREEN.
- o   NORTHERN IRELAND SMALL BUSINESS LOAN FUND.
- o   OMAGH ENTERPRISE COMPANY LTD.
- o   ORMEAU BUSINESS PARK.
- o   ORTUS GROUP.
- o   PRINCE'S TRUST NORTHERN IRELAND.
- o   QUBIS LTD.
- o   QUEEN'S UNIVERSITY BELFAST.
- o   ROE VALLEY ENTERPRISES LTD.
- o   RURAL PARTNERS ARDS & NORTH DOWN.
- o   SHELL LIVEWIRE UK.
- o   SOAR (ABC).
- o   START UP LOANS COMPANY.
- o   STRABANE ENTERPRISE AGENCY.
- o   TECHSTARTNI.
- o   TOURISM NORTHERN IRELAND.
- o   ULSTER BANK.
- o   ULSTER COMMUNITY INVESTMENT TRUST LTD.
- o   ULSTER UNIVERSITY.
- o   UNLTD.
- o   WORK WEST ENTERPRISE AGENCY.
- o   WORKSPACE ENTERPRISES LTD.

Incubation & Work space

- o   ANTRIM ENTERPRISE AGENCY LTD.
- o   ARDS BUSINESS CENTRE LTD.
- o   ARGYLE BUSINESS CENTRE LTD.
- o   ARMAGH BUSINESS CENTRE LTD.
- o   BALLYMENA BUSINESS CENTRE LTD.
- o   BANBRIDGE DISTRICT ENTERPRISES LTD.
- o   CARRICKFERGUS ENTERPRISE AGENCY LTD.
- o   CATALYST INC.

- CAUSEWAY ENTERPRISE AGENCY.
- COLLEGE FOR AGRICULTURE, FOOD & RURAL ENTERPRISE.
- COOKSTOWN ENTERPRISE CENTRE LTD.
- CRAIGAVON INDUSTRIAL DEVELOPMENT ORGANISATION LTD.
- DOWN BUSINESS CENTRE.
- DUNGANNON ENTERPRISE CENTRE LTD.
- EAST BELFAST ENTERPRISE.
- ENTERPRISE NORTH WEST.
- FERMANAGH ENTERPRISE LTD.
- FLAX TRUST.
- GLENWOOD ENTERPRISES LTD.
- INNOVATE-NI.
- INSPIRE BUSINESS CENTRE LTD.
- LISBURN ENTERPRISE ORGANISATION LTD.
- LOCAL ENTERPRISE DEVELOPMENT COMPANY LTD.
- MALLUSK ENTERPRISE PARK LTD.
- MICHELIN DEVELOPMENT.
- NEWRY & MOURNE ENTERPRISE AGENCY.
- NORTH CITY BUSINESS CENTRE LTD.
- NORTH DOWN DEVELOPMENT ORGANISATION LTD.
- NORTHERN IRELAND SCREEN.
- OMAGH ENTERPRISE COMPANY LTD.
- ORMEAU BUSINESS PARK.
- ORTUS GROUP.
- QUEEN'S UNIVERSITY BELFAST.
- ROE VALLEY ENTERPRISES LTD.
- STRABANE ENTERPRISE AGENCY.
- TOWNSEND BUSINESS PARK.
- WORK WEST ENTERPRISE AGENCY.
- WORKSPACE ENTERPRISES LTD.

Information

- ANTRIM ENTERPRISE AGENCY.
- COMPANIES HOUSE.
- EAST BELFAST ENTERPRISE.
- ENTERPRISE NORTH WEST.
- ENTERPRISE NORTHERN IRELAND.
- HEALTH & SAFETY EXECUTIVE FOR NORTHERN IRELAND.

o   HM REVENUE & CUSTOMS.
o   INTERTRADEIRELAND.
o   INVESTNI.
o   LEGAL-ISLAND.
o   LIBRARIES NI BUSINESS INFORMATION SERVICE.
o   NIBUSINESSINFO.co.uk.
o   NORTHERN IRELAND STATISTICS & RESEARCH AGENCY.

Innovation & R&D

o   ANTRIM ENTERPRISE AGENCY.
o   ARDS BUSINESS CENTRE LTD.
o   BALLYMENA BUSINESS CENTRE LTD.
o   CARRICKFERGUS ENTERPRISE AGENCY LTD.
o   CATALYST INC.
o   COLLEGE FOR AGRICULTURE, FOOD & RURAL ENTERPRISE.
o   CRAIGAVON INDUSTRIAL DEVELOPMENT ORGANISATION LTD.
o   DEPARTMENT FOR THE ECONOMY.
o   EAST BELFAST ENTERPRISE.
o   FOODOVATION.
o   INNOVATE UK.
o   INNOVATION ULSTER LTD.
o   INSPIRE BUSINESS CENTRE.
o   INTERTRADEIRELAND.
o   INVESTNI.
o   LISBURN ENTERPRISE ORGANISATION LTD.
o   LOCAL ENTERPRISE DEVELOPMENT COMPANY LTD.
o   MALLUSK ENTERPRISE PARK LTD.
o   NORTHERN IRELAND TECHNOLOGY CENTRE.
o   ORMEAU BUSINESS PARK.
o   ORTUS GROUP.
o   QUBIS LTD.
o   QUEEN'S UNIVERSITY BELFAST.
o   SHELL LIVEWIRE UK.
o   ULSTER UNIVERSITY.
o   WORK WEST ENTERPRISE AGENCY.

IP & Legal

o   INTELLECTUAL PROPERTY OFFICE.

- LABOUR RELATIONS AGENCY.
- LAW SOCIETY OF NORTHERN IRELAND.
- LEGAL-ISLAND.

Inwards Investment

- INVESTNI.

Marketing

- NORTHERN IRELAND FOOD & DRINK ASSOCIATION.
- TOURISM NORTHERN IRELAND.

Networking

- FSB NORTHERN IRELAND.
- NETWORK FOR ENTERPRISING WOMEN.
- NORTHERN IRELAND CHAMBER OF COMMERCE & INDUSTRY.
- NORTHERN IRELAND FOOD & DRINK ASSOCIATION.
- NORTHERN IRELAND RURAL WOMEN'S NETWORK.
- RURAL COMMUNITY NETWORK.
- RURAL NETWORK NI.

Policy

- CENTRE FOR CROSS-BORDER STUDIES.
- DEPARTMENT FOR THE ECONOMY.
- DEPARTMENT OF AGRICULTURE, ENVIRONMENT & RURAL AFFAIRS.
- FSB NORTHERN IRELAND.
- INTERTRADEIRELAND.

Regulation & Standards

- BRITISH STANDARDS INSTITUTION.
- COMPANIES HOUSE.
- DEPARTMENT FOR THE ECONOMY.
- DEPARTMENT OF AGRICULTURE, ENVIRONMENT & RURAL AFFAIRS.
- HEALTH & SAFETY EXECUTIVE FOR NORTHERN IRELAND.
- HM REVENUE & CUSTOMS.
- INTELLECTUAL PROPERTY OFFICE.
- TOURISM NORTHERN IRELAND.

Social Enterprise

o ANTRIM ENTERPRISE AGENCY LTD.
o CREGGAN ENTERPRISES.
o ENTERPRISE NORTH WEST.
o LOCAL ENTERPRISE DEVELOPMENT COMPANY LTD.
o NEWRY & MOURNE ENTERPRISE AGENCY.
o ORTUS GROUP.
o RURAL SUPPORT.
o SOCIAL ENTERPRISE NI.
o ULSTER COMMUNITY INVESTMENT TRUST LTD.
o UNLTD.
o WORK WEST ENTERPRISES LTD.
o WORKSPACE ENTERPRISES LTD.

Training & Mentoring

o ADVANTAGE.
o ANTRIM ENTERPRISE AGENCY LTD.
o ARDS BUSINESS CENTRE LTD.
o ARMAGH BUSINESS CENTRE LTD.
o BALLYMENA BUSINESS DEVELOPMENT CENTRE LTD.
o BANBRIDGE DISTRICT ENTERPRISES LTD.
o CARRICKFERGUS ENTERPRISE AGENCY LTD.
o CAUSEWAY ENTERPRISE AGENCY.
o CENTRE FOR CROSS-BORDER STUDIES.
o COLLEGE FOR AGRICULTURE, FOOD & RURAL ENTERPRISE.
o COOKSTOWN ENTERPRISE CENTRE LTD.
o CRAIGAVON INDUSTRIAL DEVELOPMENT ORGANISATION LTD.
o DOWN BUSINESS CENTRE.
o DUNGANNON ENTERPRISE CENTRE LTD.
o EAST BELFAST ENTERPRISE.
o ENTERPRISE NORTH WEST.
o ENTERPRISE NORTHERN IRELAND.
o FERMANAGH ENTERPRISE LTD.
o INNOVATE-NI.
o INSPIRE BUSINESS CENTRE LTD.
o LANTRA.
o LEGAL-ISLAND.
o LISBURN ENTERPRISE ORGANISATION LTD.

- LOCAL ENTERPRISE DEVELOPMENT COMPANY LTD.
- MALLUSK ENTERPRISE PARK.
- MICHELIN DEVELOPMENT
- NEWRY & MOURNE ENTERPRISE AGENCY.
- NORTH CITY BUSINESS CENTRE LTD.
- NORTH DOWN DEVELOPMENT ORGANISATION LTD.
- NORTHERN IRELAND FOOD & DRINK ASSOCIATION.
- NORTHERN IRELAND SCREEN.
- OMAGH ENTERPRISE COMPANY LTD.
- ORMEAU BUSINESS PARK.
- ORTUS GROUP.
- PRINCE'S TRUST NORTHERN IRELAND.
- ROE VALLEY ENTERPRISES LTD.
- RURAL DEVELOPMENT COUNCIL.
- SHELL LIVEWIRE UK.
- STRABANE ENTERPRISE AGENCY.
- TECHSTARTNI.
- ULSTER COMMUNITY INVESTMENT TRUST LTD.
- UNLTD.
- WORK WEST ENTERPRISE AGENCY.
- WORKSPACE ENTERPRISES LTD.

Young Enterprise

- ADVANTAGE.
- CARRICKFERGUS ENTERPRISE AGENCY LTD.
- EAST BELFAST ENTERPRISE.
- PRINCE'S TRUST NORTHERN IRELAND.
- SHELL LIVEWIRE UK.
- WORKSPACE ENTERPRISES LTD.
- YOUNG ENTERPRISE NORTHERN IRELAND.

9: IMPLEMENTATION

OK! So you're ready to go – market research done, business plan drafted, finance and supports in place. But there are a few small hurdles that could still trip you.

You ought to consider each of the following as part of your business planning:

- Bank account.
- Legal structure.
- Tax registration.
- Advisers.
- Accountants.
- Solicitors.
- Company administration.
- Accounting systems.
- Quality certification.
- Premises.

Bank Account

At least one bank account is an essential for any business, however small. Don't be tempted to run your business through your own personal bank account 'until it gets off the ground'. That is a recipe for disaster. Open a separate bank account for your business as soon as (or before) you begin to trade.

A limited company needs to pass a resolution of the Board of Directors to open a bank account. The steps involved are:

- Ask your bank manager for a copy of the form of resolution that they require. This is called a Bank Mandate because it mandates (that is, authorises) the bank to carry out the instructions of the directors regarding the operation of the account.
- Hold a meeting of the directors of the company.

- Decide what instructions you want to give the bank regarding who is authorised to sign cheques on behalf of the company, and how often you want to receive statements.
- Propose the resolution in the form required by the bank – see the mandate form for the wording – and have it adopted by the directors at a formal Board meeting.
- Complete the mandate form. Usually this is in the format of a request to the bank to open an account, and certifies that the resolution, in the prescribed wording, was passed at a meeting of the directors held on the date noted.
- Get sample signatures from each of the people authorised to sign cheques on behalf of the company.
- Return the mandate form and sample signatures to your bank manager.
- Give the bank manager a copy of your company's Constitution. This will be kept for the manager's files.
- Show the original of the company's Certificate of Incorporation to your bank manager. A copy of this will be taken for the manager's files and on the copy will be marked the fact that the original has been seen by the manager.
- Have available some money to lodge to the new account.
- If you are trading under a registered business name – that is, trading as *West Cork Forest Advisory Services* even though the company is registered in your own name as *Frank Kelly Ltd*, you will also need to show the bank manager the Certificate of Registration of Business Name for the company (note that it is no longer possible or necessary to register 'business names' in Northern Ireland).

Depending on the bank and branch, it may take a few days or a few weeks to clear all the paperwork associated with opening your company's bank account. Allow for this in your planning.

If you need immediate access to the funds you are lodging, your bank manager can usually arrange for temporary cheques to be made available while a chequebook is being printed.

Legal Structure

You have most likely already made a choice as to your legal structure (see *Chapter 2*). Now you need to implement it.

Setting Up as a Sole Trader

You automatically become a sole trader by starting up a business. Setting up as a sole trader needs almost nothing by way of legal formality. A further advantage of being a sole trader is that apart from normal tax returns, which every business must make, a sole trader is not required to make public any information on the business.

However, if you plan to run your business under a name other than your own, you must register with the COMPANIES REGISTRATION OFFICE (except in Northern Ireland, where registration of business names is not possible).

Setting Up as a Partnership

A partnership, essentially, is an agreement between two or more people to go into business together. It may be no more formal than a handshake or may run to a multi-page legal document. Whichever route you take, build the following points into your planning:

- In a partnership, each partner is liable for all the liabilities of the business. If the business fails, and your partner(s) abandon(s) you, you could be left to pay for everything out of your own pocket. Before entering a partnership, decide whether you trust your partner(s)-to-be with everything you own – because that's what you will be doing.

- If you write down nothing else, write down and have all the partners sign a document setting out how the business is to be financed, how profits and losses are to be shared, and what will happen if one of the partners decides to leave. These are important points. Failure to agree on them at an early stage can lead to difficulty later.

In Northern Ireland, it is possible to form a 'limited partnership'. Full details of the procedures involved, and implications of this, are available from COMPANIES HOUSE.

Forming an Unlimited Company

An unlimited company is formed in much the same way as a limited liability company. The principal difference is that the company's Constitution states that the liability of members is unlimited. Again, like sole traders and partnerships, this exposes your total assets in the event of the failure of the company. There seems little advantage in going through the formation requirements of a company without benefiting from limited liability.

Forming a Limited Liability Company

A limited liability company is a legal entity separate from its shareholders. The shareholders are only liable, in the event of the business becoming unable to pay its debts, for any amount outstanding on their subscribed shareholdings.

The steps involved in forming a limited company are:

- Decide on a name for your company.
- Prepare the Constitution, which states who the initial share-holders, how much they have subscribed and sets out the rules governing internal procedures of the company.
- Submit the appropriate forms, together with the Constitution and a cheque or draft for the formation fees, to the COMPANIES REGISTRATION OFFICE or COMPANIES HOUSE (Northern Ireland).

The cost of forming a limited company depends on whether you do the work yourself or ask an accountant, solicitor, or company formation agent to do it for you. Typically, using a professional adds considerably to the cost.

If your application to form a company is accepted, the Registrar will issue a Certificate of Incorporation. Only after its issue, and the first meeting of the Board of Directors of the company, may the company begin to trade.

Forming a Co-operative

A worker co-operative is where a team comes together to form and run a business according to a set of values that includes self-help, self-responsibility, democracy, equality and solidarity. The business is jointly owned and democratically controlled. Co-operative members believe in the ethical values of honesty, openness, social responsibility and caring for others. The Co-operative Principles provide guidelines on how the business should conduct itself.

Tax (Republic of Ireland)

As a first step, download the Revenue's *Starting in Business* guide (reference IT 48) and *VAT for Small Businesses* (IT 49) from its website.

The REVENUE COMMISSIONERS now use a single form to register a business for the many taxes to which it is liable. Form TR1 applies to individuals and Form TR2 to companies.

Your business's PAYE / PRSI registration number, its VAT registration number and its Corporation Tax number should be the same, though this number has nothing to do with the company's Registered Number, which is issued by the COMPANIES REGISTRATION OFFICE when the company is formed.

Employers

Employers must register for PAYE when they pay remuneration exceeding a rate of €8 a week (€36 a month) to a full-time employee or €2 a week (€9 a month) to an individual with other employment – in other words, **all** employees.

The PAYE system for employers in Ireland is changing from 1 January 2019. You can find details of the PAYE Modernisation project on the Revenue's website.

Your Own Position as an Employee

If you are a director of a limited company, then you are an employee and, with the exception of PRSI rates, which are lower for owner-directors, you will be treated on a day-to-day basis like any other PAYE employee.

However, directors are subject to self-assessment (which means you must make an annual return of income), even though their income from the company already is subject to PAYE. Directors will be liable to a surcharge where they fail to make a return of income by the appropriate date. You should discuss your own situation with your accountant.

If you are self-employed, contact your local tax office explaining your situation. You are not liable for tax payments until after the first year of trading. Two months before the first year of trading ends, you will be sent a preliminary tax notice that informs you when your first tax payment is due.

Registering for VAT

You must register your business for Value Added Tax as soon as its taxable supplies (that is, your business transactions that are liable to VAT) exceed or become likely to exceed the limits for registration. The current limits are:

- €75,000, where the supplies are of goods.
- €37,500, where the supplies are of services.

Your registration for VAT is notified to you on Form VAT 2. This will tell you:

- The date from which your business is registered for VAT. From this date onwards, you will have to charge VAT to all your customers and account to the Revenue Commissioners for it.
- Your VAT number, which you will have to quote on all invoices, statements, credit notes, etc.

In certain circumstances, you may register for VAT before you begin to trade or while your turnover is below the limits for registration. Doing so allows you to reclaim VAT paid on purchases of goods and may be of advantage to you. However, voluntary registration for VAT should not be done without professional advice. Consult your accountant and / or local tax office for further information.

Registering for Income Tax

If you choose to set up your business as a sole trader, and you have been unemployed for at least 12 months before you start, you may be entitled to Income Tax relief on income of up to €40,000 a year for the first two years of trading. Note that, at the time of writing, this relief only extended to businesses set up before 31 December 2018.

Registering for Corporation Tax

Once your new company has been registered, and you have submitted Form TR2, it will be registered for Corporation Tax, which is payable in two instalments following the end of your accounting year. Consult your accountant and / or local tax office for further information.

Note that new companies, which commenced trading on or after 1 January 2009, and whose Corporation Tax liability for each year does not exceed €40,000, are exempt from Corporation Tax (including Capital Gains Tax) in each of the first three years of trading.

Tax (Northern Ireland)

As a first step, check **www.gov.uk/topic/business-tax/self-employed**. Businesses in Northern Ireland, part of the UK, are subject to:

- Income Tax – Sole traders and partnerships on their profits.
- Corporation Tax – Limited companies on their profits.
- Value Added Tax (VAT) – All businesses with turnover over £85,000.
- National Insurance Contributions (NIC) – All businesses with employees (including owner/directors).

Registration for tax

It is your obligation to notify HM REVENUE & CUSTOMS through your local tax office of the establishment of your business and to provide them with the information required to register your business for the relevant taxes.

Corporation Tax

Limited liability companies pay Corporation Tax on the company's total profits, including any capital gains, for an accounting period – normally the period for which the company's accounts are prepared, though an accounting period cannot exceed 12 months.

A self-assessment system applies to companies. The company assesses its own liability to tax and pays it no later than nine months after the end of the accounting period. Interest will be charged if payments are made after their due date. The company will also complete a company tax return and send it to HMRC with its accounts for the period.

The current rate of Corporation Tax is 19%, which is planned to drop to 17% by 2020.

Income Tax

Income tax is payable by self-employed individuals on income earned in the tax year – that is, on annual profits or gains from an individual's trade, profession or vocation and on other income, such as investment income, rental income etc.

As soon as you start business as a self-employed person, you must tell your local tax office.

Income tax is calculated on a 12-month basis, for a year running from 6 April to the following 5 April.

HMRC requires a return of your business income and expenses in a standard format. You do not need to prepare separate accounts, although you may find that your bank wants to see formal accounts anyway.

In April, you will receive a tax return, asking you for the information needed to calculate your tax bill for the year. If you can calculate the bill yourself (the return explains how), you must send back the return by 31 January following. Alternatively, you can ask the HMRC to calculate the tax bill, based on the information on your return. In this case, you must send back your return before 30 September.

Self-employed National Insurance Contributions

Self-employed people pay National Insurance Contributions in two classes: Class 2 and Class 4 (on profits above a certain level).

PAYE & National Insurance Contributions

When you employ someone in your business, you should immediately tell your local tax office.

The Pay As You Earn (PAYE) system operates on the basis that an employer deducts tax at a specified rate from an employee's pay. The system is designed so that, as far as is possible, the correct amount of tax is deducted from an employee's pay to meet his / her tax liability for the year. To achieve this, PAYE is normally computed on a cumulative basis, from the beginning of the tax year to the date on which a payment is being made.

In addition to deducting PAYE, employers are also obliged to deduct National Insurance Contributions (NIC) from employees.

You must:

- Work out employees' PAYE and NIC each pay-day.
- Pay this amount to HMRC monthly.
- Tell your local tax office at the end of each tax year how much each employee has earned and what PAYE and NIC you have deducted.

Your local HMRC Business Support Team will advise you on the details.

Value Added Tax

Value Added Tax (VAT) is a consumer tax collected by VAT-registered traders on their supplies of taxable goods and services in the course of business.

You must register for VAT if your turnover for a 12-month period exceeds £85,000 (this amount is reviewed annually). Traders whose turnover is below this limit are not obliged to register for VAT but may do so if they wish. You should only do so on your accountant's advice.

The current rate of VAT is 20%, though some goods and services are zero-rated or taxed at a reduced rate of 5%.

HMRC offer a number of accounting schemes designed to reduce the administration required of small businesses in complying with their VAT obligations – check with HMRC or your accountant.

Information and assistance

Comprehensive guides to all aspects of business taxation may be obtained from any tax office or HMRC's website (www.hmrc.gov.uk). Your accountant will also provide advice.

HMRC is increasingly moving online. Not only are all forms and publications available on their website but, increasingly, taxpayers can make returns and payments online too.

Advisers

As you start in business, you need two key advisers: an accountant and a solicitor. In the pressures of setting up your new business, there will be a temptation to avoid finding either of these two. Not doing so saves you time and possibly money, both of which are important in a start-up situation. But it could cost you dearly later on.

Reasons for choosing a financial and a legal adviser at the start are:

- Their experience and expertise in dealing with other start-ups may save you hours of time and hundreds, or even thousands, of pounds. If they are the right advisers for you, they will be prepared to assist your enterprise with timely and constructive advice – take it and use it!

- With luck, you will never find yourself in a situation where you need to be bailed out of difficulty, but if you do, it's better to have your advisers on your team already than have to start looking for them with the millstone of your problem around your neck.

In choosing advisers, look for:

- Membership of the appropriate professional body. This is your guarantee of quality of work and source of redress, should the need ever arise (hopefully not!).

- Experience in the type of business or at least in the business area in which you intend to operate. You want to learn from your advisers' experience, not spend your time teaching them about your business.

- Adequate resources to meet your needs. What is adequate will depend on you, but don't choose a one-man band if you expect a limitless range of expertise. There is only so much one person can be expert in. Ask about the adviser's hours of business (actual hours, not published hours). Can you telephone them at 7 pm on a Sunday night? What happens when they go on holidays?

- People you can trust and work easily with. If you can't trust your advisers with your most confidential information, you shouldn't have them on your team. Find someone else.

Choosing an Accountant

If your business is set up as a limited company, your accountant will have one primary task: to carry out the annual audit (note that an audit is not required where the company's turnover is below €12 million – £10.2 million in Northern Ireland – and certain other conditions are met). An audit is a statutory inspection of the company's accounting records, which results in a formal set of accounts and an audit report.

This report is to the members (that is, the shareholders) of the company and gives the auditor's (the accountant's) opinion on:

- Whether the accounts give a true and fair view.
- Whether proper books of account have been kept.
- Whether a meeting as specified under the *Companies Act* needs to be called (this would arise where the share capital of the company amounts to less than half the net assets of the company).
- Whether all the explanations and information considered necessary for the purposes of the audit were received.

and, as a matter of fact:

- Whether the accounts agree with the books.
- Whether proper returns were received from branches (if any) not visited by the auditor.

If you do not know a suitable accountant, contact one of the following:

o   ACCA EUROPE.
o   CHARTERED ACCOUNTANTS IRELAND.
o   INSTITUTE OF CERTIFIED PUBLIC ACCOUNTANTS IN IRELAND.

Many accountants provide advice and assistance in taking a business concept from viability assessment through to the production stage and also in obtaining assistance from State and other support organisations. An initial meeting between a potential entrepreneur and the accountant is usually free and is used to gather information about the promoter and the business proposal. Based on the information available, appropriate action to advance the project will be agreed. Where further information is required, a structured feasibility study is carried out, embracing key aspects such as products, markets, competitors, technology, funding etc. A fee should be agreed before work starts. If the proposal is viable, the accountant will assist in the preparation of a comprehensive business plan, at a further agreed cost. They will make application for grants appropriate to the project and assist in raising finance from banks or private investors. They may also help to obtain commercial partners.

Choosing a Solicitor

Unlike an accountant, a solicitor has no statutory duties in relation to a company. You will, however, need a solicitor for the following:

- To sign a statutory declaration when you are forming your company.
- To check out the lease of any premises you decide to buy or rent.
- To prepare employment contracts for you and your staff.
- To draft or review contracts that you enter into with customers or suppliers.

In addition, from time to time, you may require advice on legal issues.

If you do not know a suitable solicitor, contact the LAW SOCIETY OF IRELAND or the LAW SOCIETY OF NORTHERN IRELAND.

Accounting Systems

Accounts systems provide a record of all the income and outgoings of a business and produce the basic information for the end-of-year accounts and for management information.

In a manual system, you may need some or all of the following (in varying levels of detail, depending on the size and complexity of your business – your accountant will advise):

- Cash book.
- Petty-cash book.
- Purchase day book.
- Purchase ledger.
- Sales day book.
- Sales ledger.
- Control accounts.
- Wages book / deduction sheets.
- Register of fixed assets.
- Nominal ledger.
- System for ordering goods / dealing with purchase invoices.
- System for dealing with customers' orders / sales invoices.
- Credit control procedures.
- Control of workforce and hours worked.

- Stock control procedures.
- System for regular management information.
- Adequate control procedures by management over employees.

You can also use a computerised accounting system or, indeed, an online accounting system, to be fully up-to-date – again, your accountant will advise.

Your accountant will also advise you on a system for filing and retrieving documents. You also need to consider the flow of documents and information around the business – for example, how a customer order is processed so that the goods are sent out, an invoice generated and payment received.

Whether manual or computerised, there are three simple aids that you should use to help you in the financial control of your business:

- Bank balance book.
- Still-to-be-received file.
- Still-to-be-paid file.

The 'bank balance book' does exactly what its name suggests – it tells you what your bank balance is. You need five columns – for the date, for the transaction detail (cheque or lodgement will do), for lodgements, for cheques and other withdrawals, and for the balance. If every transaction with your bank is written into this book *when it happens,* you will always know your correct bank balance. The little effort that it takes to keep this book up-to-date will be more than repaid as it keeps you out of trouble.

Cash flow is important for any business. If you sell goods on credit, you will probably find that you spend a great deal of time chasing debtors, trying to collect money. A 'still-to-be-received' file helps you by providing all the information you need on outstanding debts. Just put a copy of every invoice into the file when you issue it, and take the copy out when it is paid – then every invoice in the file represents an unpaid debt, money due to you. You can list them out, total them up, cry over them – whatever takes your fancy – but you have accurate information on which to do so.

The 'still-to-be-paid' file works in the opposite way – it reminds you of money you owe. Put a copy of every invoice you receive into it and take it out when you pay it (send the copy with your cheque so that your creditor knows which invoice you are paying!) – and what's left in the file is what you owe. So, when you get a telephone call saying that such and such an invoice is due for payment or overdue, you can check it out immediately.

Quality Certification

For some businesses in particular, and increasingly for all businesses, some form of quality certification is becoming essential. Schemes such as ISO 9000 are the norm among high-tech companies and are a minimum requirement to supply many of the foreign-owned multinationals operating in Ireland. ISO 9000 is the best known of such schemes, though the Q-Mark, awarded by EXCELLENCE IRELAND QUALITY ASSOCIATION is important in some sectors.

ISO 9000 is a standard for quality management systems, covering every stage of the production process – procurement, incoming materials, production performance, final inspection, and delivery. To implement ISO 9000 (or any quality standard):

- Management has to define clearly what is needed.
- The message must reach staff so that everybody knows what they have to do and how to do it.
- The right equipment, processes and tools must be available to do the job.
- The right information must reach the right people at the right time.
- There must be a system of management and control.

Even if your business's involvement in quality certification stems purely from a supplier-imposed requirement, keep two things in mind:

- Quality is an attitude of mind, a way of working, not just mindless compliance with written procedures. Most quality schemes involve the recording of operational procedures, together with systems to audit compliance. Beware that compliance with the system does not become the end, rather than quality itself.
- Quality involves a cost and any investment in quality systems must be justified like any other business expense. Investing in

quality for its own sake may be very noble, but it's not good business.

Premises

In the property business, they say that only three things matter: location, location, location. For certain kinds of business – shops, hotels, restaurants – location can make or break the business. But in all cases, the right working environment is important.

For workshops and factories, you need to check lay-out, logistics, transport, weight of machinery, health and safety regulations, environmental issues, availability of three-phase electricity, etc. Draw out your ideal space before starting to look for accommodation.

If you are looking for offices, and you expect to be working on your own for a while, consider serviced offices that offer secretarial support (for example, telephone answering, message-taking, fax, photocopying, reception, etc.) It will save you hiring a secretary until the workload justifies it. And you save the capital cost of little-used but essential equipment and meeting facilities – instead, you pay only as you need them.

A 'virtual office', where you only pay for the facilities as you use them, can be the ideal way to combine working from home with having top-class facilities when you need to meet visitors – or just to provide yourself with flexibility while you assess your needs. Coworking is a modern way to work as a start-up, using office facilities that you share with other businesses on a flexible basis. In addition, you also get to network with your coworkers, which may help you with useful contacts.

Wherever you locate, you need to consider insurance premiums, compliance with food hygiene and health and safety regulations, planning permission, lighting, heating, alarms, signs, locks, insurance, toilets, interior decor, fittings. And get a solicitor (see earlier) to check any lease before you sign.

10: MOVING TO IRELAND TO START A BUSINESS

Traditionally, Ireland has been associated with emigration. Images from the mid-19th century of half-starved people on coffin-ships escaping the famine back home are part and parcel of the Irish-American heritage. Many Irish men and women of that time first saw Australia from a prison-ship, courtesy of the British Government. In the 20th century, the Irish found jobs as labourers on the building sites of Britain and further afield in the United States. In the 1970s and 1980s – and again in the late 2000s, it was the educated young people, fresh from college with degrees, who 'took the boat' or increasingly the plane, in search of jobs that were not available at home.

But, in recent years, the tide has turned. Emigration has been replaced by net immigration. And, while many of the new immigrants come to fill jobs created by skills shortages, a significant number come to start their own businesses. Why?

First, put aside any preconceptions you may have of Ireland as a rural haven, populated by handsome lads and comely maidens, with dancing at the crossroads and leprechauns at every turn of the winding lane. That may be what *FÁILTE IRELAND* (the Irish Tourist Board) will sell you, though it exists only in brochures and a few select tourist enclaves. The 'real' Ireland is a modern, dynamic, European economy that is powering ahead, fuelled by export demand, deregulation and a flexible and well-educated workforce.

For the last 40 years, successive governments have pursued economic policies designed to make Ireland an attractive location for overseas investment. Their success can be seen, not just in the numbers of foreign businesses now operating in Ireland, but also in Ireland's 12th place (admittedly, down from 6th the previous year) in the *IMD World Competitiveness* rankings for 2018.

Recognising that Ireland lacks the natural resources required to support large-scale industrial development, the government has encouraged inwards investment by industries that make use of the assets available: for example, chemicals and pharmaceuticals (clustered in Cork, around the deep-water harbour), electronics and software (Ireland is now the world's largest exporter of software) and internationally traded services (in particular, financial services from the International Financial Services Centre in Dublin's revitalised Docklands). The government, in partnership with the private sector, has sought to develop Ireland's communications infrastructure to world-class standards, with bureaucrats making decisions at distinctly non-bureaucratic speeds.

Ireland is ideally situated for exporting to Europe. With the United Kingdom (at the time of writing) poised to leave the European Union in March 2019, Ireland will the only English-speaking member of the EU. Half of Irish exports already go to Europe (with a further 28% to the US), showing how important Ireland is as a gateway to the EU for many companies.

The most recent (2014) statistics show that there are 3,700 foreign-owned businesses in Ireland, employing over 300,000 people, and turning over €242bn.

Among the key attractions of Ireland for businesses are the relatively high quality, high productivity of staff and low cost of labour. But the key attraction for many businesses is the tax regime. Currently, the standard rate of tax on corporate profits is 12.5%).

Business Incentives

Incentives include grants towards capital and revenue costs (employment, training and R&D are the main categories) offered by State and State-supported agencies (see *Chapter 5*). For larger companies, moving all or a significant part of their operations to Ireland, such grants (and other assistance) are offered by IDA IRELAND, while ENTERPRISE IRELAND offers supports to start-ups and early stage companies prepared to (re)locate to Ireland.

A key determinant of government support is the location of the proposed business. Because Dublin's infrastructure is groaning at the seams, government agencies are more generous in the financial assistance they offer to businesses locating outside Dublin. Indeed, it's unusual to be offered significant financial assistance for Dublin-based start-ups.

And regional bodies are working to develop clusters of excellence in specific industries, for example, pharmaceuticals and electronics in Cork.

Business Structures and Accounting

Most trading in Ireland is carried out through private limited liability companies. Formation of such companies is straightforward (see *Chapter 9*). Where a company does not have a resident director, it must provide a bond to the value of IR£20,000. No individual may hold more than 25 directorships.

With the exception of the smallest companies, all Irish companies must have their financial statements audited annually by a chartered or certified accountant and must file these statements with the COMPANIES REGISTRATION OFFICE for public inspection. No exceptions are made for foreign-owned entities.

Requirements for Residency and Citizenship

While EU nationals may freely move to Ireland and establish a business with all the rights of Irish citizens, non-EEA nationals who wish to do so must qualify under either:

- The Immigrant Investor Programme – minimum own-funds investment €1m.
- The Start-up Entrepreneur Programme – minimum own-funds investment €50,000.

Details of both are available from the IRISH NATURALISATION & IMMIGRATION SERVICE.

Work permits are required for any non-EEA staff who move with the business and are only available where suitable Irish or EU nationals cannot be recruited for the position.

Citizenship in Ireland can be acquired through ancestry or by naturalisation. A parent or grandparent who was Irish entitles one to Irish citizenship, though the link must be proved through documentation. A foreign national resident in Ireland may apply for naturalised citizenship after seven years of residence. Where residency arises because of marriage to an Irish citizen, the waiting period for naturalisation is reduced to three years.

Personal Taxation

Foreign nationals resident in Ireland pay Irish tax on income earned by them in Ireland or the United Kingdom or income remitted to them from abroad. Income accumulated offshore, but not remitted to Ireland, is not subject to tax.

Details of the personal tax regime, which changes each year, are available from the REVENUE COMMISSIONERS.

All employees in Ireland are covered by social insurance, which is pay-related. Social insurance must be paid by all foreign employees working in Ireland for more than a year, even if they are being paid from abroad, unless they are an EU national paying social insurance in another EU member-state.

11: DIRECTORY OF SOURCES OF ASSISTANCE

The aims of this directory are:

- To highlight the many sources of assistance available to start-up and small / medium-sized enterprises in Ireland.
- To direct readers to sources appropriate to their needs.

The directory is arranged first by category and then alphabetically by organisation, with contact details (address, telephone, e-mail, website and contact name) and a summary of the assistance provided for each. Note that dialling codes are those applicable locally – readers may need to amend the code when making cross-border calls.

All the information has been checked before publication but, of course, it is subject to change. See this book's companion website, **www.startingabusinessinireland.com,** or contact the organisations directly for the most up-to-date position.

11A: DIRECTORY – BY CATEGORY

ACCOUNTING & BUSINESS PLANNING

Accountants provide a variety of services to start-ups. They can assist and advise you on:

- The legal structure, taxation and accounting systems suitable for your business.
- Business planning (though you should not let your accountant write your business plan – after all, it's your plan, not theirs!).
- Fund-raising and/or funding applications to banks, venture capitalists and grant-giving organisations.

Professional accounting bodies, accounting software providers and sources of support with business planning include:

o ACCA EUROPE.
o ADVANTAGE.
o AISLING SOFTWARE.
o BIG RED BOOK.
o BULLET.
o BYRNE & McCALL.
o CHARTERED ACCOUNTANTS IRELAND.
o CHARTERED INSTITUTE OF MANAGEMENT ACCOUNTANTS.
o ENTERPRISE NORTH WEST.
o INSTITUTE OF CERTIFIED PUBLIC ACCOUNTANTS IN IRELAND.
o INVEST-TECH.
o LIFFEY TRUST.
o LIVEPLAN.com.
o MOY VALLEY RESOURCES IRD.
o SAGE IRELAND.
o WESTBIC.

COMMUNITY & RURAL DEVELOPMENT

A sizeable element of the support for enterprise in Ireland comes from efforts towards community and rural development, often aimed at replacing industries that have closed down or relocated (or reducing dependence on them in advance). The support often also includes tourism development. Organisations in this space include:

o ACE ENTERPRISE PARK.
o ALLENWOOD COMMUNITY DEVELOPMENT ASSOCIATION LTD.
o ARDEE COMMUNITY DEVELOPMENT COMPANY LTD.
o ARDS & NORTH DOWN RURAL AREA PARTNERSHIP.
o AVONDHU BLACKWATER PARTNERSHIP CLG.
o BALLYFERMOT CHAPELIZOD PARTNERSHIP COMPANY LTD.
o BALLYHOURA DEVELOPMENT CLG.
o BRAY AREA PARTNERSHIP.
o BREFFNI INTEGRATED CLG.
o CARLOW COUNTY DEVELOPMENT PARTNERSHIP CLG.
o CAUSEWAY COAST & GLENS LOCAL ACTION GROUP.
o CLANN CREDO.
o CLARE LOCAL DEVELOPMENT COMPANY LTD.
o COLLEGE FOR AGRICULTURE, FOOD & RURAL ENTERPRISE.
o COMHAR NA NOILEÁN CTR.
o CONNEMARA WEST.
o CORK CITY PARTNERSHIP CLG.
o COUNTY KILDARE LEADER PARTNERSHIP.
o COUNTY SLIGO LEADER PARTNERSHIP COMPANY LTD.
o COUNTY WICKLOW PARTNERSHIP.
o CREGGAN ENTERPRISES LTD.
o DEPARTMENT OF AGRICULTURE, ENVIRONMENT & RURAL AFFAIRS.
o DEPARTMENT OF RURAL & COMMUNITY DEVELOPMENT.
o DERRY & STRABANE RURAL PARTNERSHIP.
o DONEGAL LOCAL DEVELOPMENT COMPANY CLG.
o DUBLIN CITY COMMUNITY CO-OP.
o DUBLIN NORTH WEST AREA PARTNERSHIP.
o DUBLIN SOUTH CITY PARTNERSHIP.
o EMPOWER.
o FÁILTE IRELAND.
o FERMANAGH & OMAGH LOCAL ACTION GROUP.

o   FINGAL LEADER PARTNERSHIP.

o   FLAX TRUST.

o   FORUM CONNEMARA CLG.

o   GALWAY CITY PARTNERSHIP.

o   GALWAY RURAL DEVELOPMENT COMPANY.

o   GROW SOUTH ANTRIM.

o   INISHOWEN DEVELOPMENT PARTNERSHIP.

o   INSTITUTE FOR MINORITY ENTREPRENEURSHIP.

o   IRD DUHALLOW LTD.

o   IRD KILTIMAGH.

o   IRISH LOCAL DEVELOPMENT NETWORK.

o   IRISH RURAL LINK LTD.

o   KILKENNY LEADER PARTNERSHIP LTD.

o   LAGAN RURAL PARTNERSHIP.

o   LAOIS PARTNERSHIP COMPANY.

o   LEADER NORTHERN IRELAND.

o   LEADER.

o   LEITRIM INTEGRATED DEVELOPMENT COMPANY LTD.

o   LIMERICK ENTERPRISE DEVELOPMENT PARTNERSHIP.

o   LOCAL ENTERPRISE DEVELOPMENT COMPANY LTD.

o   LONGFORD COMMUNITY RESOURCES LTD.

o   LOUTH LEADER PARTNERSHIP.

o   MAYO NORTH EAST LEADER PARTNERSHIP.

o   MEATH PARTNERSHIP.

o   MICHELIN DEVELOPMENT.

o   MID & EAST ANTRIM LOCAL ACTION GROUP.

o   MID ULSTER RURAL DEVELOPMENT PARTNERSHIP.

o   MONAGHAN INTEGRATED DEVELOPMENT LTD.

o   MOUNTMELLICK DEVELOPMENT ASSOCIATION.

o   MOURNE, GULLION & LECALE RURAL DEVELOPMENT PARTNERSHIP.

o   MOY VALLEY RESOURCES IRD.

o   NATIONAL RURAL NETWORK.

o   NORTH TIPPERARY LEADER PARTNERSHIP.

o   NORTH, EAST & WEST KERRY DEVELOPMENT.

o   NORTHSIDE PARTNERSHIP.

o   OFFALY INTEGRATED LOCAL DEVELOPMENT CLG.

o   PARTAS.

- o   PAUL PARTNERSHIP LIMERICK.
- o   PREMIER SERVICES.
- o   ROSCOMMON LEADER PARTNERSHIP.
- o   RURAL COMMUNITY NETWORK.
- o   RURAL DEVELOPMENT COUNCIL.
- o   RURAL NETWORK NI.
- o   RURAL PARTNERS ARDS & NORTH DOWN.
- o   RURAL SUPPORT.
- o   SCHOOL OF FOOD.
- o   SOAR (ABC).
- o   SOUTH & EAST CORK AREA DEVELOPMENT LTD.
- o   SOUTH DUBLIN COUNTY PARTNERSHIP.
- o   SOUTH KERRY DEVELOPMENT PARTNERSHIP.
- o   SOUTH TIPPERARY DEVELOPMENT CLG.
- o   SOUTH WEST MAYO DEVELOPMENT COMPANY CLG.
- o   SOUTHSIDE PARTNERSHIP DLR LTD.
- o   TALLOW ENTERPRISE CENTRE.
- o   TERENURE ENTERPRISE CENTRE.
- o   TOURISM NORTHERN IRELAND.
- o   ÚDARÁS NA GAELTACHTA.
- o   ULSTER COMMUNITY INVESTMENT TRUST LTD.
- o   WATERFORD AREA PARTNERSHIP.
- o   WATERFORD LEADER PARTNERSHIP CLG.
- o   WEST CORK DEVELOPMENT PARTNERSHIP LTD.
- o   WEST LIMERICK RESOURCES LTD.
- o   WESTERN DEVELOPMENT COMMISSION.
- o   WESTMEATH COMMUNITY DEVELOPMENT LTD.
- o   WEXFORD LOCAL DEVELOPMENT.
- o   WORKSPACE ENTERPRISES LTD.

CONSULTING

There are dozens – even hundreds – of consultants with a bewildering array of expertise, available to help you to develop your start-up business and help it grow.

Use consultants carefully. Know what you want them to do, when, and at what cost to you. Make sure they deliver before you sign off and pay their fees. Look for the consultant who thinks long-term – and is prepared to invest in you and your future success. But recognise that consultants must eat too – if you want work done, you must be prepared to pay for it. Free advice will not take you far!

Membership of the INSTITUTE OF MANAGEMENT CONSULTANTS & ADVISERS – or other relevant professional bodies – is useful as an indication of quality.

The following consultants may be able to help you:
o AMÁRACH CONSULTING.
o CENTRE FOR CO-OPERATIVE STUDIES.
o CORK BUSINESS INNOVATION CENTRE.
o ENERGY CO-OPERATIVES IRELAND.
o FOOD PRODUCT DEVELOPMENT CENTRE.
o INSTITUTE OF MANAGEMENT CONSULTANTS & ADVISERS.
o KILLARNEY TECHNOLOGY INNOVATION LTD.
o LIFFEY TRUST.
o LOCAL ENTERPRISE DEVELOPMENT COMPANY LTD.
o OPTIMUM RESULTS LTD.
o SOUTH EAST BUSINESS INNOVATION CENTRE.
o TEAGASC.

CROSS-BORDER

The following organisations assist start-ups to trade across the 'island of Ireland':
o CENTRE FOR CROSS-BORDER STUDIES.
o CO-INNOVATE PROGRAMME.
o INTERTRADEIRELAND.
o LEGAL-ISLAND.
o ULSTER COMMUNITY INVESTMENT TRUST LTD.

ENTERPRISE SUPPORT

Organisations whose support activities for entrepreneurs cannot be captured elsewhere include:
o BOLTON TRUST.
o CORK INSTITUTE OF TECHNOLOGY.
o COSME.
o DUBLIN CITY UNIVERSITY.

- o DUBLIN INSTITUTE OF TECHNOLOGY.
- o ENTERPRISE & RESEARCH INCUBATION CAMPUS.
- o ERNE ENTERPRISE DEVELOPMENT COMPANY LTD.
- o INSTITUTE OF TECHNOLOGY BLANCHARDSTOWN.
- o INSTITUTE OF TECHNOLOGY CARLOW.
- o KILKENNY LEADER PARTNERSHIP LTD.
- o MIDLANDS INNOVATION & RESEARCH CENTRE.
- o NATIONAL UNIVERSITY OF IRELAND GALWAY.
- o NATIONAL UNIVERSITY OF IRELAND MAYNOOTH.
- o POBAL.
- o RUBICON CENTRE.
- o THE LINC.
- o TRINITY COLLEGE DUBLIN.
- o UNIVERSITY COLLEGE CORK.
- o UNIVERSITY COLLEGE DUBLIN.
- o UNIVERSITY OF LIMERICK.

FRANCHISES

The following organisations can help you, if you are interested in a franchise:

- o FRANCHISE DIRECT.
- o IRISH FRANCHISE ASSOCIATION.
- o NATIONAL FRANCHISE CENTRE.
- o ULSTER BANK.

FUNDING

Sources of funding – equity, loans, grants and alternative financing – include:

- o 4th LEVEL VENTURES LTD.
- o ACT VENTURE CAPITAL LTD.
- o AIB BANK.
- o ANTRIM ENTERPRISE AGENCY LTD.
- o ARDS & NORTH DOWN RURAL AREA PARTNERSHIP.
- o ARDS BUSINESS CENTRE LTD.
- o ARMAGH BUSINESS CENTRE LTD.
- o ARTS COUNCIL OF NORTHERN IRELAND.

- ARTS COUNCIL.
- ATLANTIC BRIDGE.
- AVONDHU BLACKWATER PARTNERSHIP CLG.
- BALLYHOURA DEVELOPMENT CLG.
- BALLYMENA BUSINESS CENTRE LTD.
- BANBRIDGE DISTRICT ENTERPRISES LTD.
- BANK OF IRELAND NORTHERN IRELAND.
- BANK OF IRELAND.
- BORD BIA.
- BORD IASCAIGH MHARA.
- BREFFNI INTEGRATED CLG.
- BROADLAKE.
- BUSINESS VENTURE PARTNERS.
- CARLOW COUNTY DEVELOPMENT PARTNERSHIP CLG.
- CARRICKFERGUS ENTERPRISE AGENCY LTD.
- CATALYST INC.
- CAUSEWAY COAST & GLENS LOCAL ACTION GROUP.
- CAUSEWAY ENTERPRISE AGENCY.
- CAVAN COUNTY ENTERPRISE FUND.
- CLANCY BUSINESS FINANCE LTD.
- CLANN CREDO.
- CLARE LOCAL DEVELOPMENT COMPANY LTD.
- CLARENDON FUND MANAGERS.
- COMHAR NA NOILEÁN CTR.
- COMMUNITY FINANCE (IRELAND).
- COSME.
- COUNTY KILDARE LEADER PARTNERSHI.P
- COUNTY SLIGO LEADER PARTNERSHIP COMPANY LTD.
- COUNTY WICKLOW PARTNERSHIP.
- CRAIGAVON INDUSTRIAL DEVELOPMENT ORGANISATION LTD.
- CREDIT REVIEW OFFICE.
- CRESCENT CAPITAL.
- CROWDCUBE.
- CRUCIAL CROWDFUNDING.
- DANSKE BANK UK.
- DCU RYAN ACADEMY.
- DELTA PARTNERS.
- DEPARTMENT FOR THE ECONOMY.

- DEPARTMENT OF AGRICULTURE, ENVIRONMENT & RURAL AFFAIRS.
- DEPARTMENT OF EMPLOYMENT AFFAIRS & SOCIAL PROTECTION.
- DERRY & STRABANE RURAL PARTNERSHIP.
- DONEGAL LOCAL DEVELOPMENT COMPANY CLG.
- DONEGAL LOCAL ENTERPRISE OFFICE.
- DOWN BUSINESS CENTRE.
- DRAPER ESPRIT.
- DUBLIN BUSINESS INNOVATION CENTRE.
- DUBLIN SOUTH LOCAL ENTERPRISE OFFICE.
- DUNGANNON ENTERPRISE CENTRE LTD.
- EAST BELFAST ENTERPRISE.
- ENTERPRISE EQUITY.
- ENTERPRISE IRELAND.
- ENTERPRISE NORTHERN IRELAND.
- EUROPEAN INVESTMENT PORTAL.
- EUROPEAN SPACE AGENCY.
- EXECUTIVE AGENCY FOR SMEs.
- FERMANAGH & OMAGH LOCAL ACTION GROUP.
- FERMANAGH ENTERPRISE LTD.
- FINGAL LEADER PARTNERSHIP.
- FINISTERE VENTURES.
- FIRST TRUST BANK.
- FOCUS CAPITAL PARTNERS.
- FORUM CONNEMARA CLG.
- FOUNTAIN HEALTHCARE PARTNERS.
- FRONTLINE VENTURES.
- FUND IT.
- FUNDING COMMONS NI.
- GALWAY RURAL DEVELOPMENT COMPANY.
- GROW SOUTH ANTRIM.
- GUINNESS WORKERS' EMPLOYMENT FUND LTD.
- HALO BUSINESS ANGEL NETWORK.
- HORIZON 2020.
- INISHOWEN DEVELOPMENT PARTNERSHIP.
- INNER CITY ENTERPRISE.
- INNOVATE UK.
- INNOVATE-NI.
- INNOVATION ULSTER LTD.

- o   INSPIRE BUSINESS CENTRE.
- o   INTERTRADEIRELAND.
- o   INVESTNI.
- o   IRD DUHALLOW LTD.
- o   IRISH LEAGUE OF CREDIT UNIONS.
- o   IRISH VENTURE CAPITAL ASSOCIATION.
- o   KERNEL CAPITAL PARTNERS.
- o   KERRY LOCAL ENTERPRISE OFFICE.
- o   KICKSTARTER.
- o   KILKENNY LEADER PARTNERSHIP LTD.
- o   LAGAN RURAL PARTNERSHIP.
- o   LAOIS PARTNERSHIP COMPANY.
- o   LEADER NORTHERN IRELAND.
- o   LEADER.
- o   LEITRIM LOCAL ENTERPRISE OFFICE.
- o   LINKEDFINANCE
- o   LISBURN ENTERPRISE ORGANISATION LTD.
- o   LOCAL ENTERPRISE DEVELOPMENT COMPANY LTD.
- o   LOCAL ENTERPRISE OFFICE CARLOW.
- o   LOCAL ENTERPRISE OFFICE CAVAN.
- o   LOCAL ENTERPRISE OFFICE CLARE.
- o   LOCAL ENTERPRISE OFFICE CORK CITY.
- o   LOCAL ENTERPRISE OFFICE CORK NORTH & WEST.
- o   LOCAL ENTERPRISE OFFICE DUBLIN CITY.
- o   LOCAL ENTERPRISE OFFICE DUN LAOGHAIRE-RATHDOWN.
- o   LOCAL ENTERPRISE OFFICE FINGAL.
- o   LOCAL ENTERPRISE OFFICE GALWAY.
- o   LOCAL ENTERPRISE OFFICE KILDARE.
- o   LOCAL ENTERPRISE OFFICE KILKENNY.
- o   LOCAL ENTERPRISE OFFICE LAOIS.
- o   LOCAL ENTERPRISE OFFICE LIMERICK.
- o   LOCAL ENTERPRISE OFFICE LOUTH.
- o   LOCAL ENTERPRISE OFFICE MAYO.
- o   LOCAL ENTERPRISE OFFICE MONAGHAN.
- o   LOCAL ENTERPRISE OFFICE OFFALY.
- o   LOCAL ENTERPRISE OFFICE ROSCOMMON.
- o   LOCAL ENTERPRISE OFFICE SLIGO.
- o   LOCAL ENTERPRISE OFFICE SOUTH CORK.

- LOCAL ENTERPRISE OFFICE WESTMEATH.
- LOCAL ENTERPRISE OFFICE WICKLOW.
- LOCAL ENTERPRISE OFFICES.
- LOMBARD.
- LONGFORD COMMUNITY RESOURCES LTD.
- LONGFORD LOCAL ENTERPRISE OFFICE.
- LOUGH SHORE INVESTMENTS.
- LOUTH CRAFTMARK.
- LOUTH LEADER PARTNERSHIP.
- MALLUSK ENTERPRISE PARK.
- MAYO NORTH EAST LEADER PARTNERSHIP.
- MEATH LOCAL ENTERPRISE OFFICE.
- MEATH PARTNERSHIP.
- MICHELIN DEVELOPMENT.
- MICROFINANCE IRELAND.
- MID & EAST ANTRIM LOCAL ACTION GROUP.
- MID ULSTER RURAL DEVELOPMENT PARTNERSHIP.
- MML GROWTH CAPITAL PARTNERS.
- MOURNE, GULLION & LECALE RURAL DEVELOPMENT PARTNERSHIP.
- MOY VALLEY RESOURCES IRD.
- NDRC.
- NEW FRONTIERS.
- NEWRY & MOURNE ENTERPRISE AGENCY.
- NORTH CITY BUSINESS CENTRE LTD.
- NORTH DOWN DEVELOPMENT ORGANISATION LTD.
- NORTH TIPPERARY LEADER PARTNERSHIP.
- NORTH, EAST & WEST KERRY DEVELOPMENT.
- NORTHERN IRELAND SCREEN.
- NORTHERN IRELAND SMALL BUSINESS LOAN FUND.
- OFFALY INTEGRATED LOCAL DEVELOPMENT CLG.
- OMAGH ENTERPRISE COMPANY LTD.
- ORMEAU BUSINESS PARK.
- ORTUS GROUP.
- OYSTER CAPITAL PARTNERS.
- PERMANENT TSB.
- POLARIS PARTNERS.
- POWERSCOURT CAPITAL PARTNERS.

- PRINCE'S TRUST NORTHERN IRELAND.
- QUBIS LTD.
- QUEEN'S UNIVERSITY BELFAST.
- ROE VALLEY ENTERPRISES LTD.
- ROSCOMMON LEADER PARTNERSHIP.
- RURAL PARTNERS ARDS & NORTH DOWN.
- SCREEN IRELAND.
- SEEDUPS.ie.
- SEROBA LIFE SCIENCES LTD.
- SHELL LIVEWIRE UK.
- SOAR (ABC).
- SOCIAL ENTREPRENEURS IRELAND.
- SOCIAL INNOVATION FUND IRELAND.
- SOS VENTURES.
- SOUTH & EAST CORK AREA DEVELOPMENT LTD.
- SOUTH KERRY DEVELOPMENT PARTNERSHIP.
- SOUTH TIPPERARY DEVELOPMENT CLG.
- SOUTH WEST MAYO DEVELOPMENT COMPANY CLG.
- SPARK CROWDFUNDING.
- START UP LOANS COMPANY.
- START-UP REFUNDS FOR ENTREPRENEURS.
- STRABANE ENTERPRISE AGENCY.
- STRATEGIC BANKING CORPORATION OF IRELAND.
- SUIR VALLEY VENTURES.
- TECHSTARTNI.
- TIPPERARY LOCAL ENTERPRISE OFFICE.
- TOURISM NORTHERN IRELAND.
- ÚDARÁS NA GAELTACHTA.
- ULSTER BANK.
- ULSTER COMMUNITY INVESTMENT TRUST LTD.
- ULSTER UNIVERSITY.
- UNLTD.
- WATERFORD LEADER PARTNERSHIP CLG.
- WATERFORD LOCAL ENTERPRISE OFFICE.
- WEST LIMERICK RESOURCES LTD.
- WESTERN DEVELOPMENT COMMISSION.
- WESTMEATH COMMUNITY DEVELOPMENT LTD.
- WEXFORD LOCAL DEVELOPMENT.

○ WEXFORD LOCAL ENTERPRISE OFFICE.
○ WHITEROCK CAPITAL PARTNERS.
○ WORK WEST ENTERPRISE AGENCY.
○ WORKSPACE ENTERPRISES LTD.

INCUBATION & WORK SPACE

A large number of organisations provide (as part of a support package or separately on a commercial basis) incubation or work space tailored to the needs of a start-up, including:

○ ACE ENTERPRISE PARK.
○ ALLENWOOD COMMUNITY DEVELOPMENT ASSOCIATION LTD.
○ ANTRIM ENTERPRISE AGENCY LTD.
○ ARCLABS.
○ ARDEE COMMUNITY DEVELOPMENT COMPANY LTD.
○ ARDS BUSINESS CENTRE LTD.
○ ARGYLE BUSINESS CENTRE LTD.
○ ARKLOW BUSINESS ENTERPRISE CENTRE.
○ ARMAGH BUSINESS CENTRE LTD.
○ ATHLONE INSTITUTE OF TECHNOLOGY.
○ ATHY COMMUNITY ENTERPRISE COMPANY LTD.
○ BAILIEBOROUGH BUSINESS CENTRE.
○ BALBRIGGAN ENTERPRISE & TRAINING CENTRE.
○ BALBRIGGAN ENTERPRISE DEVELOPMENT GROUP.
○ BALLINAMORE ENTERPRISE CENTRE.
○ BALLINASLOE AREA COMMUNITY DEVELOPMENT LTD.
○ BALLYHAUNIS ENTERPRISE CENTRE.
○ BALLYHOURA DEVELOPMENT CLG.
○ BALLYMENA BUSINESS CENTRE LTD.
○ BANBRIDGE DISTRICT ENTERPRISES LTD.
○ BANK OF IRELAND WORKBENCH.
○ BASE ENTERPRISE CENTRE CLG.
○ BNEST.
○ BOLTON TRUST.
○ BOYLE ENTERPRISE & MORE.
○ BUSINESS INCUBATION CENTRE.
○ BUSINESS INNOVATION CENTRE NUI GALWAY.
○ BUSINESS INNOVATION CENTRES.

- CARLOW COMMUNITY ENTERPRISE CENTRES LTD.
- CARRICK BUSINESS CENTRE.
- CARRICKFERGUS ENTERPRISE AGENCY LTD.
- CASTLEBLAYNEY ENTERPRISE CENTRE.
- CASTLECOMER ENTERPRISE GROUP LTD.
- CATALYST INC.
- CAUSEWAY ENTERPRISE AGENCY.
- CAVAN COUNTY ENTERPRISE FUND.
- CAVAN INNOVATION & TECHNOLOGY CENTRE.
- CLANE PROJECT CENTRE.
- COLAB LYIT.
- COLLEGE FOR AGRICULTURE, FOOD & RURAL ENTERPRISE.
- CONVOY ENTERPRISE CENTRE.
- COOKSTOWN ENTERPRISE CENTRE LTD.
- COOLOCK DEVELOPMENT COUNCIL.
- CORK BUSINESS INNOVATION CENTRE.
- CORK INCUBATOR KITCHEN.
- CORK INSTITUTE OF TECHNOLOGY.
- COWORKING IN IRELAND.
- CRAIGAVON INDUSTRIAL DEVELOPMENT ORGANISATION LTD.
- CREATIVE SPARK CLG.
- CROOM COMMUNITY ENTERPRISE CENTRE.
- DCU ALPHA INNOVATION CAMPUS.
- DCU INVENT.
- DIGITAL HUB DEVELOPMENT AGENCY.
- DIT HOTHOUSE.
- DOGPATCH LABS.
- DOWN BUSINESS CENTRE.
- DRINAN ENTERPRISE CENTRE.
- DRUMSHANBO ENTERPRISE CENTRE.
- DUBLIN BUSINESS INNOVATION CENTRE.
- DUBLIN CITY UNIVERSITY.
- DUBLIN INSTITUTE OF TECHNOLOGY.
- DÚN LAOIRE ENTERPRISE CENTRE.
- DUNDALK INSTITUTE OF TECHNOLOGY.
- DUNGANNON ENTERPRISE CENTRE LTD.
- DUNGARVAN ENTERPRISE CENTRE.
- DUNHILL ECOPARK.

- EAST BELFAST ENTERPRISE.
- ENTERPRISE & RESEARCH INCUBATION CAMPUS.
- ENTERPRISE NORTH WEST.
- ENTERPRISE YOUGHAL.
- ENTERPRISING MONAGHAN.
- FERBANE BUSINESS & TECHNOLOGY PARK.
- FERBANE FOOD CAMPUS.
- FERMANAGH ENTERPRISE LTD.
- FIONTARLANN TEO.
- FLAX TRUST.
- FOOD HUB.
- FUMBALLY EXCHANGE.
- GALWAY TECHNOLOGY CENTRE.
- GALWAY–MAYO INSTITUTE OF TECHNOLOGY.
- GATEWAY UCC.
- GLENWOOD ENTERPRISES LTD.
- GMIT INNOVATION HUBS.
- GUINNESS ENTERPRISE CENTRE.
- HARTNETT ENTERPRISE ACCELERATION CENTRE.
- HOUR KITCHEN.
- IADT MEDIA CUBE.
- INNOVATE-NI.
- INNOVATION CENTRE.
- INSPIRE BUSINESS CENTRE.
- INSTITUTE OF ART, DESIGN & TECHNOLOGY.
- INSTITUTE OF TECHNOLOGY BLANCHARDSTOWN.
- INSTITUTE OF TECHNOLOGY CARLOW.
- INSTITUTE OF TECHNOLOGY SLIGO.
- INSTITUTE OF TECHNOLOGY TRALEE.
- IRD KILTIMAGH.
- ITT DUBLIN.
- JOE GILMORE ENTERPRISE CENTRE.
- KELLS ENTERPRISE & TECHNOLOGY CENTRE.
- KILLARNEY TECHNOLOGY INNOVATION LTD.
- LETTERKENNY INSTITUTE OF TECHNOLOGY.
- LIFFEY TRUST.
- LIMERICK ENTERPRISE DEVELOPMENT PARTNERSHIP.
- LIMERICK INSTITUTE OF TECHNOLOGY.

- o LISBURN ENTERPRISE ORGANISATION LTD.
- o LOCAL ENTERPRISE DEVELOPMENT COMPANY LTD.
- o LUDGATE HUB.
- o MACROOM E BUSINESS CENTRE.
- o MALLUSK ENTERPRISE PARK.
- o MAYNOOTHWORKS.
- o MEATH ENTERPRISE.
- o MIDLANDS INNOVATION & RESEARCH CENTRE.
- o MOHILL ENTERPRISE CENTRE.
- o MOUNTMELLICK DEVELOPMENT ASSOCIATION.
- o MOY VALLEY RESOURCES IRD.
- o MULLINGAR EMPLOYMENT ACTION GROUP.
- o NATIONAL ASSOCIATION OF COMMUNITY ENTERPRISE CENTRES.
- o NATIONAL COLLEGE OF IRELAND.
- o NATIONAL FRANCHISE CENTRE.
- o NATIONAL UNIVERSITY OF IRELAND GALWAY.
- o NATIONAL UNIVERSITY OF IRELAND MAYNOOTH.
- o NEWMARKET KITCHEN.
- o NEWRY & MOURNE ENTERPRISE AGENCY.
- o NEXUS INNOVATION CENTRE.
- o NORTH CITY BUSINESS CENTRE LTD.
- o NORTH DOWN DEVELOPMENT ORGANISATION LTD.
- o NORTH TIPPERARY FOODWORKS.
- o NORTHERN IRELAND SCREEN.
- o NORTHSIDE ENTERPRISE CENTRE.
- o NOVAUCD.
- o NSC CAMPUS.
- o NUTGROVE ENTERPRISE PARK.
- o OMAGH ENTERPRISE COMPANY LTD.
- o ORIGIN8.
- o ORMEAU BUSINESS PARK.
- o ORTUS GROUP.
- o PARTAS.
- o PILTOWN COMMUNITY ENTERPRISE.
- o PLUS 10.
- o PORTARLINGTON ENTERPRISE CENTRE.
- o PORTLAOISE ENTERPRISE CENTRE.
- o PREMIER BUSINESS CENTRES.

- QUEEN'S UNIVERSITY BELFAST.
- QUESTUM ACCELERATION CENTRE.
- REGIONAL DEVELOPMENT CENTRE.
- REPUBLIC OF WORK.
- ROE VALLEY ENTERPRISES LTD.
- RUBICON CENTRE.
- SCCUL ENTERPRISE CENTRE.
- SCHOOL OF FOOD.
- SHANNON COMMERCIAL PROPERTIES.
- SHANNON GROUP PLC.
- SLIGO ENTERPRISE & TECHNOLOGY CENTRE.
- SOUTH EAST BUSINESS INNOVATION CENTRE.
- SPADE ENTERPRISE CENTRE.
- STRABANE ENTERPRISE AGENCY.
- SYNERGY CENTRE.
- SYNERGY GLOBAL.
- TALENT GARDEN DUBLIN.
- TALLOW ENTERPRISE CENTRE.
- TERENURE ENTERPRISE CENTRE.
- THE BASE ENTERPRISE CENTRE.
- THE HIVE.
- THE LINC.
- TOM CREAN BUSINESS CENTRE.
- TOWNSEND BUSINESS PARK.
- TRINITY COLLEGE DUBLIN.
- TRINITY TECHNOLOGY & ENTERPRISE CAMPUS.
- ÚDARÁS NA GAELTACHTA.
- UNIVERSITY COLLEGE CORK.
- UNIVERSITY COLLEGE DUBLIN.
- UNIVERSITY OF LIMERICK.
- WATERFORD INSTITUTE OF TECHNOLOGY.
- WESTBIC.
- WESTMEATH COMMUNITY DEVELOPMENT LTD.
- WEXFORD ENTERPRISE CENTRE.
- WICKLOW ENTERPRISE CENTRE.
- WORK WEST ENTERPRISE AGENCY.
- WORKSPACE ENTERPRISES LTD.

INFORMATION

Information is critical to a good business plan and a well-managed start-up. Many potential sources of market research information were identified in *Chapter 2* and are listed below.

Recognise that some of these organisations are member-based and thus restrict their services to members only, or charge fees to non-members for access to training and other supports. Most of the organisations listed are key players in their own industries, with a good finger on what's happening – so it may be well worth your while paying for their specialist insight.

o AIB BANK.
o ANTRIM ENTERPRISE AGENCY LTD.
o BeSMART.ie.
o BORD BIA.
o BORDBIAVANTAGE.
o BUSINESS INFORMATION CENTRE.
o BUSINESS PLUS.
o BUSINESS POST.
o BUSINESSACHIEVERS.com.
o BUSINESSREGULATION.IE.
o CENTRAL STATISTICS OFFICE.
o COMPANIES HOUSE.
o COMPANIES REGISTRATION OFFICE.
o CREATIVEIRELAND.com.
o CRUCIAL CROWDFUNDING.
o DCCOIENTERPRISE.ie.
o DEPARTMENT OF EMPLOYMENT AFFAIRS & SOCIAL PROTECTION.
o DONEGAL LOCAL ENTERPRISE OFFICE.
o DUBLIN SOUTH LOCAL ENTERPRISE OFFICE.
o EAST BELFAST ENTERPRISE.
o ENERGY CO-OPERATIVES IRELAND.
o ENTERPRISE EUROPE NETWORK.
o ENTERPRISE IRELAND.
o ENTERPRISE NORTH WEST.
o ENTERPRISE NORTHERN IRELAND.
o ENVIRONMENTAL PROTECTION AGENCY.
o EUROPA.

- ○ EUROPEDIRECT.ie.
- ○ FÁILTE IRELAND.
- ○ FOOD SAFETY AUTHORITY OF IRELAND.
- ○ FOUNTAIN RESOURCE GROUP.
- ○ FRANCHISE DIRECT.
- ○ GOV.ie.
- ○ GOVERNMENT PUBLICATIONS OFFICE.
- ○ HEALTH & SAFETY AUTHORITY.
- ○ HEALTH & SAFETY EXECUTIVE FOR NORTHERN IRELAND.
- ○ HM REVENUE & CUSTOMS.
- ○ INSTITUTE OF MANAGEMENT CONSULTANTS & ADVISERS.
- ○ INSTITUTE OF PUBLIC ADMINISTRATION.
- ○ INTERTRADEIRELAND.
- ○ INVESTNI.
- ○ IRISH SINGLE POINT OF CONTACT.
- ○ KERRY LOCAL ENTERPRISE OFFICE.
- ○ KNOWLEDGE TRANSFER IRELAND.
- ○ LEGAL-ISLAND.
- ○ LEITRIM LOCAL ENTERPRISE OFFICE.
- ○ LIBRARIES NI BUSINESS INFORMATION SERVICE.
- ○ LOCAL ENTERPRISE OFFICE CARLOW.
- ○ LOCAL ENTERPRISE OFFICE CAVAN.
- ○ LOCAL ENTERPRISE OFFICE CLARE.
- ○ LOCAL ENTERPRISE OFFICE CORK CITY.
- ○ LOCAL ENTERPRISE OFFICE CORK NORTH & WEST.
- ○ LOCAL ENTERPRISE OFFICE DUBLIN CITY.
- ○ LOCAL ENTERPRISE OFFICE DUN LAOGHAIRE-RATHDOWN.
- ○ LOCAL ENTERPRISE OFFICE FINGAL.
- ○ LOCAL ENTERPRISE OFFICE GALWAY.
- ○ LOCAL ENTERPRISE OFFICE KILDARE.
- ○ LOCAL ENTERPRISE OFFICE KILKENNY.
- ○ LOCAL ENTERPRISE OFFICE LAOIS.
- ○ LOCAL ENTERPRISE OFFICE LIMERICK.
- ○ LOCAL ENTERPRISE OFFICE LOUTH.
- ○ LOCAL ENTERPRISE OFFICE MAYO.
- ○ LOCAL ENTERPRISE OFFICE MONAGHAN.
- ○ LOCAL ENTERPRISE OFFICE OFFALY.
- ○ LOCAL ENTERPRISE OFFICE ROSCOMMON.

o　LOCAL ENTERPRISE OFFICE SLIGO.
o　LOCAL ENTERPRISE OFFICE SOUTH CORK.
o　LOCAL ENTERPRISE OFFICE WESTMEATH.
o　LOCAL ENTERPRISE OFFICE WICKLOW.
o　LOCAL ENTERPRISE OFFICES.
o　LONGFORD LOCAL ENTERPRISE OFFICE.
o　MEATH LOCAL ENTERPRISE OFFICE.
o　NATIONAL STANDARDS AUTHORITY OF IRELAND.
o　NIBUSINESSINFO.CO.UK.
o　NORTHERN IRELAND STATISTICS & RESEARCH AGENCY.
o　OAK TREE PRESS.
o　OFFICE OF THE DIRECTOR OF CORPORATE ENFORCEMENT.
o　PATENTS OFFICE.
o　REVENUE COMMISSIONERS.
o　SENIOR ENTERPRISE.
o　SILICONREPUBLIC.com.
o　START UP EUROPE CLUB.
o　STARTUPS.ie.
o　SUPPORTINGSMES.ie.
o　TERENURE ENTERPRISE CENTRE.
o　THINKBUSINESS.IE.
o　TIPPERARY LOCAL ENTERPRISE OFFICE.
o　WATERFORD LOCAL ENTERPRISE OFFICE.
o　WEXFORD LOCAL ENTERPRISE OFFICE.
o　WOMENMEANBUSINESS.com.
o　WORKPLACERELATIONS.ie.
o　YOUR EUROPE.

INNOVATION & R&D

Innovation – though it need not always be high tech innovation – is key to success in business today. The following organisations assist start-ups in the areas of innovation and / or R&D:

o　ANTRIM ENTERPRISE AGENCY LTD.
o　ARCLABS.
o　ARDS BUSINESS CENTRE LTD.
o　ATHLONE INSTITUTE OF TECHNOLOGY.
o　BALLYHOURA DEVELOPMENT CLG.

- o BALLYMENA BUSINESS CENTRE LTD.
- o CARRICKFERGUS ENTERPRISE AGENCY LTD.
- o CATALYST INC.
- o CO-INNOVATE PROGRAMME.
- o COLAB LYIT.
- o COLLEGE FOR AGRICULTURE, FOOD & RURAL ENTERPRISE.
- o CRAIGAVON INDUSTRIAL DEVELOPMENT ORGANISATION LTD.
- o DCU INVENT.
- o DEPARTMENT FOR THE ECONOMY.
- o DIT HOTHOUSE.
- o DUBLIN INSTITUTE OF TECHNOLOGY.
- o EAST BELFAST ENTERPRISE.
- o EDEN CENTRE FOR ENTREPRENEURSHIP, DESIGN & INNOVATION.
- o EUROPEAN SPACE AGENCY.
- o FOOD HUB.
- o FOOD PRODUCT DEVELOPMENT CENTRE.
- o FOODOVATION.
- o GALWAY–MAYO INSTITUTE OF TECHNOLOGY.
- o GATEWAY UCC.
- o GMIT INNOVATION HUBS.
- o HORIZON 2020.
- o INNOVATE UK.
- o INNOVATION CENTRE.
- o INNOVATION ULSTER LTD.
- o INSPIRE BUSINESS CENTRE.
- o INSTITUTE OF TECHNOLOGY BLANCHARDSTOWN.
- o INSTITUTE OF TECHNOLOGY CARLOW.
- o INSTITUTE OF TECHNOLOGY SLIGO.
- o INSTITUTE OF TECHNOLOGY TRALEE.
- o INTERTRADEIRELAND.
- o INVESTNI.
- o ITT DUBLIN.
- o KILKENNY RESEARCH & INNOVATION CENTRE.
- o LETTERKENNY INSTITUTE OF TECHNOLOGY.
- o LIMERICK INSTITUTE OF TECHNOLOGY.
- o LISBURN ENTERPRISE ORGANISATION LTD.
- o LOCAL ENTERPRISE DEVELOPMENT COMPANY LTD.
- o MALLUSK ENTERPRISE PARK.

o   MARINE INSTITUTE.
o   MEATH ENTERPRISE.
o   NATIONAL UNIVERSITY OF IRELAND GALWAY.
o   NATIONAL UNIVERSITY OF IRELAND MAYNOOTH.
o   NORTHERN IRELAND TECHNOLOGY CENTRE.
o   NOVA UCD.
o   ORIGIN8.
o   ORMEAU BUSINESS PARK.
o   ORTUS GROUP.
o   QUBIS LTD.
o   QUEEN'S UNIVERSITY BELFAST.
o   SHELL LIVEWIRE UK.
o   TEAGASC.
o   TECHNOLOGY IRELAND INNOVATION FORUM.
o   TECHNOLOGY IRELAND.
o   TRINITY COLLEGE DUBLIN.
o   TYNDALL NATIONAL INSTITUTE.
o   ULSTER UNIVERSITY.
o   UNIVERSITY COLLEGE CORK.
o   UNIVERSITY COLLEGE DUBLIN.
o   UNIVERSITY OF LIMERICK.
o   WATERFORD INSTITUTE OF TECHNOLOGY.
o   WORK WEST ENTERPRISE AGENCY.
o   WORKPLACE INNOVATION TOOLKIT.
o   YOUNG SOCIAL INNOVATORS.

IP & LEGAL

Intellectual property (IP) describes the various rights conferred by patents, trade marks, copyright, etc. Under Irish, UK and EU law, you can protect your 'rights' in inventions and so on (but not in ideas alone). You can then exploit these rights yourself or license or sell them to others – this is sometimes called 'technology transfer'. Often technology transfer works on an inwards basis, with Irish businesses acquiring rights to use technologies developed elsewhere. It's a specialist area in which you should take advice and proceed with caution.

Consider these sources of assistance:

o   ANNE RYAN & CO.

- o CHARTERED INSTITUTE OF PERSONNEL & DEVELOPMENT.
- o COMPANY FORMATIONS INTERNATIONAL LTD.
- o COMPANY SETUP.
- o CRUICKSHANK & CO.
- o DEFINITION IP.
- o EUROPEAN IPR HELP DESK.
- o FF GORMAN & CO.
- o FR KELLY & CO.
- o HANNA MOORE & CURLEY.
- o INTELLECTUAL PROPERTY OFFICE.
- o ISLAND PATENTS.
- o LABOUR RELATIONS AGENCY.
- o LAW SOCIETY OF IRELAND.
- o LAW SOCIETY OF NORTHERN IRELAND.
- o LEGAL-ISLAND.
- o MacLACHLAN & DONALDSON.
- o MURGITROYD.
- o O'BRIEN (JOHN A.) & ASSOCIATES.
- o O'CONNOR INTELLECTUAL PROPERTY.
- o OFFICE OF THE DIRECTOR OF CORPORATE ENFORCEMENT.
- o PATENTS OFFICE.
- o PURDYLUCEY.
- o RDJSTARTUPS.ie.
- o SMALL FIRMS ASSOCIATION.
- o TOMKINS.
- o WELDON (MICHAEL) & CO.
- o WORKPLACERELATIONS.ie.

INWARDS INVESTMENT

Bringing Foreign Direct Investment to the country is primarily a State responsibility, though some private sector advisers assist here too:

- o BYRNE & McCALL.
- o IDA IRELAND.
- o INVESTNI.
- o IRISH NATURALISATION & IMMIGRATION SERVICE.

MARKETING

A consistent failing of Irish business has been – and still is, sadly – its lack of emphasis on, and commitment to, marketing. That this is changing is shown by the number of organisations committed to helping small businesses succeed at marketing, including:

o   AMÁRACH CONSULTING.
o   ASPIRE! MANAGEMENT CONSULTANTS.
o   BORD BIA.
o   BORD IASCAIGH MHARA.
o   DESIGN & CRAFTS COUNCIL OF IRELAND.
o   DUBLIN FOOD CHAIN.
o   EXCELLENCE IRELAND QUALITY ASSOCIATION.
o   FÁILTE IRELAND.
o   GUARANTEED IRISH LTD.
o   LIFFEY TRUST.
o   LOUTH CRAFTMARK.
o   MARKETING INSTITUTE OF IRELAND.
o   NORTHERN IRELAND FOOD & DRINK ASSOCIATION.
o   PUBLIC RELATIONS CONSULTANTS ASSOCIATION OF IRELAND.
o   PUBLIC RELATIONS INSTITUTE OF IRELAND.
o   SALES INSTITUTE OF IRELAND.
o   TOURISM NORTHERN IRELAND.
o   WESTBIC.

NETWORKING

If you're not out and about meeting people for some part of your time, you're probably missing opportunities to meet potential customers, to find out what competitors are up to, or to spot new business leads.

Here are some sources of networking opportunities:

o   BANK OF IRELAND WORKBENCH.
o   BUSINESSACHIEVERS.com.
o   CHAMBERS IRELAND.
o   COLAB LYIT.
o   CREATIVEIRELAND.com.
o   DUBLIN BUSINESS INNOVATION CENTRE.
o   DUBLIN FOOD CHAIN.

- ○ ENTREPRENEURS ANONYMOUS.
- ○ FSB NORTHERN IRELAND.
- ○ INNOVATION CENTRE.
- ○ INSTITUTE OF DIRECTORS IN IRELAND.
- ○ IRISH COUNTRYWOMEN'S ASSOCIATION.
- ○ IRISH EXPORTERS ASSOCIATION.
- ○ IRISH INSTITUTE OF TRAINING & DEVELOPMENT.
- ○ IRISH INTERNET ASSOCIATION.
- ○ IRISH MANAGEMENT INSTITUTE.
- ○ IRISH SMALL & MEDIUM ENTERPRISES ASSOCIATION.
- ○ LOUTH CRAFTMARK.
- ○ LUDGATE HUB.
- ○ MAYNOOTHWORKS.
- ○ NATIONAL GUILD OF MASTER CRAFTSMEN.
- ○ NETWORK FOR ENTERPRISING WOMEN.
- ○ NETWORK IRELAND.
- ○ NORTHERN IRELAND CHAMBER OF COMMERCE & INDUSTRY.
- ○ NORTHERN IRELAND FOOD & DRINK ASSOCIATION.
- ○ NORTHERN IRELAND RURAL WOMEN'S NETWORK.
- ○ REPUBLIC OF WORK.
- ○ RURAL COMMUNITY NETWORK.
- ○ RURAL NETWORK NI.
- ○ SALES INSTITUTE OF IRELAND.
- ○ SMALL FIRMS ASSOCIATION.
- ○ START UP EUROPE CLUB.
- ○ TALENT GARDEN DUBLIN.
- ○ TECHNOLOGY IRELAND INNOVATION FORUM.
- ○ TECHNOLOGY IRELAND.
- ○ WESTBIC.
- ○ WOMENMEANBUSINESS.com.

POLICY

Although well-removed from the day-to-day concerns of entrepreneurs, policy is critical to a flourishing economy. Organisations active in this area include:

- ○ CENTRE FOR CROSS-BORDER STUDIES.
- ○ DEPARTMENT FOR THE ECONOMY.

o   DEPARTMENT OF AGRICULTURE, ENVIRONMENT & RURAL AFFAIRS.
o   DEPARTMENT OF AGRICULTURE, FOOD & THE MARINE.
o   DEPARTMENT OF BUSINESS, ENTERPRISE & INNOVATION.
o   DEPARTMENT OF EMPLOYMENT AFFAIRS & SOCIAL PROTECTION.
o   DEPARTMENT OF HOUSING, PLANNING & LOCAL GOVERNMENT.
o   DEPARTMENT OF JUSTICE & EQUALITY.
o   DEPARTMENT OF RURAL & COMMUNITY DEVELOPMENT.
o   EASTERN & MIDLAND REGIONAL ASSEMBLY.
o   FSB NORTHERN IRELAND.
o   IBEC.
o   INTERTRADEIRELAND.
o   IRISH SMALL & MEDIUM ENTERPRISES ASSOCIATION.
o   MARINE INSTITUTE.
o   NORTHERN & WESTERN REGIONAL ASSEMBLY.
o   SMALL FIRMS ASSOCIATION.
o   SOUTHERN REGIONAL ASSEMBLY.
o   WESTERN DEVELOPMENT COMMISSION.

REGULATION & STANDARDS

Organisations that are engaged in setting, monitoring or enforcing regulation or standards include:

o   BORD BIA.
o   BORD IASCAIGH MHARA.
o   BRITISH STANDARDS INSTITUTION.
o   BUSINESSREGULATION.ie.
o   COMPANIES HOUSE.
o   COMPANIES REGISTRATION OFFICE.
o   COMPETITION & CONSUMER PROTECTION COMMISSION.
o   CREDIT REVIEW OFFICE.
o   DATA PROTECTION COMMISSION.
o   DEPARTMENT FOR THE ECONOMY.
o   DEPARTMENT OF AGRICULTURE, ENVIRONMENT & RURAL AFFAIRS.
o   DEPARTMENT OF AGRICULTURE, FOOD & THE MARINE.
o   DEPARTMENT OF BUSINESS, ENTERPRISE & INNOVATION.
o   DEPARTMENT OF EMPLOYMENT AFFAIRS & SOCIAL PROTECTION.
o   DEPARTMENT OF HOUSING, PLANNING & LOCAL GOVERNMENT.
o   DEPARTMENT OF JUSTICE & EQUALITY.

- o DEPARTMENT OF RURAL & COMMUNITY DEVELOPMENT.
- o ENVIRONMENTAL PROTECTION AGENCY.
- o EXCELLENCE IRELAND QUALITY ASSOCIATION.
- o FOOD SAFETY AUTHORITY OF IRELAND.
- o HEALTH & SAFETY AUTHORITY.
- o HEALTH & SAFETY EXECUTIVE FOR NORTHERN IRELAND.
- o HM REVENUE & CUSTOMS.
- o IE DOMAIN REGISTRY CLG.
- o INTELLECTUAL PROPERTY OFFICE.
- o IRISH NATURALISATION & IMMIGRATION SERVICE.
- o IRISH ORGANIC ASSOCIATION.
- o LICENCES.ie.
- o NATIONAL GUILD OF MASTER CRAFTSMEN.
- o NATIONAL STANDARDS AUTHORITY OF IRELAND.
- o OFFICE OF THE DIRECTOR OF CORPORATE ENFORCEMENT.
- o PATENTS OFFICE.
- o REVENUE COMMISSIONERS.
- o SEA-FISHERIES PROTECTION AUTHORITY.
- o TOURISM NORTHERN IRELAND.

SOCIAL ENTERPRISE

Social enterprise (including co-operatives) is the 'third way', balancing a profitability with social objectives. Organisations that support social enterprises include:

- o ANTRIM ENTERPRISE AGENCY LTD.
- o BNEST.
- o CENTRE FOR CO-OPERATIVE STUDIES.
- o CLANE PROJECT CENTRE.
- o CLANN CREDO.
- o CO-OPERATIVE HOUSING IRELAND.
- o COMMUNITY FINANCE (IRELAND).
- o CREGGAN ENTERPRISES.
- o DONEGAL LOCAL DEVELOPMENT COMPANY CLG.
- o DUBLIN CITY COMMUNITY CO-OP.
- o DUNHILL ECOPARK.
- o ENACTUS IRELAND.
- o ENERGY CO-OPERATIVES IRELAND.

- o   ENTERPRISE NORTH WEST.
- o   FORUM CONNEMARA CLG.
- o   GALWAY CITY PARTNERSHIP.
- o   INNER CITY ENTERPRISE.
- o   IRISH CO-OPERATIVE SOCIETY LTD.
- o   IRISH LEAGUE OF CREDIT UNIONS.
- o   IRISH SOCIAL ENTERPRISE NETWORK.
- o   LOCAL ENTERPRISE DEVELOPMENT COMPANY LTD.
- o   MOY VALLEY RESOURCES IRD.
- o   NEWRY & MOURNE ENTERPRISE AGENCY.
- o   NORTHSIDE PARTNERSHIP.
- o   ORTUS GROUP.
- o   PARTAS.
- o   PAUL PARTNERSHIP LIMERICK.
- o   RURAL SUPPORT.
- o   SOCIAL ENTERPRISE DEVELOPMENT COMPANY LTD.
- o   SOCIAL ENTERPRISE NI.
- o   SOCIAL ENTREPRENEURS IRELAND.
- o   SOCIAL INNOVATION FUND IRELAND.
- o   SOUTH DUBLIN COUNTY PARTNERSHIP.
- o   SOUTHSIDE PARTNERSHIP DLR LTD.
- o   ULSTER COMMUNITY INVESTMENT TRUST LTD.
- o   UNLTD.
- o   WEXFORD ENTERPRISE CENTRE.
- o   WORK WEST ENTERPRISE AGENCY.
- o   WORKSPACE ENTERPRISES LTD.
- o   YOUNG SOCIAL INNOVATORS.

TRAINING & MENTORING

It's not enough to start a business – in some ways, that's actually the easy bit! – you also have to keep it going. And as you do, you will discover that you need new skills or need to further develop existing skills. Most professional bodies have made continuing training a condition of membership. You could do worse than adopt the same high standards for your new profession of entrepreneur.

The following organisations offer training and / or mentoring – in start-up skills and across a wide range of other, often specialist, topics – to entrepreneurs:

o   ACE ENTERPRISE PARK.
o   ADVANTAGE.
o   ALLENWOOD COMMUNITY DEVELOPMENT ASSOCIATION LTD.
o   ANTRIM ENTERPRISE AGENCY LTD.
o   ARCLABS.
o   ARDEE COMMUNITY DEVELOPMENT COMPANY LTD.
o   ARDS BUSINESS CENTRE LTD.
o   ARKLOW BUSINESS ENTERPRISE CENTRE.
o   ARMAGH BUSINESS CENTRE LTD.
o   ASPIRE! MANAGEMENT CONSULTANTS.
o   ATHLONE INSTITUTE OF TECHNOLOGY.
o   BALBRIGGAN ENTERPRISE & TRAINING CENTRE.
o   BALBRIGGAN ENTERPRISE DEVELOPMENT GROUP.
o   BALLYFERMOT CHAPELIZOD PARTNERSHIP COMPANY LTD.
o   BALLYMENA BUSINESS CENTRE LTD .
o   BANBRIDGE DISTRICT ENTERPRISE.
o   BIZMENTORS.ie.
o   BLACKSTONE LAUNCHPAD.
o   BNEST.
o   BORD BIA.
o   BORD IASCAIGH MHARA.
o   BORDBIAVANTAGE.
o   BRAY AREA PARTNERSHIP.
o   BREFFNI INTEGRATED CLG.
o   BUSINESS INCUBATION CENTRE.
o   BUSINESS INNOVATION CENTRE NUI GALWAY.
o   BUSINESS INNOVATION CENTRES.
o   CARLOW COUNTY DEVELOPMENT PARTNERSHIP CLG.
o   CARRICKFERGUS ENTERPRISE AGENCY LTD.
o   CASTLEBLAYNEY ENTERPRISE CENTRE.
o   CAUSEWAY ENTERPRISE AGENCY.
o   CAVAN INNOVATION & TECHNOLOGY CENTRE.
o   CENTRE FOR CO-OPERATIVE STUDIES.
o   CENTRE FOR CROSS-BORDER STUDIES.

o CHARTERED INSTITUTE OF PERSONNEL & DEVELOPMENT.

o CLARE LOCAL DEVELOPMENT COMPANY LTD.

o COLAB LYIT.

o COLLEGE FOR AGRICULTURE, FOOD & RURAL ENTERPRISE.

o COOKSTOWN ENTERPRISE CENTRE LTD.

o CORK BUSINESS INNOVATION CENTRE.

o CORK CITY PARTNERSHIP CLG.

o CORK INSTITUTE OF TECHNOLOGY.

o COUNTY SLIGO LEADER PARTNERSHIP COMPANY LTD.

o CRAIGAVON INDUSTRIAL DEVELOPMENT ORGANISATION LTD.

o DCCOIENTERPRISE.ie.

o DCU INVENT.

o DCU RYAN ACADEMY.

o DESIGN & CRAFTS COUNCIL OF IRELAND.

o DIT HOTHOUSE.

o DONEGAL LOCAL DEVELOPMENT COMPANY CLG.

o DONEGAL LOCAL ENTERPRISE OFFICE.

o DOWN BUSINESS CENTRE.

o DRUMSHANBO ENTERPRISE CENTRE.

o DUBLIN BUSINESS INNOVATION CENTRE.

o DUBLIN CITY UNIVERSITY.

o DUBLIN FOOD CHAIN.

o DUBLIN INSTITUTE OF TECHNOLOGY.

o DUBLIN NORTH WEST AREA PARTNERSHIP.

o DUBLIN SOUTH CITY PARTNERSHIP.

o DUBLIN SOUTH LOCAL ENTERPRISE OFFICE.

o DUNDALK INSTITUTE OF TECHNOLOGY.

o DUNGANNON ENTERPRISE CENTRE LTD.

o DUNGARVAN ENTERPRISE CENTRE.

o DUNHILL ECOPARK.

o EAST BELFAST ENTERPRISE.

o EDEN CENTRE FOR ENTREPRENEURSHIP, DESIGN & INNOVATION.

o EMPOWER.

o ENNISCORTHY ENTERPRISE & TECHNOLOGY CENTRE.

o ENNISTYMON ENTERPRISE CENTRE LTD.

o ENTERPRISE & RESEARCH INCUBATION CAMPUS.

o ENTERPRISE IRELAND.

o ENTERPRISE NORTH WEST.

- ENTERPRISE NORTHERN IRELAND.
- FÁILTE IRELAND.
- FERMANAGH ENTERPRISE LTD.
- FINGAL LEADER PARTNERSHIP.
- FOOD ACADEMY.
- FOOD HUB.
- FOOD PRODUCT DEVELOPMENT CENTRE.
- FOOD SAFETY AUTHORITY OF IRELAND.
- FOODWORKS.
- FOUNTAIN RESOURCE GROUP.
- GALWAY CITY PARTNERSHIP.
- GALWAY RURAL DEVELOPMENT COMPANY.
- GALWAY–MAYO INSTITUTE OF TECHNOLOGY.
- GATEWAY UCC.
- GMIT INNOVATION HUBS.
- GOOGLE.
- HARTNETT ENTERPRISE ACCELERATION CENTRE.
- HEALTH & SAFETY AUTHORITY.
- HSALEARNING.ie.
- IADT MEDIA CUBE.
- INISHOWEN DEVELOPMENT PARTNERSHIP.
- INNOVATE-NI.
- INNOVATION CENTRE.
- INSPIRE BUSINESS CENTRE.
- INSTITUTE FOR MINORITY ENTREPRENEURSHIP.
- INSTITUTE OF ART, DESIGN & TECHNOLOGY.
- INSTITUTE OF DIRECTORS IN IRELAND.
- INSTITUTE OF TECHNOLOGY BLANCHARDSTOWN.
- INSTITUTE OF TECHNOLOGY CARLOW.
- INSTITUTE OF TECHNOLOGY SLIGO.
- INSTITUTE OF TECHNOLOGY TRALEE.
- IRD DUHALLOW LTD.
- IRD KILTIMAGH.
- IRISH COUNTRYWOMEN'S ASSOCIATION.
- IRISH EXPORTERS ASSOCIATION.
- IRISH INSTITUTE OF TRAINING & DEVELOPMENT.
- IRISH MANAGEMENT INSTITUTE.
- IRISH SMALL & MEDIUM ENTERPRISES ASSOCIATION.

- o ITT DUBLIN.
- o KELLS ENTERPRISE & TECHNOLOGY CENTRE.
- o KERRY LOCAL ENTERPRISE OFFICE.
- o LANTRA.
- o LARKIN UNEMPLOYED CENTRE.
- o LEGAL-ISLAND.
- o LEITRIM INTEGRATED DEVELOPMENT COMPANY LTD.
- o LEITRIM LOCAL ENTERPRISE OFFICE.
- o LETTERKENNY INSTITUTE OF TECHNOLOGY.
- o LIFFEY TRUST.
- o LIMERICK INSTITUTE OF TECHNOLOGY.
- o LISBURN ENTERPRISE ORGANISATION LTD.
- o LOCAL ENTERPRISE DEVELOPMENT COMPANY LTD.
- o LOCAL ENTERPRISE OFFICE CARLOW.
- o LOCAL ENTERPRISE OFFICE CAVAN.
- o LOCAL ENTERPRISE OFFICE CLARE.
- o LOCAL ENTERPRISE OFFICE CORK CITY.
- o LOCAL ENTERPRISE OFFICE CORK NORTH & WEST.
- o LOCAL ENTERPRISE OFFICE DUBLIN CITY.
- o LOCAL ENTERPRISE OFFICE DUN LAOGHAIRE-RATHDOWN.
- o LOCAL ENTERPRISE OFFICE FINGAL.
- o LOCAL ENTERPRISE OFFICE GALWAY.
- o LOCAL ENTERPRISE OFFICE KILDARE.
- o LOCAL ENTERPRISE OFFICE KILKENNY.
- o LOCAL ENTERPRISE OFFICE LAOIS.
- o LOCAL ENTERPRISE OFFICE LIMERICK.
- o LOCAL ENTERPRISE OFFICE LOUTH.
- o LOCAL ENTERPRISE OFFICE MAYO.
- o LOCAL ENTERPRISE OFFICE MONAGHAN.
- o LOCAL ENTERPRISE OFFICE OFFALY.
- o LOCAL ENTERPRISE OFFICE ROSCOMMON.
- o LOCAL ENTERPRISE OFFICE SLIGO.
- o LOCAL ENTERPRISE OFFICE SOUTH CORK.
- o LOCAL ENTERPRISE OFFICE WESTMEATH.
- o LOCAL ENTERPRISE OFFICE WICKLOW.
- o LOCAL ENTERPRISE OFFICES.
- o LONGFORD LOCAL ENTERPRISE OFFICE.
- o MACROOM E BUSINESS CENTRE.

- MALLUSK ENTERPRISE PARK.
- MARKETING INSTITUTE OF IRELAND.
- MAYNOOTHWORKS.
- MAYO NORTH EAST LEADER PARTNERSHIP.
- MEATH ENTERPRISE.
- MEATH LOCAL ENTERPRISE OFFICE.
- MEATH PARTNERSHIP.
- MICHELIN DEVELOPMENT.
- MICROFINANCE IRELAND.
- MIDLANDS INNOVATION & RESEARCH CENTRE.
- MOHILL ENTERPRISE CENTRE.
- MOY VALLEY RESOURCES IRD.
- MULLINGAR EMPLOYMENT ACTION GROUP.
- NATIONAL COLLEGE OF IRELAND.
- NATIONAL FRANCHISE CENTRE.
- NATIONAL UNIVERSITY OF IRELAND GALWAY.
- NATIONAL UNIVERSITY OF IRELAND MAYNOOTH.
- NDRC.
- NETWORK IRELAND.
- NEW FRONTIERS.
- NEWMARKET KITCHEN.
- NEWRY & MOURNE ENTERPRISE AGENCY.
- NEXUS INNOVATION CENTRE.
- NORTH CITY BUSINESS CENTRE LTD.
- NORTH DOWN DEVELOPMENT ORGANISATION LTD.
- NORTH TIPPERARY LEADER PARTNERSHIP.
- NORTH, EAST & WEST KERRY DEVELOPMENT.
- NORTHERN IRELAND FOOD & DRINK ASSOCIATION.
- NORTHERN IRELAND SCREEN.
- NORTHSIDE PARTNERSHIP.
- OAK TREE PRESS.
- OFFALY INTEGRATED LOCAL DEVELOPMENT CLG.
- OMAGH ENTERPRISE COMPANY LTD.
- OPTIMUM RESULTS LTD.
- ORGANIC COLLEGE.
- ORMEAU BUSINESS PARK.
- ORTUS GROUP.
- PARTAS.

- PAUL PARTNERSHIP LIMERICK.
- PLATO DUBLIN.
- PORTARLINGTON ENTERPRISE CENTRE.
- PRINCE'S TRUST NORTHERN IRELAND.
- REGIONAL DEVELOPMENT CENTRE.
- ROE VALLEY ENTERPRISES LTD.
- ROSCOMMON LEADER PARTNERSHIP.
- RUBICON CENTRE.
- RURAL DEVELOPMENT COUNCIL.
- SCHOOL OF FOOD.
- SHELL LIVEWIRE UK.
- SMALL BUSINESS ADVICE.
- SMALL FIRMS ASSOCIATION.
- SMILE.
- SOLAS.
- SOUTH & EAST CORK AREA DEVELOPMENT LTD.
- SOUTH EAST BUSINESS INNOVATION CENTRE.
- SOUTHSIDE PARTNERSHIP DLR LTD.
- STRABANE ENTERPRISE AGENCY.
- SUSTAINABLE ENERGY AUTHORITY OF IRELAND.
- SYNERGY CENTRE.
- TALENT GARDEN DUBLIN.
- TALLOW ENTERPRISE CENTRE.
- TEAGASC.
- TECHSTARTNI.
- TERENURE ENTERPRISE CENTRE.
- THE LINC.
- TIPPERARY LOCAL ENTERPRISE OFFICE.
- TOM CREAN BUSINESS CENTRE.
- TRINITY COLLEGE DUBLIN.
- ULSTER COMMUNITY INVESTMENT TRUST LTD.
- UNIVERSITY COLLEGE CORK.
- UNIVERSITY COLLEGE DUBLIN.
- UNIVERSITY OF LIMERICK.
- UNLTD.
- WATERFORD INSTITUTE OF TECHNOLOGY.
- WATERFORD LOCAL ENTERPRISE OFFICE.
- WESTBIC.

- WESTERN MANAGEMENT CENTRE.
- WESTMEATH COMMUNITY DEVELOPMENT LTD.
- WEXFORD LOCAL DEVELOPMENT.
- WEXFORD LOCAL ENTERPRISE OFFICE.
- WICKLOW ENTERPRISE CENTRE.
- WORK WEST ENTERPRISE AGENCY.
- WORKSPACE ENTERPRISES LTD.
- YOUNG SOCIAL INNOVATORS.

YOUNG ENTERPRISE

The following organisations support young entrepreneurs:

- ADVANTAGE.
- CARRICKFERGUS ENTERPRISE AGENCY LTD.
- DONEGAL LOCAL ENTERPRISE OFFICE.
- DUBLIN SOUTH LOCAL ENTERPRISE OFFICE.
- EAST BELFAST ENTERPRISE.
- ENTERPRISE IRELAND.
- KERRY LOCAL ENTERPRISE OFFICE.
- LEITRIM LOCAL ENTERPRISE OFFICE.
- LOCAL ENTEPRRISE OFFICES.
- LOCAL ENTERPRISE OFFICE CARLOW.
- LOCAL ENTERPRISE OFFICE CAVAN.
- LOCAL ENTERPRISE OFFICE CLARE.
- LOCAL ENTERPRISE OFFICE CORK CITY.
- LOCAL ENTERPRISE OFFICE CORK NORTH & WEST.
- LOCAL ENTERPRISE OFFICE DUBLIN CITY.
- LOCAL ENTERPRISE OFFICE DUN LAOGHAIRE-RATHDOWN.
- LOCAL ENTERPRISE OFFICE FINGAL.
- LOCAL ENTERPRISE OFFICE GALWAY.
- LOCAL ENTERPRISE OFFICE KILDARE.
- LOCAL ENTERPRISE OFFICE KILKENNY.
- LOCAL ENTERPRISE OFFICE LAOIS.
- LOCAL ENTERPRISE OFFICE LIMERICK.
- LOCAL ENTERPRISE OFFICE LOUTH.
- LOCAL ENTERPRISE OFFICE MAYO.
- LOCAL ENTERPRISE OFFICE MONAGHAN.
- LOCAL ENTERPRISE OFFICE OFFALY.

- o LOCAL ENTERPRISE OFFICE ROSCOMMON.
- o LOCAL ENTERPRISE OFFICE SLIGO.
- o LOCAL ENTERPRISE OFFICE SOUTH CORK.
- o LOCAL ENTERPRISE OFFICE WESTMEATH.
- o LOCAL ENTERPRISE OFFICE WICKLOW.
- o LONGFORD LOCAL ENTERPRISE OFFICE.
- o MEATH LOCAL ENTERPRISE OFFICE.
- o PRINCE'S TRUST NORTHERN IRELAND.
- o SHELL LIVEWIRE UK.
- o TIPPERARY LOCAL ENTERPRISE OFFICE.
- o WATERFORD LOCAL ENTERPRISE OFFICE.
- o WEXFORD LOCAL ENTERPRISE OFFICE.
- o WORKSPACE ENTERPRISES LTD.
- o YOUNG ENTERPRISE NORTHERN IRELAND.
- o YOUNG SOCIAL INNOVATORS.

11B: DIRECTORY – ALPHABETICAL

4TH LEVEL VENTURES LTD

75 St. Stephen's Green, Dublin 2 T: (01) 633 3627 E: info@4thlevelventures.ie W: www.4thlevelventures.ie

Funding

4th Level Ventures is a €20 million venture capital fund focused on investing in research-based commercial opportunities.

ACCA EUROPE

9 Leeson Park, Dublin 6 E: info@accaglobal.com W: www.accaglobal.com/ie

Accounting & Business Planning

ACCA is one of the accountancy bodies whose members are permitted to audit company accounts in Ireland. If you're looking for an accountant, ACCA can direct you to one of its members.

ACE ENTERPRISE PARK

Bawnogue Road, Clondalkin, Dublin 22 T: (01) 457 9662 E: info@acepark.ie W: www.acepark.ie

Community & Rural Development; Incubation & Work space; Training & Mentoring

ACE Enterprise Park is a Clondalkin-based community enterprise centre, established in 1995. It offers business space and business training to SMEs in Bawnogue and Neilstown. It is a member of the NATIONAL ASSOCIATION OF COMMUNITY ENTERPRISE CENTRES.

ACT VENTURE CAPITAL LTD

6 Richview Office Park, Clonskeagh, Dublin 14 T: (01) 260 0966 E: info@actvc.ie W: www. actventure.com

Funding

ACT Venture Capital provides capital in the range of €1m to €10 million, to growth-oriented private companies in ICT, medical devices and life sciences.

ADVANTAGE

Sloefield Business Park, Sloefield Drive, Carrickfergus, Co. Antrim BT38 8GX T: (028) 9335 6730 E: info@advantage-ni.com W: advantageni.com

Accounting & Business Planning; Training & Mentoring; Young Enterprise

Advantage provides services for young people and an online business planning tool.

AIB BANK

Bankcentre, Ballsbridge, Dublin 4 T: (1890) 478833 W: www.business.aib.ie/my-business-is/business-start-up-package#Starting%20up

Funding; Information

AIB Bank is Ireland's largest bank, providing a full range of banking services to business customers. It operates in Northern Ireland as FIRST TRUST BANK.

AISLING SOFTWARE

Unit 3B, KTI Centre, Deer Park, Killarney, Co. Kerry T: (1890) 767848 E: contact@sortmybooks.ie W: www.sortmybooks.com

Accounting & Business Planning

Aisling Software is an Irish software company, specialising in accounting packages for small businesses and owner / managers.

ALLENWOOD COMMUNITY DEVELOPMENT ASSOCIATION LTD

Allenwood North, Allenwood, Co. Kildare T: (045) 870804 E: reception@acdal.ie W: www.acdal.ie

Community & Rural Development; Incubation & Work space; Training & Mentoring

ACDAL is a community development centre that facilitates the development of small businesses by providing industrial and office accommodation.

AMÁRACH CONSULTING

11 Kingswood Business Centre, Kingswood Road, Citywest Campus, Dublin D24 KT63 T: (01) 410 5200 E: info@amarach.com W: www.amarach.com

Consulting; Marketing

Amárach ('tomorrow') uses market research to look ahead – to what will happen.

ANNE RYAN & CO.

2 Crofton Terrace, Dun Laoire, Co. Dublin A96 V6P7 T: (01) 668 0094 E: mailroom@anneryanip.com W: www.anneryanip.com

IP & Legal

Anne Ryan & Co. are patents, trade marks and designs specialists.

ANTRIM ENTERPRISE AGENCY LTD

58 Greystone Road, Antrim BT41 1JZ T: (028) 9446 7774 E: admin@antrimenterprise.com W: www.antrimenterprise.com

Funding; Incubation & Work space; Information; Innovation & R&D; Social Enterprise; Training & Mentoring

Antrim Enterprise Agency is a member of ENTERPRISE NORTHERN IRELAND. It offers workspace, start-up and ongoing training and loans.

ARCLABS

Waterford Institute of Technology West Campus, Carriganore, Co. Waterford T: (051) 302900 E: ccullen@wit.ie W: www.arclabs.ie

Incubation & Work space; Innovation & R&D; Training & Mentoring

Arclabs is the research and innovation centre at WATERFORD INSTITUTE OF TECHNOLOGY. It provides work space and business supports, as well as access to WIT's research community.

ARDEE COMMUNITY DEVELOPMENT COMPANY LTD

Hale Street, Ardee, Co. Louth T: (041) 685 7680 E: ardbuspark@eircom.net W: www.ardeebusinesspark.ie

Community & Rural Development; Incubation & Work space; Training & Mentoring

Ardee Community Development is a community-owned project, whose objective is to assist local entrepreneurs and businesses to boost employment in the region. It operates the Ardee Business Park and is a member of the NATIONAL ASSOCIATION OF COMMUNITY ENTERPRISE CENTRES.

ARDS & NORTH DOWN RURAL AREA PARTNERSHIP

Ards & North Down Borough Council, Town Hall, The Castle, Bangor BT20 4B T: (0300) 013 3333 E: info@ruralpartnersand.co.uk W: www.ruralpartnersand.co.uk

Community & Rural Development; Funding

Ards & North Down Rural Partnership is the Local Action Group responsible for rural development in the area, delivering the LEADER and Rural Development programmes through RURAL PARTNERS ARDS & NORTH DOWN. It provides funding and other supports for rural development.

ARDS BUSINESS CENTRE LTD

Sketrick House, 16 Jubilee Road, Newtownards, Co. Down BT23 4YH T: (028) 9181 9787 E: info@ardsbusiness.com W: www.ardsbusiness.com

Funding; Incubation & Work space; Innovation & R&D; Training & Mentoring

Ards Business Centre is a member of ENTERPRISE NORTHERN IRELAND and is the local enterprise agency for the Ards Borough Council area. It provides support to businesses through advice to those forming and growing their businesses and through the provision of property.

ARGYLE BUSINESS CENTRE LTD

39 North Howard Street, Belfast BT13 2AP T: (028) 9023 3777 E: info@abcni.net W: www.argylebusinesscentre.com

Incubation & Workspace

Argyle Business Centre offers managed work space, close to Belfast city centre.

ARKLOW BUSINESS ENTERPRISE CENTRE

Kilbride Industrial Estate, Kilbride, Arklow, Co. Wicklow Y14 T440 T: (0402) 26900 E: info@abec.ie W: www.abec.ie

Incubation & Work space; Training & Mentoring

ABEC offers co-working and office space, as well as mentoring. It is a member of the NATIONAL ASSOCIATION OF COMMUNITY ENTERPRISE CENTRES.

ARMAGH BUSINESS CENTRE LTD

2 Loughgall Road, Armagh BT61 7NH T: (028) 3752 5050 E: info@abcarmagh.com W: www.abcarmagh.com

Funding; Incubation & Workspace; Training & Mentoring

Armagh Business Centre is a member of ENTERPRISE NORTHERN IRELAND and is the local enterprise agency for business start-up advice and business development support in Armagh.

ARTS COUNCIL

Arts Council, 70 Merrion Square, Dublin D02 NY52 T: (01) 618 0200 E: reception@artscouncil.ie W: www.artscouncil.ie

Funding

The Arts Council is the national agency for funding, developing and promoting the arts in Ireland and the primary source of financial and other support for individual creative and interpretative artists.

ARTS COUNCIL OF NORTHERN IRELAND

1 The Sidings, Antrim Road, Lisburn BT28 3AJ T: (028) 9262 3555 E: info@artscouncil-ni.org W: www.artscouncil-ni.org

Funding

The Arts Council of Northern Ireland is the lead development agency for the arts in Northern Ireland. It distributes public money and National Lottery funds to develop and deliver a wide variety of arts projects, events and initiatives.

ASPIRE! MANAGEMENT CONSULTANTS

Fastnet House, Schull, Co. Cork T: (087) 251 3306 E: simon.okeeffe@aspire.ie W: www.aspire.ie

Marketing; Training & Mentoring

Aspire! provides marketing strategy and branding expertise and works with clients to support them in executing their strategies and plans. It also provides mentoring.

ATHLONE INSTITUTE OF TECHNOLOGY

Dublin Road, Athlone, Co. Westmeath T: (090) 646 8000 E: receeption@ait.ie W: www.ait.ie

Incubation & Work space; Innovation & R&D; Training & Mentoring

AIT supports entrepreneurs through its MIDLANDS INNOVATION & RESEARCH CENTRE.

ATHY COMMUNITY ENTERPRISE COMPANY LTD

Woodstock South, Kilkenny Road, Athy, Co. Kildare T: (059) 863 4534 E: hdowling@kildarecoco.ie W: www.athycec.com

Incubation & Work space

Athy Community Enterprise Centre provides incubation space for new and emerging businesses. It is an initiative of the Athy Investment Development & Employment Forum and is a member of the NATIONAL ASSOCIATION OF COMMUNITY ENTERPRISE CENTRES.

ATLANTIC BRIDGE

31 Kildare Street, Dublin 2 T: (01) 603 4450 E: info@abven.com W: www.abven.com

Funding

Atlantic Bridge provides venture funding of up to €15m to companies in the ICT, semiconductor and software sectors. It also runs the University Bridge Fund, a €60m fund to accelerate the commercialisation of ground-breaking research.

AVONDHU BLACKWATER PARTNERSHIP CLG

The Old Mill, Castletownroche, Co. Cork T: (022) 46580 E: info@avondhublackwater.com W: www.avondhublackwater.com

Community & Rural Development; Funding

Avondhu Blackwater Partnership is the integrated LEADER Partnership Company for North County Cork and is a member of the IRISH LOCAL DEVELOPMENT NETWORK. It delivers the Rural Development Programme / LEADER and the Social Inclusion & Community Activation Programme.

BAILIEBOROUGH BUSINESS CENTRE

Shercock Road, Bailieborough, Co. Cavan T: (042) 969 4716 E: bda@bailieborough.com

Incubation & Work space

The Bailieborough Business Centre offers hot desk facilities, as well units to rent.

BALBRIGGAN ENTERPRISE & TRAINING CENTRE

Stephenstown Industrial Estate, Balbriggan, Co. Dublin T: (01) 802 0400 E: info@beat.ie W: www.beat.ie

Incubation & Work space; Training & Mentoring

BEaT offers work / office space, as well as virtual office space. It is a member of the NATIONAL ASSOCIATION OF COMMUNITY ENTERPRISE CENTRES.

BALBRIGGAN ENTERPRISE DEVELOPMENT GROUP

Unit 9, The BEaT Centre, Stephenstown Industrial Estate, Balbriggan, Co. Dublin
T: (01) 802 0417 E: info@bedg.ie W: www.bedg.ie

Incubation & Work space; Training & Mentoring

BEDG's objective is to create an enterprise culture in the community by
encouraging initiatives specifically geared towards supporting existing and new
enterprises. To achieve this, it provides support and training.

BALLINAMORE ENTERPRISE CENTRE

Willowfield Road, Ballinamore, Co. Leitrim T: (071) 964 4881

Incubation & Work space

Ballinamore Enterprise Centre offers units to rent for local businesses.

BALLINASLOE AREA COMMUNITY DEVELOPMENT LTD

Ballinasloe Enterprise Centre, Creagh, Ballinasloe. Co. Galway T: (090) 964 6516
E: info@ballinasloeenterprisecentre.ie W: www.ballinasloeenterprisecentre.ie

Incubation & Work space

Ballinasloe Enterprise Centre provides flexible workspace and support services to
encourage early stage and developing enterprises. It is managed by Ballinasloe Area
Community Development Ltd, which is a member of the NATIONAL
ASSOCIATION OF COMMUNITY ENTERPRISE CENTRES.

BALLYFERMOT CHAPELIZOD PARTNERSHIP COMPANY LTD

4 Drumfinn Park, Ballyfermot, Dublin 10 T: (01) 623 5612 E:
info@bcpartnership.ie W: www.bcpartnership.ie

Community & Rural Development; Training & Mentoring

Ballyfermot Chapelizod Partnership is supported under the Social Inclusion &
Community Activation Programme and is a member of the IRISH LOCAL
DEVELOPMENT NETWORK. It offers a start-your-own-business support service.

BALLYHAUNIS ENTERPRISE CENTRE

Clare Road, Ballyhaunis, Co. Mayo T: (094) 963 0311 E:
ballyhaunischamber@gmail.com W: www.ballyhaunischamber.ie

Incubation & Work space

Ballyhaunis Enterprise Centre offers work space to rent. It is a member of the
NATIONAL ASSOCIATION OF COMMUNITY ENTERPRISE CENTRES.

BALLYHOURA DEVELOPMENT CLG

Main Street, Kilfinane, Co. Limerick T: (063) 91300 E: info@ballyhoura.org W: www.ballyhouradevelopment.com

Community & Rural Development; Funding; Incubation & Work space; Innovation & R&D

Ballyhoura Development is supported under LEADER and the Social Inclusion & Community Activation Programme and is a member of the IRISH LOCAL DEVELOPMENT NETWORK. Among other supports, it offers access to food preparation facilities at four locations.

BALLYMENA BUSINESS CENTRE LTD

62 Fenaghy Road, Galgorm Industrial Estate, Ballymena BT42 1FL T: (028) 2565 8616 E: info@ballymenabusiness.co.uk W: www.ballymenabusiness.co.uk

Funding; Incubation & Work space; Innovation & R&D; Training & Mentoring

Ballymena Business Centre is a member of ENTERPRISE NORTHERN IRELAND and offers advice, guidance, training, workspace and networking opportunities.

BANBRIDGE DISTRICT ENTERPRISE

Scarva Road Industrial Estate, Scarva Road, Banbridge, Co. Down BT32 3QD T: (028) 4066 2260 E: info@bdelonline.com W: www.bdelonline.com

Funding; Incubation & Work space; Training & Mentoring

Banbridge District Enterprises is a member of ENTERPRISE NORTHERN IRELAND. It supports the development of businesses in the Banbridge District through a partnership approach between the public, private and voluntary sectors.

BANK OF IRELAND

Bank of Ireland Business Banking, 40 Mespil Road, Dublin 4 T: (01) 661 5933 W: businessbanking.bankofireland.com

Funding

Bank of Ireland provides a full range of banking services to business customers. It operates in Northern Ireland as BANK OF IRELAND NORTHERN IRELAND. Bank of Ireland also provides advice to entrepreneurs through THINKBUSINESS.ie.

BANK OF IRELAND NORTHERN IRELAND

1 Donegall Square South, Belfast, BT1 5LR T: (028) 9043 3000 W: www.bankofirelanduk.com

Funding

Bank of Ireland in Northern Ireland is a full service bank with a 28 strong branch network, including business centres, as well as direct, phone and online services.

BANK OF IRELAND WORKBENCH

W: www.businessbanking.bankofireland.com/campaigns/bank-of-ireland-workbench/

Incubation & Work space; Networking

Bank of Ireland Workbench connects entrepreneurs, branch, and community by offering free dedicated space for co-working, seminars, clinics and events to encourage innovation and new ideas. Workbenchs are located at 1 Grand Canal Square (Dublin), Trinity (Dublin), Montrose (Dublin), Mainguard Street (Galway), O'Connell Street (Limerick) and Patrick Street (Cork).

BASE ENTERPRISE CENTRE CLG

Damastown Road, Mulhuddart, Dublin 15 T: (01) 820 3020 E: reception@base-centre.com W: www.baseenterprisecentre.com

Incubation & Work space

The BASE (Blanchardstown Area Small Enterprises) Centre offers incubation units (including food units) and supports to SMEs. It is a member of the NATIONAL ASSOCIATION OF COMMUNITY ENTERPRISE CENTRES.

BeSMART.IE

W: www.besmart.ie

Information

BeSmart is a free online safety management and risk assessment tool from the HEALTH & SAFETY AUTHORITY.

BIG RED BOOK

Rathdown Hall, Upper Glenageary Road, Glenageary, Co. Dublin A96 VY20 T: (01) 204 8300 E: info@bigredbook.com W: www.bigredbook.com

Accounting & Business Planning

Big Red Book offers accounting and payroll software, designed by professional accountants, ideal for small businesses.

BIZMENTORS.IE

SCCUL Enterprise Centre, Castlepark Road, Ballybane, Galway T: (091) 386004 E: info@bizmentors.ie W: www.bizmentors.ie

Training & Mentoring

Bizmentors.ie offers mentoring to new and existing businesses to help further develop local businesses.

BLACKSTONE LAUNCHPAD

W: www.blackstonelaunchpad.org

Training & Mentoring

Blackstone LaunchPad is an international campus-based entrepreneurship program, accessed by over 500,000 students globally. In Ireland, it is available in NATIONAL UNIVERSITY OF IRELAND GALWAY, TRINITY COLLEGE DUBLIN and UNIVERSITY COLLEGE CORK.

BNEST

Nexus Innovation Centre, Tierney Building, University of Limerick, Plassey, Limerick T: (061) 332929 E: info@bnest.ie W: www.bnest.ie

Incubation & Work space; Social Enterprise; Training & Mentoring

BNest is a social enterprise incubator.

BOLTON TRUST

128-130 East Wall Road, Dublin 3 T: (01) 240 1377 E: info@docklandsinnovation.ie W: www.docklandsinnovation.ie

Enterprise Support; Incubation & Work space

The Bolton Trust is an independent voluntary trust, established in 1986 by staff of the DUBLIN INSTITUTE OF TECHNOLOGY, that assists people to create sustainable businesses and runs the Docklands Innovation Park. It is a member of the NATIONAL ASSOCIATION OF COMMUNITY ENTERPRISE CENTRES.

BORD BIA

Clanwilliam Court, Lower Mount Street, Dublin D02 A344 T: (01) 668 5155 E: info@bordbia.ie W: www.bordbia.ie

Funding; Information; Marketing; Regulation & Standards; Training & Mentoring

Bord Bia (The Irish Food Board) is the Irish government agency charged with the promotion, trade development and marketing of the Irish food, drink and horticulture industry. Its supports for food producers are showcased on its online support website, BORDBIAVANTAGE.ie.

BORD IASCAIGH MHARA

PO Box 12, Crofton Road, Dún Laoire, Co. Dublin A96 E5A0 T: (01) 214 4100 E: info@bim.ie W: www.bim.ie

Funding; Marketing; Regulation & Standards; Training & Mentoring

Bord Iascaigh Mhara helps to develop the Irish seafood industry by providing technical expertise, business support, funding, training and promoting responsible environmental practice.

BORDBIAVANTAGE.IE

Bord Bia Vantage, Clanwilliam Court, Lower Mount Street, Dublin 2 T: (01) 668 5155 E: vantage@bordbia.ie W: www.bordbiavantage.ie

Information; Training & Mentoring

An online resource for small food businesses.

BOYLE ENTERPRISE & MORE

Boyle, Co. Roscommon E: info@boyleenterprise.com W: www.boyleenterprise.com

Incubation & Work space

Boyle Enterprise is a member of the NATIONAL ASSOCIATION OF COMMUNITY ENTERPRISE CENTRES. It offers enterprise space for all stages of business.

BRAY AREA PARTNERSHIP

4 Prince of Wales Terrace, Quinsboro Road, Bray, Co. Wicklow A98 E8H4 T: (01) 286 8266 E: info@brayareapartnership.org W: www.brayareapartnership.ie

Community & Rural Development; Training & Mentoring

Supported under the Social Inclusion & Community Activation Programme, Bray Area Partnership offers training and one-to-one supports for entrepreneurs and is a member of the IRISH LOCAL DEVELOPMENT NETWORK.

BREFFNI INTEGRATED CLG

Unit 6a, Corlurgan Business Park, Ballinagh Road, Cavan H12 DP86 T: (049) 433 1029 E: info@breffniint.ie W: www.breffniint.ie

Community & Rural Development; Funding; Training & Mentoring

Breffni Integrated CLG is a community-led Local Development Company that delivers rural, social and economic programmes across Co. Cavan. It is supported under LEADER and the Social Inclusion & Community Activation Programme and is a member of the IRISH LOCAL DEVELOPMENT NETWORK.

BRITISH STANDARDS INSTITUTION

389 Chiswick High Road, London W4 4AL T: (0345) 086 9001 W: www.bsigroup.com

Regulation & Standards

BSI is the UK's national standards body, recognised worldwide.

BROADLAKE

Hilton House, Ardee Road, Rathmines, Dublin 6 T: (01) 598 9400 E: info@broadlake.ie W: www.broadlake.ie

Funding

Broadlake invests between €1m and €10m in established companies.

BULLET

E: hello@bullethq.com W: bullethq.com

Accounting & Business Planning

An Irish company, Bullet offers free cloud-based accounting software for small businesses.

BUSINESS INCUBATION CENTRE

National College of Ireland, Mayor Street, IFSC, Dublin D01 Y300 T: (01) 449 8704 E: bkelly@ncirl.ie W: www.ncirl.ie/Campus/Services-to-Business/Business-Incubation-Centre

Incubation & Work space; Training & Mentoring

NATIONAL COLLEGE OF IRELAND's Business Incubation Centre supports the development of knowledge-intensive start-up companies.

BUSINESS INFORMATION CENTRE

Dublin City Public Library, ILAC Shopping Centre, Henry Street, Dublin D01 DY80 T: (01) 873 4333 E: businesslibrary@dublincity.ie W: www.dublincitypubliclibraries.ie

Information

A reference service specialising in company and market research information. It stocks books, reports, directories, journals / periodicals, databases, newspapers / press cuttings (from the late 1970s) on Irish companies and organisations and a wide range of business-related subjects.

BUSINESS INNOVATION CENTRE NUI GALWAY

National University of Ireland Galway, University Road, Galway H91 TK33 T: (091) 524411 W: www.nuigalway.ie/innovation/business-innovation-centre/

Incubation & Work space; Training & Mentoring

NATIONAL UNIVERSITY OF IRELAND GALWAY provides offices, hot-desks, co-working spaces and access to laboratories, as well as business development supports, mentoring and access to academic expertise through its Business Innovation Centre.

BUSINESS INNOVATION CENTRES

W: www.irishbics.ie

Incubation & Work space; Training & Mentoring

See individual entries for:

o CORK BUSINESS INNOVATION CENTRE.
o DUBLIN BUSINESS INNOVATION CENTRE.
o INNOVATE NI (formerly NORIBIC).
o SOUTH-EAST BUSINESS INNOVATION CENTRE.
o WESTBIC.

BUSINESS PLUS

30 Morehampton Road, Dublin 4 T: (01) 660 8400 E: info@businessplus.ie W: www.bizplus.ie

Information

Good business magazine, with strong focus on e-business / e-commerce issues, and a useful website. The magazine is available at newsagents or on subscription.

BUSINESS POST

T: (01) 602 6000 W: www.businesspost.ie

Information

The Business Post digital platform provides independent insight, commentary and analysis of the important stories and issues across a broad spectrum of topics: business, finance, politics, technology, markets, media, marketing and personal finance – from the publishers of the *Sunday Business Post* newspaper.

BUSINESS VENTURE PARTNERS

Unit 23, The Cubes 2, Beacon South Quarter, Sandyford, Dublin D18 K6Y6 T: (01) 657 2900 W: bvp.ie

Funding

BVP helps clients raise funds and advises on strategic growth. It focuses on renewable energy, energy efficiency, agri-tech and industrial companies.

BUSINESSACHIEVERS.COM

W: www.business-achievers.com

Information; Networking

BusinessAchievers.com is a business portal and networking hub, powered by ULSTER BANK, to connect business owners and entrepreneurs to industry thought-leaders and to generate new business opportunities and connections.

BUSINESSREGULATION.IE

W: www.businessregulation.ie

Information; Regulation & Standards

BusinessRegulation.ie – an initiative of the DEPARTMENT OF BUSINESS, ENTERPRISE & INNOVATION – helps entrepreneurs identify the main regulations that affect their business and provides links to the relevant agencies and their guidance, tools and contact points – see also SUPPORTINGSMES.IE

BYRNE & McCALL

Core B, Block 71, The Plaza, Park West, Dublin 12 T: (01) 612 0580 E: info@byrnemccall.ie W: www.byrnemccall.ie

Accounting & Business Planning; Inwards Investment

Byrne & McCall is a firm of accountants and tax advisors who specialise in providing tax advice and accounting services to overseas companies. A sister company, Modern Management, provides management and support services to e-commerce and direct selling companies.

CARLOW COMMUNITY ENTERPRISE CENTRES LTD

Enterprise House, O'Brien Road, Carlow T: (059) 912 9783 E: info@enterprisehouse.ie W: www.enterprisehouse.ie

Incubation & Work space

Enterprise House offers accommodation and business support services to start-up and growing businesses. It also operates the Tinteán Training & Community Centre in Pollerton, Co. Carlow and is a member of the NATIONAL ASSOCIATION OF COMMUNITY ENTERPRISE CENTRES.

CARLOW COUNTY DEVELOPMENT PARTNERSHIP CLG

Main Street, Bagnelstown, Co. Carlow T: (059) 972 0733 E:
info@carlowdevelopment.ie W: www.carlowdevelopment.ie

Community & Rural Development; Funding; Training & Mentoring

Carlow County Development Partnership is the Local Development Company for
Carlow. It is supported under LEADER and the Social Inclusion & Community
Activation Programme and is a member of the IRISH LOCAL DEVELOPMENT
NETWORK. It provides advice and mentoring to unemployed persons seeking to set
up their own business and grant funding.

CARRICK BUSINESS CENTRE

Carrick-on-Suir Community Resource Centre, William Street, Carrick-on-Suir, Co.
Tipperary T: (051) 649502 E: info@carrickbusinesscentre.ie W:
www.carrickbusinesscentre.ie

Incubation & Work space

The Carrick Business Centre provides a range of facilities for hire available to both
the education and commercial sectors. It is a member of the NATIONAL
ASSOCIATION OF COMMUNITY ENTERPRISE CENTRES.

CARRICKFERGUS ENTERPRISE AGENCY LTD

8 Meadowbank Road, Carrickfergus, Co. Antrim BT38 8YF T: (028) 9336 9528
E: info@ceal.co.uk W: www.ceal.co.uk

*Funding; Incubation & Work space; Innovation & R&D; Training & Mentoring;
Young Enterprise*

CEAL is a member of ENTERPRISE NORTHERN IRELAND and offers workspace, as
well as start-up and ongoing training.

CASTLEBLAYNEY ENTERPRISE CENTRE

Dublin Road, Co. Monaghan T: (042) 974 6087 E: cceltd@castleblayney.ie W:
www.castleblayney.ie/index.php/castleblayney-enterprise-centre

Incubation & Work space; Training & Mentoring

Castleblayney Enterprise Centre supports local businesses by offering office / work
space for rent and a range of training courses. It is a member of the NATIONAL
ASSOCIATION OF COMMUNITY ENTERPRISE CENTRES.

CASTLECOMER ENTERPRISE GROUP LTD

Castlecomer Enterprise Centre, Kilkenny Road, Castlecomer, Co. Kilkenny T:
(056) 440 0734 W: www.castlecomerenterprise.ie

Incubation & Work space

Castlecomer Enterprise Group operates the Castlecomer Enterprise Centre, through
which it promotes employment opportunities and business start-ups. It is a member
of the NATIONAL ASSOCIATION OF COMMUNITY ENTERPRISE CENTRES.

CATALYST INC

The Innovation Centre, Queen's Road, Belfast BT3 9DT T: (028) 9073 7800
E: enquiries@catalyst-inc.org W: www.catalyst-inc.org

Funding; Incubation & Work space; Innovation & R&D

Catalyst Inc is Northern Ireland's next generation science park. It operates
Connect, a community of innovators, and Capital Match, which identifies potential
sources of funding, as well providing work space.

CAUSEWAY COAST & GLENS LOCAL ACTION GROUP

Causeway Coast & Glens Borough Council, Cloonavin, 66 Portstewart Road,
Coleraine BT52 1EY T: (028) 7034 7016 E: rdp@causewaycoastandglens.gov.uk
W: www.causewaycoastandglens.gov.uk/work/rural-development

Community & Rural Development; Funding

The Causeway Coast & Glens LAG is responsible for delivering LEADER / Priority
6 of the Rural Development Programme 2014-2020 in its area.

CAUSEWAY ENTERPRISE AGENCY

Loughanhill Industrial Estate, Coleraine, Co. Londonderry BT52 2NR T: (028)
7035 6318 E: info@causeway-enterprise.co.uk W: www.causeway-enterprise.co.uk

Funding; Incubation & Work space; Training & Mentoring

Causeway Enterprise Agency is a not-for-profit company delivering business
support, workspace units and enterprise education in the boroughs of Coleraine
and Moyle, and is a member of ENTERPRISE NORTHERN IRELAND.

CAVAN COUNTY ENTERPRISE FUND

Cavan Innovation & Technology Centre, Dublin Road, Cavan T: (049) 437 7277
E: info@ccef.ie W: www.cavanenterprisefund.ie

Funding; Incubation & Workspace

Cavan County Enterprise Fund offers funding and manages enterprise centres in
Killygarry (outside Monaghan town), Cootehill, Killeshandra and Blacklion, as
well as the CAVAN INNOVATION & TECHNOLOGY CENTRE. It is a member of the
NATIONAL ASSOCIATION OF COMMUNITY ENTERPRISE CENTRES.

CAVAN INNOVATION & TECHNOLOGY CENTRE

Dublin Road, Cavan T: (049) 437 7277 E: info@cavanitc.ie W: www.cavanitc.ie

Incubation & Work space; Training & Mentoring

Cavan Innovation & Technology Centre is a state-of-the-art innovation, education
and meeting facility, whose mission is to promote innovation, learning and
economic growth in the Cavan and Border region. It is a member of the NATIONAL
ASSOCIATION OF COMMUNITY ENTERPRISE CENTRES.

CENTRAL STATISTICS OFFICE

Skehard Road, Mahon, Cork T12 X00E T: (021) 453 5000 E: information@cso.ie
W: www.cso.ie

Information

The Central Statistics Office is Ireland's national statistical office. It collects,
compiles, analyses and disseminates statistical information relating to the economic
and social life of Ireland and thus is a key source of market research information.

CENTRE FOR CO-OPERATIVE STUDIES

O'Rahilly Building, University College Cork, College Road, Cork T: (021) 490
2570 E: foodbusiness@ucc.ie W: www.ucc.ie/en/ccs/

Consulting; Social Enterprise; Training & Mentoring

CCS is a university research centre that promotes education and training and
independent research and consultancy in all aspects of co-operative organisation.

CENTRE FOR CROSS-BORDER STUDIES

39 Abbey Street, Armagh BT61 7EB T: (028) 3751 1550 W: www.crossborder.ie

Cross-Border; Policy; Training & Mentoring

The Centre is a policy research and development institute, which commissions and
publishes research on issues related to opportunities for, and obstacles to, cross-
border co-operation in all fields of society and economy. It also provides services to
cross-border projects and networks – for example, training and mentoring using
the tools developed as part of its research programme.

CHAMBERS IRELAND

11 St. Stephen's Green, Dublin D02 FY84 T: (01) 400 4300 E: info@chambers.ie
W: www.chambers.ie

Networking

Chambers Ireland is Ireland's largest business organisation with a network of
Chambers of Commerce in every major town and region in the country. Each
chamber consists of local business representatives who join together to promote the
economic and social development of their community in order to make it a better
place in which to live, work and do business.

CHARTERED ACCOUNTANTS IRELAND

Chartered Accountants House, 47-49 Pearse Street, Dublin 2 T: (01) 637 7200 E:
ca@charteredaccountants.ie W: www.charteredaccountants.ie

Accounting & Business Planning

Chartered Accountants Ireland is one of the accountancy bodies whose members
are permitted to audit company accounts in Ireland. It has 26,000 members
worldwide. If you're looking for an accountant, Chartered Accountants Ireland's
website can direct you to one of its members.

CHARTERED INSTITUTE OF MANAGEMENT ACCOUNTANTS

Block E – 5th Floor, Iveagh Court, Harcourt Road, Dublin 2 T: (01) 643 0400 E: cima.ireland@aicpa-cima.com W: www.cimaglobal.com/Our-locations/Ireland/

Accounting & Business Planning

Chartered Management Accountants assist SMEs in a wide variety of ways, although CIMA members do not audit limited companies' accounts. If you are looking for a Chartered Management Accountant, see **www.cimaglobal.com/About-us/Find-a-CIMA-Accountant/**.

CHARTERED INSTITUTE OF PERSONNEL & DEVELOPMENT

A3 The Locks, Charlotte Quay Dock, Dublin 4 T: (01) 678 0090 W: cipd.ie

IP & Legal; Training & Mentoring

CIPD Ireland is the professional membership body for those involved in the management and development of people. It offers training and other supports to its members, while providing research and reports more widely.

CLANCY BUSINESS FINANCE LTD

33 Carysfort Avenue, Blackrock, Co. Dublin T: (01) 438 6462 E: lucinda@clancybusiness.com W: www.clancybusinessfinance.com

Funding

Based on your funding requirements, Clancy Business Finance identifies the suitable funders and products, facilitates meetings with potential funders, co-ordinates the application process and negotiates with lenders on your behalf.

CLANE PROJECT CENTRE

Unit 1A, Thompson Enterprise Centre, Clane Business Park, College Road, Clane, Co. Kildare T: (045) 861500 E: info@claneprojectcentre.ie W: www.claneprojectcentre.ie

Incubation & Work space; Social Enterprise

Clane Project Centre provides workspace and support services for commercial and community ventures in North Kildare. It is a member of the NATIONAL ASSOCIATION OF COMMUNITY ENTERPRISE CENTRES.

CLANN CREDO

Irish Social Finance Centre, 10 Grattan Crescent, Inchicore, Dublin D08 R240 T: (01) 400 2100 E: info@clanncredo.ie W: www.clanncredo.ie

Community & Rural Development; Funding; Social Enterprise

Clann Credo is a leading provider of social finance to community organisations.

CLARE LOCAL DEVELOPMENT COMPANY LTD

1 Westgate Business Park, Kilrush Road, Ennis, Co. Clare T: (065) 686 6800 E: info@cldc.ie W: www.cldc.ie

Community & Rural Development; Funding; Training & Mentoring

Clare Local Development is supported under LEADER and the Social Inclusion & Community Activation Programme and is a member of the IRISH LOCAL DEVELOPMENT NETWORK. It provides start-your-own-business training and mentoring, as well as access to funding.

CLARENDON FUND MANAGERS

City Exchange, 11/13 Gloucester Street, Belfast BT1 4LS T: (028) 9032 6465 E: info@clarendon-fm.co.uk W: www.clarendon-fm.co.uk

Funding

Clarendon Fund Managers Limited is a venture capital fund manager whoseinvestment focus is on innovative SMEs based in Northern Ireland. It manages the Co-Investment Fund, which matches private investment into high-growth potential businesses based in Northern Ireland.

CO-INNOVATE PROGRAMME

InterTradeIreland, The Old Gasworks Business Park, Kilmorey Street, Newry, Co. Down BT34 2DE T: (028) 3083 4197 W: www.co-innovateprogramme.eu

Cross-Border; Innovation & R&D

The Co-Innovate programme is a cross-border research and innovation initiative funded under the European INTERREG VA Programme, which aims to increase the proportion of SMEs engaged in cross-border research and innovation.

CO-OPERATIVE HOUSING IRELAND

33 Lower Baggot Street, Dublin 2 T: (01) 661 2877 E: admin@cooperativehousing.ie W: www.cooperativehousing.ie

Social Enterprise

Co-operative Housing Ireland is Ireland's national federation for the co-operative housing sector.

COLAB LYIT

Port Road, Ballyraine, Letterkenny, Co. Donegal T: (074) 918 6703 E: W: www.co-lab.ie

Incubation & Work space; Innovation & R&D; Networking; Training & Mentoring

Colab is LETTERKENNY INSTITUTE OF TECHNOLOGY's incubation centre, providing a supportive environment for entrepreneurs and researchers.

COLLEGE FOR AGRICULTURE, FOOD & RURAL ENTERPRISE

Loughry Campus, 76 Dungannon Road, Cookstown, Co. Tyrone BT80 9AA T: (028) 8676 8101 E: enquiries@cafre.ac.uk W: www.cafre.ac.uk

Community & Rural Development; Incubation & Work space; Innovation & R&D; Training & Mentoring

CAFRE provides a range of training programmes aimed at farmers, farm family members and those who work in food and land-based industries. It also has dedicated teams devoted to food business development, innovation, energy and waste management and operates a Food Business Incubation Centre.

COMHAR NA NOILEÁN CTR

Inis Oírr, Oileáin Árainn, Co. na Gaillimhe H91 D27X T: (099) 75096 E: fios@oileain.ie / T: (026) 45366 E: corcaigh@udaras.ie W: www.oileain.ie

Community & Rural Development; Funding

Comhar na nOileán is supported under LEADER and the Social Inclusion & Community Activation Programme and is a member of the IRISH LOCAL DEVELOPMENT NETWORK.

COMMUNITY FINANCE (IRELAND)

Unit 16, Ardee Business Park, Hale Street, Ardee, Co. Louth, A92 XN79 T: (041) 685 8637 E: mariecarpenter@communityfinance.ie W: www.communityfinance.ie

Funding; Social Enterprise

Community Finance (Ireland), formerly UCIT (Ireland), is a charity that provides loans to other third sector organisations such as community groups, charities, sports clubs and social enterprises in the Republic of Ireland. It is a sister-company of the ULSTER COMMUNITY INVESTMENT TRUST.

COMPANIES HOUSE

The Linenhall – 2nd Floor, 32-38 Linenhall Street, Belfast BT2 8BG T: (0303) 1234 500 E: enquiries@companieshouse.gov.uk W: www.gov.uk/government/organisations/companies-house

Information; Regulation & Standards

The registry for all Northern Ireland companies.

COMPANIES REGISTRATION OFFICE

Bloom House, Gloucester Place Lower, Dublin 1 / O'Brien Road, Carlow (postal address) T: (01) 804 5200 E: info@cro.ie W: www.cro.ie

Information; Regulation & Standards

The core functions of the Companies Registration Office are the incorporation of new companies and the registration of business names, the receipt and registration of post-incorporation documents, enforcement of the filing requirements of the *Companies Act 2014*, and provision of information to the public. Almost all of the information filed with the CRO is available for public inspection – often free, sometimes for a small fee.

COMPANY FORMATIONS INTERNATIONAL LTD

22 Northumberland Road, Ballsbridge, Dublin 4 T: (01) 664 1177 E: cfi@formations.ie W: www.formations.ie

IP & Legal

CFI is a specialist in company formation and secretarial / business information.

COMPANY SETUP

Coliemore House, Coliemore Road, Dalkey, Co. Dublin T: (01) 284 8911 E: info@companysetup.ie W: www.companysetup.ie

IP & Legal

Company Setup is a specialist in company formation and secretarial / business information.

COMPETITION & CONSUMER PROTECTION COMMISSION

Bloom House, Railway Street, Dublin D01 C576 T: (01) 402 5000 E: W: www.ccpc.ie

Regulation & Standards

The CCPC is an independent statutory body whose mandate is to enforce competition and consumer protection law in Ireland.

CONNEMARA WEST

Connemara West Centre, Letterfrack, Co. Galway T: (095) 41047 E: reception@connemarawest.ie W: www.connemarawest.ie

Community & Rural Development

Connemara West plc is a community development company and is a member of the NATIONAL ASSOCIATION OF COMMUNITY ENTERPRISE CENTRES.

CONVOY ENTERPRISE CENTRE

Convoy, Co. Donegal F93 YP22 T: (074) 914 7456 E: phil@convoyenterprise.com W: www.convoyenterprise.com

Incubation & Work space

Formerly the Convoy Woollen Mills, Convoy Enterprise Centre offers state-of-the-art office and industrial space, as well as advice and support.

COOKSTOWN ENTERPRISE CENTRE LTD

Derryloran Industrial Estate, Sandholes Road, Cookstown, Co. Tyrone BT80 9LU T: (028) 8676 3660 E: info@cookstownenterprise.com W: www.cookstownenterprise.com

Incubation & Work space; Training & Mentoring

Cookstown Enterprise Centre promotes urban and rural regeneration by offering industrial, commercial and office units available for rent, complemented by advice, support and training for start-up and expanding businesses. It is a member of ENTERPRISE NORTHERN IRELAND.

COOLOCK DEVELOPMENT COUNCIL

Northside Enterprise Centre, Bunratty Drive, Coolock, Dublin 17 T: (01) 867 5200 W: www.nec.ie

Incubation & Work space

The Coolock Development Council established the Coolock Development Centre in 1990, with small business incubator units available from 1994. The NORTHSIDE ENTERPRISE CENTRE was built in 2001. It is a member of the NATIONAL ASSOCIATION OF COMMUNITY ENTERPRISE CENTRES.

CORK BUSINESS INNOVATION CENTRE

NSC Campus, Mahon, Cork T: (021) 230 7005 E: info@corkbic.com W: www.corkbic.com

Consulting; Incubation & Work space; Training & Mentoring

CorkBIC identifies and builds knowledge-intensive companies based on promising technology and capable, innovative people. It is a leading interdisciplinary venture consultancy that provides an integrated process for incubating and growing high potential technology-driven companies.

CORK CITY PARTNERSHIP CLG

Heron House, Blackpool Park, Cork T: (021) 430 2310 E: info@partnershipcork.ie W: www.corkcitypartnership.ie

Community & Rural Development; Training & Mentoring

Cork City Partnership is supported under the Social Inclusion & Community Activation Programme and is a member of the IRISH LOCAL DEVELOPMENT NETWORK. It provides start-your-own-business support to local entrepreneurs.

CORK INCUBATOR KITCHEN

Units 1 & 2, J Street, Carrigaline Industrial Estate, Kilnagleary, Carrigaline, Co. Cork

Incubation & Work space

Cork Incubator Kitchens, a Cork County Council initiative, assists emerging and existing food ventures to start, grow and expand. The facility offers modern kitchen equipment and kitchen spaces which are approved for food production for rent to registered FBOs, eliminating the high cost of setting up a kitchen.

CORK INSTITUTE OF TECHNOLOGY

Rossa Avenue, Bishopstown, Cork T12 P928 T: (021) 432 6100 E: info@cit.ie W: www.cit.ie

Enterprise Support; Incubation & Work space; Training & Mentoring

CIT provides supports to entrepreneurs through its on-campus RUBICON CENTRE.

COSME

W: https://ec.europa.eu/growth/smes/cosme_en

Enterprise Support; Funding

COSME (Competitiveness of Enterprises and Small & Medium-sized Enterprises) is an EU programme, managed by the EXECUTIVE AGENCY FOR SMES, to make it easier for SMEs to access finance and open new markets. It supports entrepreneurs through entrepreneurship education and improving business conditions.

COUNTY KILDARE LEADER PARTNERSHIP

Jigginstown Commercial Centre, Old Limerick Road, Naas, Co. Kildare T: (045) 895450 E: info@countykildarelp.ie W: www.countykildarelp.ie

Community & Rural Development; Funding

County Kildare LEADER Partnership is supported under the Social Inclusion & Community Activation Programme and LEADER and is a member of the IRISH LOCAL DEVELOPMENT NETWORK.

COUNTY SLIGO LEADER PARTNERSHIP COMPANY LTD

Sligo Development Centre, Cleveragh Road, Sligo T: (071) 914 1138 E: info@sligoleader.ie W: www.sligoleader.com

Community & Rural Development; Funding; Training & Mentoring

County Sligo LEADER Partnership is supported under LEADER, the Rural Development Programme and the Social Inclusion & Community Activation Programme and is a member of the IRISH LOCAL DEVELOPMENT NETWORK. It supports entrepreneurs through training, mentoring and funding.

COUNTY WICKLOW PARTNERSHIP

Avoca River House – 3rd Floor, Bridgewater Centre, Arklow, Co. Wicklow T: (0402) 20955 E: info@wicklowpartnership.ie W: www.wicklowpartnership.ie

Community & Rural Development; Funding; Training & Mentoring

County Wicklow Partnership is supported under the Social Inclusion & Community Activation Programme and the Rural Development Programme / LEADER and is a member of the IRISH LOCAL DEVELOPMENT NETWORK.

COWORKING IN IRELAND

W: www.coworking.ie

Incubation & Work space

Use this site to help you find a great place to work, as well as sharing office space, resources and ideas.

CRAIGAVON INDUSTRIAL DEVELOPMENT ORGANISATION LTD

CIDO Innovation Centre, 73 Charlestown Road, Portadown, Craigavon BT63 5RH T: (028) 3839 6520 E: info@cido.co.uk W: www.cido.co.uk

Funding; Incubation & Work space; Innovation & R&D; Training & Mentoring

CIDO is a member of ENTERPRISE NORTHERN IRELAND. It assists the formation of new business and the development of existing small businesses, by providing support in the form of premises, training, guidance and advocacy.

CREATIVE SPARK CLG

Clontygora Drive, Muirhevnamor, Dundalk, Co. Louth A91 HF77 T: (042) 938 5720 E: hello@creativespark.ie W: www.creativespark.ie

Incubation & Work space

Creative Spark is a not-for-profit social enterprise that aims to develop the local creative industries sector and support new and established innovative enterprises in County Louth. Creative Spark is a member of the NATIONAL ASSOCIATION OF COMMUNITY ENTERPRISE CENTRES.

CREATIVEIRELAND.COM

W: www.creativeireland.com

Information; Networking

Creative Ireland is the online home for the Irish creative design community. It provides news, a directory of designers, a jobs desk for those looking for work or designers, and a gateway to essential design resources on the Internet.

CREDIT REVIEW OFFICE

The Plaza, East Point Business Park, Dublin D03 E5R6 T: 1850 211 789 E: info@creditreview.ie W: www.creditreview.ie

Funding; Regulation & Standards

The Credit Review Office provides an independent, impartial credit appeals process for SMEs, sole traders and farm enterprises that have had requests for credit refused or had existing credit facilities reduced or withdrawn.

CREGGAN ENTERPRISES LTD

Ráth Mór Business & Community Enterprise Centre, Bligh's Lane, Derry BT48 0LZ T: (028) 7137 3170 E: info@rathmor.com W: www.rathmor.com/cel_intro.html

Community & Rural Development; Social Enterprise

Creggan Enterprises works to address the social and economic needs of the local community and operates the Ráth Mór Business & Community Enterprise Centre.

CRESCENT CAPITAL

7 Upper Crescent, Belfast BT7 1NT T: (028) 9023 3633 E:
oonagh@crescentcapital.co.uk W: www.crescentcapital.co.uk

Funding

Crescent Capital funds early-stage to MBO investments in IT, life sciences and
manufacturing in Northern Ireland.

CROOM COMMUNITY ENTERPRISE CENTRE

Croom Enterprise Park, Hospital Road, Croom, Co. Limerick V35 WF77 T: (061)
602000 E: info@croomenterprisecentre.ie W: www.croomenterprisecentre.ie

Incubation & Work space

Croom Community Centre was established by the Croom Community
Development Association and is part of LIMERICK INSTITUTE OF TECHNOLOGY's
Enterprise Ladder, which includes enterprise programmes and enterprise centres.

CROWDCUBE

Broadwalk House – South Entrance / 4th Floor, Southernhay, Exeter EX1 1TS W:
www.crowdcube.com

Funding

CrowdCube is one of Europe's leading equity crowdfunding platforms.

CRUCIAL CROWDFUNDING

T: (044) 934 3444 E: info@meag.ie W: www.crucialcrowdfunding.com

Funding; Information

CRUCIAL Crowdfunding is an ERASMUS+ supported project, designed to de-
mystify crowdfunding for entrepreneurs and SMEs seeking financial support. It
provides a list of European crowdfunding platforms.

CRUICKSHANK & CO

8a Sandyford Business Centre, Sandyford, Dublin D18 R2NB T: (01) 299 2222 E:
post@cruickshank.ie W: www.cruickshank.ie

IP & Legal

Cruickshank & Co is a multidisciplinary patent and trade mark practice.

DANSKE BANK UK

Donegall Square West, Belfast BT1 6JS T: (028) 9024 5277 W:
www.danskebank.co.uk

Funding

Danske Bank UK (formerly Northern Bank) offers a full range of business banking
services in Northern Ireland.

DATA PROTECTION COMMISSION

Canal House, Station Road, Portarlington, Co. Laois R32 AP23 T: (057) 868 4800
E: info@dataprotection.ie W: www.dataprotection.ie

Regulation & Standards

The Commission is responsible for monitoring the application of the GDPR in
order to protect the rights and freedoms of individuals in relation to processing. Its
tasks include promoting public awareness and understanding of the risks, rules,
safeguards and rights in relation to processing, handling complaints lodged by data
subjects and cooperating with (which includes sharing information with) other data
protection authorities in other EU Member States.

DCCOIENTERPRISE.IE

W: www.dccoienterprise.ie

Information; Training & Mentoring

A dedicated design / craft enterprise website from the DESIGN & CRAFTS COUNCIL
OF IRELAND.

DCU ALPHA INNOVATION CAMPUS

Old Finglas Road, Glasnevin, Dublin 11 T: (01) 907 2760 E: ronan.furlong@dcu.ie
W: www.dcualpha.ie

Incubation & Work space

DCU ALPHA is a commercial innovation campus that promotes the growth of
research-intensive businesses creating the technologies and services of tomorrow.

DCU INVENT

Dublin City University, Glasnevin, Dublin 9 T: (01) 700 7777 E:
info@invent.dcu.ie W: www.dcuinvent.ie

Incubation & Work space; Innovation & R&D; Training & Mentoring

DCU Invent is DUBLIN CITY UNIVERSITY's commercialisation and technology
transfer unit, working with companies to bring university research to the market.

DCU RYAN ACADEMY

3013 Lake Drive, Citywest Business Campus, Dublin 24 T: (01) 700 6786 E:
info@ryanacademy.ie W: www.ryanacademy.ie

Funding; Training & Mentoring

DCU Ryan Academy offers a number of cutting-edge incubation and accelerator
programmes, some of which provide access to funding. Startup Lighthouse, in
association with STARTUP EUROPE CLUB, aims to connect Irish start-ups with
others across Europe.

DEFINITION IP

Creative Dock, Malahide Marina Village, Malahide, Co. Dublin K36 W540 T: (01) 969 7808 E: info@definitionip.com W: www.definitionip.com

IP & Legal

Definition IP is a firm of intellectual property attorneys providing expert advice and services across all aspects of the intellectual property system including patents, trade marks, registered designs, copyright and trade secrets.

DELTA PARTNERS

Media House, South County Business Park, Leopardstown, Dublin 18 T: (01) 294 0870 E: info@deltapartners.com W: www.deltapartners.com

Funding

Delta Partners is a venture capital firm investing in Ireland and the UK, with €250 million under management and a strong focus on investing in early stage technology companies in technology and healthcare.

DEPARTMENT FOR THE ECONOMY

Netherleigh, Massey Avenue, Belfast BT4 2JP T: (028) 9052 9900 E: dfemail@economy-ni.gov.uk W: www.economy-ni.gov.uk

Funding; Innovation & R&D; Policy; Regulation & Standards

The Department is responsible for economic strategy, regulation, innovation, enterprise and social economy policy across Northern Ireland, acting through a number of agencies.

DEPARTMENT OF AGRICULTURE, ENVIRONMENT & RURAL AFFAIRS

Dundonald House, Upper Newtownards Road, Belfast BT4 3SB T: (028) 9049 5780 E: daera.helpline@daera-ni.gov.uk W: www.daera-ni.gov.uk

Community & Rural Development; Funding; Policy; Regulation & Standards

DAERA has responsibility for food, farming, environmental, fisheries, forestry and sustainability policy and the development of the rural sector in Northern Ireland. DAERA acts as the managing authority for the Rural Development Programme in Northern Ireland and is responsible for its implementation.

DEPARTMENT OF AGRICULTURE, FOOD & THE MARINE

Agriculture House, Kildare Street, Dublin D02 WK12 T: (01) 607 2000 E: info@agriculture.gov.ie W: www.agriculture.gov.ie

Policy; Regulation & Standards

DAFM is responsible for regulating and developing the agri-food sector in Ireland.

DEPARTMENT OF BUSINESS, ENTERPRISE & INNOVATION

23 Kildare Street, Dublin D02 TD30 T: (01) 631 2121 E: info@dbei.gov.ie W: www.dbei.gov.ie

Policy; Regulation & Standards

The Department's mandate is to implement Government policy in the development of enterprise and trade, employment promotion, protection of workers and regulation of businesses.

DEPARTMENT OF EMPLOYMENT AFFAIRS & SOCIAL PROTECTION

Áras Mhic Dhiarmada, Store Street, Dublin 1 T: (01) 704 3000 E: info@welfare.ie W: www.welfare.ie

Funding; Information; Policy; Regulation & Standards

The Department plays a key role in policy relating to the distribution and re-distribution of income to assure social cohesion and equity of economic outcomes, and the efficient operation of the supply side of the labour market. It also operates the Back to Work Allowance and Short-term Enterprise Allowance for unemployed people who wish to start a business.

DEPARTMENT OF HOUSING, PLANNING & LOCAL GOVERNMENT

Custom House, Dublin D01 W6X0 T: (01) 888 2000 E: qcsofficer@housing.gov.ie W: www.housing.gov.ie

Policy; Regulation & Standards

The Department's mission is to support the sustainable and efficient delivery of well-planned homes and effective local government.

DEPARTMENT OF JUSTICE & EQUALITY

51 St. Stephen's Green, Dublin D02 HK52 T: (01) 602 8202 E: info@justice.ie W: www.justice.ie

Policy; Regulation & Standards

The Department is responsible for making Ireland a safe, fair and inclusive place to live and work. It provides strategic and policy direction and delivery.

DEPARTMENT OF RURAL & COMMUNITY DEVELOPMENT

Trinity Point, 10-11 Leinster Street South, Dublin D02 EF85 T: (076) 106 4900 E: info@drcd.gov.ie W: www.drcd.gov.ie

Community & Rural Development; Policy; Regulation & Standards

The Department's mission is "to promote rural and community development and to support vibrant, inclusive and sustainable communities throughout Ireland".

DERRY & STRABANE RURAL PARTNERSHIP

Derry City & Strabane District Council, 98 Strand Road, Derry BT48 7NN T: (028) 71253253 x 6917 E: rural.development@derrystrabane.com W: www.derrystrabane.com/Subsites/Rural/Derry-and-Strabane-Rural-Partnership

Community & Rural Development; Funding

Derry & Strabane Rural Partnership delivers the LEADER elements (Priority 6) of the Northern Ireland Rural Development Programme.

DESIGN & CRAFTS COUNCIL OF IRELAND

Castle Yard, Kilkenny T: (056) 776 1804 E: info@dccoi.ie W: www.dccoi.ie

Marketing; Training & Mentoring

DCCoI is the national agency for the commercial development of Irish designers and makers. It has a craft enterprise website, **www.dccoienterprise.ie.**

DIGITAL HUB DEVELOPMENT AGENCY

The Digital Hub, Dublin D08 TCV4 T: (01) 480 6200 E: info@thedigitalhub.com W: www.digitalhub.com

Incubation & Work space

The Digital Hub is the largest cluster of technology, digital media and internet companies in Ireland, offering a collaborative space for digital businesses to grow.

DIT HOTHOUSE

Greenway Hub, Dublin Institute of Technology, Grangegorman Lower, Dublin, D07 H6K8 T: (01) 402 5328 W: www.dit.ie/hothouse

Incubation & Work space; Innovation & R&D; Training & Mentoring

DIT Hothouse is the knowledge transfer and incubation centre at DUBLIN INSTITUTE OF TECHNOLOGY, responsible for the commercialisation of intellectual property arising from DIT research and for supporting start-ups.

DOGPATCH LABS

The CHQ Building, Custom House Quay, Dublin 1 E: info@dogpatchlabs.com W: www.dogpatchlabs.com

Incubation & Work space

Dogpatch Labs is a start-up hub, whose mission is to accelerate the development of Ireland's start-up ecosystem by providing a community from where businesses can grow, share knowledge and form connections.

DONEGAL LOCAL DEVELOPMENT COMPANY CLG

1 Millennium Court, Pearse Road, Letterkenny, Co. Donegal F92 W50R T: (091) 27056 E: info@dldc.org W: www.dldc.org

Community & Rural Development; Funding; Social Enterprise; Training & Mentoring

DLDC is a community-led local development organisation, supported under the Social Inclusion & Community Activation Programme and LEADER, and is a member of the IRISH LOCAL DEVELOPMENT NETWORK. It offers training and other supports for entrepreneurs starting businesses or social enterprises.

DONEGAL LOCAL ENTERPRISE OFFICE

Enterprise Fund Business Centre, Ballyraine, Letterkenny, Co. Donegal T: (074) 916 0735 E: info@leo.donegalcoco.ie W: www.localenterprise.ie/donegal

Funding; Information; Training & Mentoring; Young Enterprise

Donegal Local Enterprise Office provides both direct supports (feasibility, priming or business expansion grants) and indirect supports (mentoring, management development, or other capacity building programmes).

DOWN BUSINESS CENTRE

46 Belfast Road, Downpatrick, Co. Down BT30 9UP T: (028) 4461 6416 E: reception@downbc.co.uk W: www.downbc.co.uk

Funding; Incubation & Work space; Training & Mentoring

Down Business Centre is a member of ENTERPRISE NORTHERN IRELAND and provides training, support and workspace for start-up and existing businesses.

DRAPER ESPRIT

Merrion Buildings, 18/20 Merrion Street, Dublin D02 XH98 T: (+44 207) 931 8800 W: www.draperesprit.com

Funding

The European arm of a global network of venture funds, unusually Draper Esprit is listed on the stock market. It invests between €1m and €15m in companies in digital media / web 2.0, electronics, energy, energy, environmental, ICT, life sciences, medical devices, photonics, semi-conductors, software and telecoms.

DRINAN ENTERPRISE CENTRE

Swords Enterprise Park, Feltrim Road, Swords, Fingal, Co. Dublin T: (01) 892 8000 W: www.drinanenterprisecentre.ie

Incubation & Work space

The Drinan Enterprise Centre provides enterprise space to start-up businesses and growing businesses to help facilitate their expansion. It is a member of the NATIONAL ASSOCIATION OF COMMUNITY ENTERPRISE CENTRES.

DRUMSHANBO ENTERPRISE CENTRE

Hill Road, Drumshanbo, Co. Leitrim T: (091) 964 1577

Incubation & Work space; Training & Mentoring

Drumshanbo Enterprise Centre offers work space and training.

DUBLIN BUSINESS INNOVATION CENTRE

The Tower, Trinity Technology & Enterprise Centre, Grand Canal Quay, Dublin 2 T: (01) 671 3111 E: startup@dublinbic.ie W: www.dublinbic.ie

Funding; Incubation & Work space; Networking; Training & Mentoring

Dublin BIC empowers entrepreneurs to start and scale by providing a comprehensive range of programmes designed to advance the ambitions of early-stage companies, focusing on access to finance, investor-ready preparation, incubation space and community and collaboration. It also runs a number of funds, including the €30m Irish Smart Tech fund.

DUBLIN CITY COMMUNITY CO-OP

Unit 1, Killarney Court, Buckingham Street, Dublin 1 T: (01) 855 7105 E: info@dublincitycommunitycoop.ie W: www.dublincitycommunitycoop.ie

Community & Rural Development; Social Enterprise

Dublin City Community Co-op is an alliance of 13 grassroots, Dublin inner city, community development organisations working together to ensure the development and delivery of social, economic and cultural services. It is a member of the IRISH LOCAL DEVELOPMENT NETWORK and provides support to people setting up their own business, both for-profit and social enterprises.

DUBLIN CITY UNIVERSITY

Glasnevin, Dublin 9 T: (01) 700 5000 W: www.dcu.ie

Enterprise Support; Incubation & Work space; Training & Mentoring

DCU provides supports to entrepreneurs through DCU INVENT and DCU ALPHA INNOVATION CAMPUS.

DUBLIN FOOD CHAIN

W: www.dublinfoodchain.ie

Marketing; Networking; Training & Mentoring

The Dublin Food Chain is a marketing and networking forum that helps members to grow their food sector business through new sales contacts, networking, training, and agency support. It is supported by the LOCAL ENTERPRISE OFFICES in Dublin and BORD BIA.

DUBLIN INSTITUTE OF TECHNOLOGY

T: (01) 402 3000 W: www.dit.ie

Enterprise Support; Incubation & Work space; Innovation & R&D; Training & Mentoring

DIT supports the development of new business ventures through DIT HOTHOUSE.

DUBLIN NORTH WEST AREA PARTNERSHIP

Rosehill House, Finglas Road, Dublin 11 T: (01) 868 3806 W: www.dnwap.ie

Community & Rural Development; Training & Mentoring

Dublin North West Area Partnership offers training, mentoring, business information and advice to businesses in its catchment area. It is funded under the Social Inclusion & Community Activation Programme and is a member of the IRISH LOCAL DEVELOPMENT NETWORK.

DUBLIN SOUTH CITY PARTNERSHIP

3/4 St. Agnes Road, Crumlin, Dublin 12 T: (01) 473 2196 E: info@dscp.ie W: www.dublinsouthcitypartnership.ie

Community & Rural Development; Training & Mentoring

Dublin South City Partnership assists people interested in starting their own business through individual mentoring and training programmes. It is funded under the Social Inclusion & Community Activation Programme and is a member of the IRISH LOCAL DEVELOPMENT NETWORK.

DUBLIN SOUTH LOCAL ENTERPRISE OFFICE

County Hall, Tallaght, Dublin 24 T: (01) 414 9000 E: info@leo.sdublincoco.ie W: www.localenterprise.ie/southdublin

Funding; Information; Training & Mentoring; Young Enterprise

Dublin South Local Enterprise Office provides both direct supports (feasibility, priming or business expansion grants) and indirect supports (mentoring, management development, or other capacity building programmes).

DÚN LAOIRE ENTERPRISE CENTRE

The Old Firestation, George's Place, Dún Laoire, Co. Dublin T: (01) 202 0056 E: dlenterprisecebtre1@gmail.com

Incubation & Work space

An incubation centre offering workspace, which is a member of the NATIONAL ASSOCIATION OF COMMUNITY ENTERPRISE CENTRES.

DUNDALK INSTITUTE OF TECHNOLOGY

Dublin Road, Dundalk, Co. Louth T: (042) 937 0200 E: info@dkit.ie W: www.dkit.ie

Incubation & Work space; Training & Mentoring

Dundalk IT supports entrepreneurs through its REGIONAL DEVELOPMENT CENTRE.

DUNGANNON ENTERPRISE CENTRE LTD

2 Coalisland Road, Dungannon, Co. Tyrone BT71 6JT T: (028) 8772 3489 E: info@dungannonenterprise.com W: www.dungannonenterprise.com

Funding; Incubation & Workspace; Training & Mentoring;

Dungannon Enterprise Centre supports the development of micro-businesses, through estate management, ICT, marketing and business / financial planning. It is a member of ENTERPRISE NORTHERN IRELAND.

DUNGARVAN ENTERPRISE CENTRE

Old Friary Building, Lower Main Street, Dungarvan, Co. Waterford T: (058) 23598 E: info@dungarvanec.com W: www.dungarvanec.com

Incubation & Work space; Training & Mentoring

The Centre provides business services, office space, conference facilities, training and mentoring to small and growing businesses locally. It is a member of the NATIONAL ASSOCIATION OF COMMUNITY ENTERPRISE CENTRES.

DUNHILL ECOPARK

Dunhill Rural Enterprises Ltd, Ballyphilip, Dunhill, Co. Waterford T: (051) 396622: E: senan@dunhillecopark.com W: www.dunhillecopark.ie

Incubation & Work space; Social Enterprise; Training & Mentoring

Dunhill Ecopark is a social enterprise whose mission is to cultivate an entrepreneurial culture and facilitate job creation. It is a member of the NATIONAL ASSOCIATION OF COMMUNITY ENTERPRISE CENTRES.

EAST BELFAST ENTERPRISE

City East Business centre, 68/72 Newtownards Road, Belfast BT4 1GW T: (028) 9094 2010 E: info@eastbelfast.org W: www.eastbelfast.org

Funding; Incubation & Work space; Information; Innovation & R&D; Training & Mentoring; Young Enterprise

East Belfast Enterprise is a member of ENTERPRISE NORTHERN IRELAND and is the Local Enterprise Agency for East Belfast. It supports entrepreneurs through free pre-start mentoring, support and workshops, shared offices for freelancers to fully serviced premises for established companies.

EASTERN & MIDLAND REGIONAL ASSEMBLY

Ballymun Civic Centre – 3rd Floor North, Main Street, Ballymun, Dublin D09 C8P5 T: (01) 807 4482 E: info@emra.ie W: www.emra.ie

Policy

The Eastern & Midland Regional Assembly implements appropriate Regional Planning Guidelines operational within its geographical area; prepares, adopts and implements Regional Spatial and Economic Strategies; participates on EU operational programme monitoring committees; and identifies, participates in and co-ordinates certain EU projects.

EDEN CENTRE FOR ENTREPRENEURSHIP, DESIGN & INNOVATION

BL1.19 Rowan House, North Campus, NUI Maynooth, Maynooth, Co. Kildare
T: (01) 708 6634 E: eden@mu.ie W: www.maynoothuniversity.ie/eden

Innovation & R&D; Training & Mentoring

EDEN helps NATIONAL UNIVERSITY OF IRELAND MAYNOOTH students to
develop their creative confidence and turn their creative ideas into action that will
add value to the world.

EMPOWER

Dillon House, 106 Coolmine Industrial Estate, Dublin 15 T: (01) 820 9550 W:
www.empower.ie

Community & Rural Development; Training & Mentoring

Formerly the Blanchardstown Area Partnership, Empower is supported under the
Social Inclusion & Community Activation Programme and is a member of the
IRISH LOCAL DEVELOPMENT NETWORK. Empower provides one-to-one supports
for entrepreneurs, as well as training.

ENACTUS IRELAND

35 Exchequer Street, Dublin 2 T: (01) 670 8795 E: ireland@enactus.org W:
www.enactusireland.org

Social Enterprise

Enactus Ireland is a charity that develops future talent by enabling third-level
students to create and implement social entrepreneurial projects and by showcasing
them in an annual national competition, the winner of which goes on to represent
Ireland at the Enactus World Cup.

ENERGY CO-OPERATIVES IRELAND

6 St. Gall's Gardens North, Windy Arbour, Dublin D14 FX46 T: (086) 678 4063
E: info@energyco-ops.ie W: www.energyco-ops.ie

Consulting; Information; Social Enterprise

Energy Co-operatives Ireland supports community-based renewable energy co-
operatives, guiding them through the legal process of setting up a co-operative,
advising them on their dealings with State agencies, introducing them to a network
of co-operatives where they can learn from best practice examples, and helping
them communicate their message locally and nationally.

ENNISCORTHY ENTERPRISE & TECHNOLOGY CENTRE

Milehouse Road, Enniscorthy, Co. Wexford Y21 D8W6 T: (053) 923 7499
E: info@eetc.ie W: www.eetc.ie

Incubation & Workspace; Training & Mentoring

Enniscorthy Enterprise & Technology Centre supports local business, through
mentoring, advice, training and incubation space. It is a member of the NATIONAL
ASSOCIATION OF COMMUNITY ENTERPRISE CENTRES.

ENNISTYMON ENTERPRISE CENTRE LTD

Deerpark West, Ennistymon, Co. Clare T: (065) 707 2999
E: ennistymon@eircom.net W: www.projectennistymon.com

Incubation & Workspace; Training & Mentoring

Ennistymon Enterprise Centre supports local business, through mentoring, advice,
training and incubation space. It is a member of the NATIONAL ASSOCIATION OF
COMMUNITY ENTERPRISE CENTRES.

ENTERPRISE & RESEARCH INCUBATION CAMPUS

IT Carlow, Kilkenny Road, Carlow T: (059) 917 5200 E:
maresa.fitzhenry@itcarlow.ie W: www.itcarlow.ie/industry-innovation/sme-
entrepreneurial-supports.htm

Enterprise Support; Incubation & Work space; Training & Mentoring

Located on the INSTITUTE OF TECHNOLOGY CARLOW campus, ERIC accelerates
the development of start-up companies through a combination of infrastructure,
business support services, training and specialised resources.

ENTERPRISE EQUITY

The Media Cube, Kill Avenue, Dun Laoire, Co. Dublin T: (01) 214 5606 E:
info@enterpriseequity.ie W: www.enterpriseequity.ie

Funding

Established by the International Fund for Ireland, Enterprise Equity provides
venture capital of between €250,000 and €1.5 million to new and expanding
businesses in software, high-tech manufacturing and medical technologies.

ENTERPRISE EUROPE NETWORK

W: https://een.ec.europa.eu/about/branches/ireland

Information

Enterprise Europe Network's services in Ireland are delivered by Enterprise Ireland,
together with the CHAMBERS OF COMMERCE in Cork and Dublin and the LOCAL
ENTERPRISE OFFICES.

ENTERPRISE IRELAND

The Plaza, East Point Business Park, Dublin 3 T: (01) 727 2000 E: client.service@enterprise-ireland.com W: www.enterprise-ireland.com

Funding; Information; Training & Mentoring; Young Enterprise

Enterprise Ireland is the government organisation responsible for the development and growth of Irish enterprises in world markets. Its High Potential Start-Up (HPSU) team provides hands-on support and advice to entrepreneurs and early stage companies considered to have an innovative product, service or technology, and have the potential to achieve international sales and create employment. It funds the NEW FRONTIERS programmes, delivered by the INSTITUTES OF TECHNOLOGY nationwide.

ENTERPRISE NORTH WEST

NW Business Complex, Skeoge Industrial Park, Beraghmore Road, Derry BT48 8SE T: (028) 7135 2693 E: info@enterprisenw.com W: www.enterprisenw.com

Accounting & Business Planning; Incubation & Work space; Information; Social Enterprise; Training & Mentoring

Enterprise North West provides confidential and impartial advice on a one-to-one basis, helps with producing a business plan and financial projections, training, signposting to other support organisations and help with identifying appropriate sources of financial support. It also supports social enterprises and is a member of ENTERPRISE NORTHERN IRELAND.

ENTERPRISE NORTHERN IRELAND

Aghanloo Industrial Estate, Aghanloo Road, Limavady BT49 0HE T: (028) 7776 3555 E: pa@enterpriseni.com W: www.enterpriseni.com

Funding; Information; Training & Mentoring

Enterprise Northern Ireland is the umbrella body for the Local Enterprise Agencies in Northern Ireland, which offer advice on business start-up, accessing business investment and training. It also offers funding from the START UP LOANS COMPANY, accessed through the LEAs. See individual entries for:

- ANTRIM ENTERPRISE AGENCY LTD.
- ARDS BUSINESS CENTRE LTD.
- ARMAGH BUSINESS CENTRE LTD.
- BALLYMENA BUSINESS CENTRE LTD.
- BANBRIDGE DISTRICT ENTERPRISES LTD.
- CARRICKFERGUS ENTERPRISE AGENCY LTD.
- CAUSEWAY ENTERPRISE AGENCY LTD.
- COOKSTOWN ENTERPRISE CENTRE LTD.
- CRAIGAVON INDUSTRIAL DEVELOPMENT ORGANISATION LTD.
- DOWN BUSINESS CENTRE.
- DUNGANNON ENTERPRISE CENTRE LTD.
- EAST BELFAST ENTERPRISE.
- ENTERPRISE NORTH WEST.

- ○ FERMANAGH ENTERPRISE LTD.
- ○ INSPIRE BUSINESS CENTRE LTD.
- ○ LISBURN ENTERPRISE ORGANISATION LTD.
- ○ LOCAL ENTERPRISE DEVELOPMENT COMPANY LTD.
- ○ MALLUSK ENTERPRISE PARK.
- ○ NEWRY & MOURNE ENTERPRISE AGENCY.
- ○ NORTH CITY BUSINESS CENTRE LTD.
- ○ NORTH DOWN DEVELOPMENT ORGANISATION LTD.
- ○ OMAGH ENTERPRISE COMPANY LTD.
- ○ ORMEAU BUSINESS PARK.
- ○ ORTUS GROUP.
- ○ ROE VALLEY ENTERPRISES LTD.
- ○ STRABANE ENTERPRISE AGENCY.
- ○ WORK WEST ENTERPRISE AGENCY.
- ○ WORKSPACE ENTERPRISES LTD.

ENTERPRISE YOUGHAL

St. Mary's College, Emmet Place, Youghal, Co. Cork T: (024) 81800
E: info@enterpriseyoughal.ie W: www.enterpriseyoughal.ie

Incubation & Work space

Enterprise Youghal offers state-of-the-art office space to rent. It is a member of the NATIONAL ASSOCIATION OF COMMUNITY ENTERPRISE CENTRES.

ENTERPRISING MONAGHAN

M:TEK 1 Building, Knockaconny, Monaghan T: (047) 75255
E: info@enterprisingmonaghan.ie W: www.monaghancef.ie

Incubation & Work space

Enterprising Monaghan provides flexible, affordable offices to rent in Co. Monaghan, assisting or building directly M:TEK I, M:TEK II, Clones Business Technology Park, Ballybay Business Centre, and CTEK, as well as an Enterprise Centre in Emyvale. It is a member of the NATIONAL ASSOCIATION OF COMMUNITY ENTERPRISE CENTRES.

ENTREPRENEURS ANONYMOUS

W: www.entanon.com

Networking

Entrepreneurs Anonymous is a Europe-wide community of like-minded people where founders, both new and experienced, can connect, learn and get inspired. Membership is free.

ENVIRONMENTAL PROTECTION AGENCY

PO Box 3000, Johnstown Castle Estate, Co. Wexford Y35 W821 T: (053) 916 0600 E: info@epa.ie W: www.epa.ie

Information; Regulation & Standards

The EPA is responsible for licensing, enforcement, monitoring and assessment of environmental protection and has a key role in environmental legislation, provision of knowledge and advocacy for the environment.

ERNE ENTERPRISE DEVELOPMENT COMPANY LTD

Lakeside Community Centre, Belleek Road, Ballyhanna, Ballyshannon, Co. Donegal T: (071) 985 2822

Enterprise Support

Erne Enterprise is a local community development company that offers incubation and office space at the Tirhugh Resource Centre, the Finner Business Park and Portnason IT Centre. It is supported by POBAL and is a member of the NATIONAL ASSOCIATION OF COMMUNITY ENTERPRISE CENTRES.

EUROPA

W: europa.eu

Information

The European Union's website, Europa, features information on the objectives of the EU, details on its agencies and the latest news. The website **https://europa.eu/european-union/business/startups_en** is specific to start-ups.

EUROPEAN INVESTMENT PORTAL

W: https://ec.europa.eu/eipp/desktop/en/index.html

Funding

By registering a project on the European Investment Project Portal, a promoter can boost its visibility to a large network of international investors – though the minimum project size is now €1 million!

EUROPEAN IPR HELP DESK

T: (+352 25) 22 33 333 W: www.iprhelpdesk.eu

IP & Legal

The European IPR Helpdesk offers free-of-charge, first-line support on IP matters to beneficiaries of EU-funded research projects and EU SMEs involved in transnational partnership agreements.

EUROPEAN SPACE AGENCY

8/10 rue Mario Nikis, 75738 Paris, France T: (+33 1) 5369 7155 W: www.esa.int / business.esa.int

Funding; Innovation & R&D

The ESA is Europe's gateway to space. Its mission is to shape the development of Europe's space capability and ensure that investment in space continues to deliver benefits to the citizens of Europe and the world. ESA Business Applications enables and supports businesses in the short-term commercialisation and application of space data and technology for everyday services.

EUROPEDIRECT.ie

W: www.europedirect.ie

Information

Europe Direct Ireland is delivered by the public libraries service on behalf of the European Commission Representation in Ireland.

EXCELLENCE IRELAND QUALITY ASSOCIATION

Q Mark House, 68 Pembroke Road, Ballsbridge, Dublin D04 A3T6 T: (01) 660 4100 E: info@eiqa.com W: www.eiqa.com

Marketing; Regulation & Standards

EIQA is the Irish national quality association and operates the Q-Mark schemes.

EXECUTIVE AGENCY FOR SMEs

W: ec.euopa.eu/easme/

Funding

EASME manages several EU programmes, including COSME, ENTERPRISE EUROPE NETWORK, YOUR EUROPE and part of HORIZON 2020 (especially the Innovation in SMEs element) on behalf of the European Commission.

FÁILTE IRELAND

88-95 Amiens Street, Dublin D01 WR86 T: (01) 884 7700 E: customersupport@failteireland.ie W: www.failteireland.ie

Community & Rural Development; Information; Marketing; Training & Mentoring

As the national tourism development authority, Fáilte Ireland supports the tourism industry and works to sustain Ireland as a high-quality and competitive tourism destination. It provides a range of practical business supports to help tourism businesses better manage and market their products and services.

FERBANE BUSINESS & TECHNOLOGY PARK

Ballycumber Road, Co. Offaly T: (090) 645 3926 E: donal@ferbanefoodcampus.ie
W: www.ferbanefoodcampus.ie

Incubation & Work space

Ferbane Business and Technology Park is a community-owned not-for-profit
organisation aimed at generating employment opportunities in the locality. The
Park is home to the FERBANE FOOD CAMPUS. It is a member of the NATIONAL
ASSOCIATION OF COMMUNITY ENTERPRISE CENTRES.

FERBANE FOOD CAMPUS

Ballycumber Road, Co. Offaly T: (090) 645 3926 E: donal@ferbanefoodcampus.ie
W: www.ferbanefoodcampus.ie

Incubation & Work space

Ferbane Food Campus is a state-of-the-art food product development, timeshare
production and training facility.

FERMANAGH & OMAGH LOCAL ACTION GROUP

The Sperrin Centre, 1 Market Street, Omagh, Co. Tyrone BT78 1EE T: (028) 8225
0202 W: www.fermanaghomagh.com/business-services/fermanagh-omagh-lag-
local-action-group/

Community & Rural Development; Funding

The Fermanagh & Omagh LAG administers the Rural Business Investment Scheme
under the NI Rural Development Programme 2014-2020 / LEADER.

FERMANAGH ENTERPRISE LTD

Enniskillen Business Centre, 21 Lackaghboy Road, Enniskillen BT74 4RL T: (028)
6632 3117 E: info@fermanaghenterprise.com W: www.fermanaghenterprise.com

Funding; Incubation & Work space; Training & Mentoring

Fermanagh Enterprise is a member of ENTERPRISE NORTHERN IRELAND and
helps individuals set up and grow their own businesses.

FF GORMAN & CO

15 Clanwilliam Terrace, Grand Canal Dock, Dublin 2 T: (01) 676 0363 E:
ffgorman@indigo.ie

IP & Legal

A firm of patent and trade mark agents.

FINGAL LEADER PARTNERSHIP

DSV House, Swords Business Park, Swords, Co. Dublin K67 K8Y2 T: (01) 807 4282 E: rdinfo@fingalleaderpartnership.ie W: fingalleaderpartnership.ie

Community & Rural Development; Funding; Training & Mentoring

Fingal LEADER Partnership promotes social inclusion, provides supports for enterprise development and employment creation, as well as education opportunities reducing climate change, and assists community groups to find local solutions to local problems. It is supported under LEADER and is a member of the IRISH LOCAL DEVELOPMENT NETWORK.

FINISTERE VENTURES

The Academy, 42 Pearse Street, Dublin 2 T: (01) 556 3630 E: info@finistere.com W: www.finistere.com

Funding

Finistere has partnered with the Ireland Strategic Investment Fund to create the €20m Ireland AgTech Fund, to invest in start-up and early-stage agri-tech companies that can generate significant economic impact.

FIONTARLANN TEO

Baile Mún, Cill Chartha, Co. Dhún na nGall T: (074) 973 8333 E: ecunningham@westbic.ie W: www.fiontarlann.com

Incubation & Work space

Fiontarlann is a new state-of-the-art incubation and enterprise centre, suitable for knowledge-based and office businesses. It is a member of the NATIONAL ASSOCIATION OF COMMUNITY ENTERPRISE CENTRES.

FIRST TRUST BANK

92 Ann Street, Belfast BT1 3HH T: (0345) 6005 925 W: www.firsttrustbank.co.uk

Funding

First Trust Bank is AIB BANK's Northern Ireland business banking service.

FLAX TRUST

Brookfield Business Centre, 333 Crumlin Road, Belfast BT14 7EA T: (028) 9074 5241 E: marie@flaxtrust.com W: www.flaxtrust.com

Community & Rural Development; Incubation & Work space

The Flax Trust is one of the largest and longest-established community regeneration projects in Ireland and is committed to the "reconciliation of a divided community through economic and social development, bringing peace to both communities, one person and one job at a time".

FOCUS CAPITAL PARTNERS

Pepper Canister House, Mount Street Crescent, Dublin, D02 WC63 T: (01) 905 2970 E: enquire@focuscapital.ie W: www.focuscapitalpartners.ie

Funding

Focus Capital Partners is a boutique corporate finance firm that provides a broad suite of corporate financing and capital-raising services.

FOOD ACADEMY

W: http://www.bordbiavantage.ie/business-development/irish-retail-programme-2/food-academy/ ; https://www.localenterprise.ie/Discover-Business-Supports/Training-Programmes/Food-Academy-Programme/ ; https://supervalu.ie/real-people/food-academy-programme

Training & Mentoring

Food Academy – a joint initiative of BORD BIA, LOCAL ENTERPRISE OFFICES and SuperValu – works with and nurtures small businesses through their journey from start-up to getting their products on supermarket shelves.

FOOD HUB

Carrick Road, Drumshanbo, Co. Leitrim T: (071) 964 1848 W: www.thefoodhub.com

Incubation & Work space; Innovation & R&D; Training & Mentoring

The Food Hub is a best practice food production and education facility that provides 14 individual food business units. It is operated by the Drumshanbo Community Council, which is a member of the NATIONAL ASSOCIATION OF COMMUNITY ENTERPRISE CENTRES.

FOOD PRODUCT DEVELOPMENT CENTRE

Dublin Institute of Technology, Cathal Brugha Street, Dublin 1 T: (01) 814 6080 E: fpdc@dit.ie W: www.fpdc.dit.ie

Consulting; Innovation & R&D; Training & Mentoring

The Food Product Development Centre at the DUBLIN INSTITUTE OF TECHNOLOGY develops innovative food concepts through investigating value-added opportunities in Irish and European markets. Its confidential development work includes: idea generation; concept and prototype development; ingredient sourcing and testing; shelf-life studies; sensory assessment and market research; nutritional declaration; and labelling. It also offers training.

FOOD SAFETY AUTHORITY OF IRELAND

Abbey Court, Lower Abbey Street, Dublin D01 W2H4 T: (01) 817 1300 E: info@fsai.ie W: www.fsai.ie

Information; Regulation & Standards; Training & Mentoring

The FSAI's mission is to protect consumers' health by ensuring that food consumed, distributed, marketed or produced in Ireland meets the highest standards of food safety and hygiene. FSAI offers a fact sheet outlining the steps to be taken when starting a food business in Ireland, as well as a guide to food law for start-ups and elearning on aspects of food production.

FOODOVATION

North West Regional College, Northland Building, Asylum Road, Derry-Londonderry BT48 7EA T: (028) 7127 6408 E: brian.mcdermott@nwrc.ac.uk W: www.foodovation.co.uk

Innovation & R&D

Foodovation is a business centre of excellence for food development and technology that nurtures small to medium-sized food businesses and provides industry specialists with technical advice to ensure their route to market is successful and sustainable.

FOODWORKS

Bord Bia, Clanwilliam Court, Lower Mount Street, Dublin D02 A344 E: info@foodworksireland.ie W: www.foodworksireland.ie

Training & Mentoring

Food Works is an accelerator programme that helps develop the next generation of scalable and export-driven Irish food businesses. It is run by BORD BIA, ENTERPRISE IRELAND and TEAGASC.

FORUM CONNEMARA CLG

Letterfrack, Connemara, Co. Galway T: (095) 41116 E: info@forumconnemara.ie W: www.forumconnemara.ie

Community & Rural Development; Funding; Social Enterprise

Forum Connemara is a Local Development Company whose main aim is the economic and social development of the Connemara region. It is supported under LEADER and is a member of the IRISH LOCAL DEVELOPMENT NETWORK.

FOUNTAIN HEALTHCARE PARTNERS

Guild House – 4th Floor, Guild Street, IFSC, Dublin D01 K2C5 T: (01) 522 5100 E: info@fh-partners.com W: www.fh-partners.com

Funding

Fountain Healthcare Partners provides risk capital and expertise to ambitious entrepreneurs developing outstanding life sciences companies – in particular, specialty pharma, biopharmaceuticals, medical devices and diagnostics.

FOUNTAIN RESOURCE GROUP

St. James' Presbytery, James Street, Dublin 8 T: (01) 454 6753 E:
fountainresourceltd@gmail.com W: www.frg.ie

Information; Training & Mentoring

Fountain Resource group is a non-profit community organisation providing a range
of free community services in the Dublin 8 area. Its Enterprise Officer provides
advice and guidance to entrepreneurs in the inner city, in conjunction with the
LARKIN UNEMPLOYED CENTRE.

FR KELLY & CO.

27 Clyde Road, Ballsbridge, Dublin D04 F838 T: (01) 231 4848 E:
info@frkelly.com W: www.frkelly.com

IP & Legal

FR Kelly & Co. offers expertise and experience in all aspects of intellectual
property law, trade marks and brand name protection.

FRANCHISE DIRECT

Suite 106, The Capel Building, Capel Street, Dublin 7 T: (01) 865 6370 W:
www.franchisedirect.ie

Franchises; Information

FranchiseDirect is a leading international franchising resource, which provides
views, news and advice to entrepreneurs and franchisers.

FRONTLINE VENTURES

26-28 Lombard Street East, Dublin 2 E: info@frontline.vc W: www.frontline.vc

Funding

Frontline is an early-stage VC firm, based in London and Dublin, with strong links
into the US, that invests €100,000 to €2m in software, digital media / Web 2.0 and
fintech companies.

FSB NORTHERN IRELAND

Cathedral Chambers – 1st Floor, 143 Royal Avenue, Belfast BT1 1FH T: (028)
9032 6035 E: FSBNI@fsb.org.uk W: www.fsb.org.uk/standing-up-for-
you/national-offices/northern-ireland

Networking; Policy

FSB Northern Ireland has around 6,000 business-owner members in Northern
Ireland and campaigns on their behalf.

FUMBALLY EXCHANGE

5 Dame Lane, Dublin 2 T: (086) 809 8205 E: hello@fumballyexchange.com
W: www.fumballyexchange.com

Incubation & Work space

Fumbally Exchange is a not-for-profit movement of creative and innovative
professionals who share co-working spaces. It has three hubs: Dublin city centre,
Balbriggan (North County Dublin) and Waterford city centre.

FUND IT

Business to Arts, 17 Kildare Street – Lower Ground Floor, Dublin D02 CY90
E: info@businesstoarts.ie W: www.fundit.ie
Funding
Fund It is an Ireland-based, Ireland-wide crowdfunding website.

FUNDING COMMONS NI

W: www.thefundingcommons.com
Funding
The Funding Commons was created to help businesses and start-ups in Northern
Ireland to better navigate funding opportunities, based on their technology
readiness level and funding requirements. It is funded by QUEEN'S UNIVERSITY
BELFAST and ULSTER UNIVERSITY, in partnership with CATALYST INC.

GALWAY CITY PARTNERSHIP

3 The Plaza, Headford Road, Galway T: (091) 773466 E: info@gcp.ie W:
www.gcp.ie
Community & Rural Development; Social Enterprise; Training & Mentoring
Galway City Partnership is supported under the Social Inclusion & Community
Activation Programme and is a member of the IRISH LOCAL DEVELOPMENT
NETWORK. It offers a range of supports for businesses and social enterprises.

GALWAY RURAL DEVELOPMENT COMPANY

Mellows Campus, Athenry, Co. Galway T: (091) 844335 E: grd@grd.ie /
leader@grd.ie W: www.grd.ie
Community & Rural Development; Funding; Training & Mentoring
Galway Rural Development is supported under LEADER and the Social Inclusion &
Community Activation Programme and is a member of the IRISH LOCAL
DEVELOPMENT NETWORK.

GALWAY TECHNOLOGY CENTRE

Mervue Business Park, Galway T: (091) 730700 W: www.gtc.ie
Incubation & Work space
Galway Technology Centre provides serviced office space to companies in the ICT,
digital media and other knowledge- and service-based sectors. GTC also provides a
range of business start-up services and is a member of the NATIONAL
ASSOCIATION OF COMMUNITY ENTERPRISE CENTRES.

GALWAY–MAYO INSTITUTE OF TECHNOLOGY

Dublin Road, Galway H91 T8NW T: (091) 753161 E: info@gmit.ie W:
www.gmit.ie
Incubation & Work space; Innovation & R&D; Training & Mentoring
GMIT operates the GMIT INNOVATION HUBS at its campuses in Galway and
Mayo, which offer incubation facilities and a supportive environment to potential
entrepreneurs to help them take their ideas from concept to commercialisation.

GATEWAY UCC

Western Gateway Building, Western Road, Cork T: (021) 420 5885 E: myriam.cronin@ucc.ie W: www.ucc.ie/en/gateway/

Incubation & Work space; Innovation & R&D; Training & Mentoring

Gateway UCC is a state-of-the-art innovation and incubation centre that supports the development of knowledge-based indigenous companies arising from UNIVERSITY COLLEGE CORK's research.

GLENWOOD ENTERPRISES LTD

Glenwood Business Centre, 57/60 Springbank Industrial Estate, Dunmurry, Belfast BT17 0YU T: (028) 9061 0311 E: info@glenwoodbc.com W: www.glenwoodbc.com

Incubation & Work space

Glenwood Enterprises was the first Enterprise Agency in Belfast. It now offers incubation and work space.

GMIT INNOVATION HUBS

Galway Mayo Institute of Technology, Dublin Road, Galway T: (091) 742822 E: ihubgalway@gmit.ie W: www.gmit.ie/gmit-innovation-hubs

Incubation & Work space: Innovation & R&D; Training & Mentoring

The GMIT Innovation Hubs in Galway and Mayo provide support and facilities for start-up businesses.

GOOGLE

Gordon House, Barrow Street, Dublin 4 W: https://events.withgoogle.com/adoptastartup/

Training & Mentoring

Best-known for its search engine, Google Ireland also runs an Adopt A Start-up programme annually, which offers hands-on mentoring from Google consultants and workshops to help ambitious start-ups to scale their business further.

GOV.ie

W: www.gov.ie

Information

Gov.ie provides information on the operation of the State, with links to Government departments and local authorities.

GOVERNMENT PUBLICATIONS OFFICE

T: (076) 110 6834 E: publications@opw.ie W: www.opw.ie/en/governmentpublications/

Information

All Government publications are available from the sales office, including CENTRAL STATISTICS OFFICE reports, which are useful for market research.

GROW SOUTH ANTRIM

Mossley Mill, Carnmoney Road North, Newtownabbey BT36 5QA T: (028) 9448 1311 E: grow@antrimandnewtownabbey.gov.uk W: www.growsouthantrim.com

Community & Rural Development; Funding

GROW South Antrim has been appointed by Antrim & Newtownabbey Borough Council to implement LEADER / Priority 6 of the Northern Ireland Rural Development Programme 2014-2020 in rural South Antrim.

GUARANTEED IRISH LTD

1 Fitzwilliam Place, Dublin 2 T: (01) 661 2607 E: info@guaranteedirish.ie W: www.guaranteedirish.ie

Marketing

Guaranteed Irish awards the Guaranteed Irish symbol – widely recognised by consumers and businesses as the national symbol of provenance and trust – to indigenous and international companies operating in Ireland, across all sectors, which provide quality jobs, support local communities and are committed to Irish provenance, thus helping its members to expand at home and abroad.

GUINNESS ENTERPRISE CENTRE

Taylor's Lane, Dublin 8 T: (01) 410 0600 E: startup@gec.ie W: www.gec.ie

Incubation & Work space

Managed by DUBLIN BUSINESS INNOVATION CENTRE, the GEC is a not-for-profit, world-class enterprise centre for ambitious and innovative companies. It provides private, shared or co-working office space, plus business support services.

GUINNESS WORKERS' EMPLOYMENT FUND LTD

St James's Gate, Dublin 8 T: (01) 453 6700

Funding

Funded by Guinness workers and pensioners, the Fund provides start-ups with financial assistance, and supports expansion of existing businesses, usually by way of a term loan, at interest rates below those charged by banks. Entrepreneurs must submit applications on the fund's official application form. GWEF also helped to fund the development of the GUINNESS ENTERPRISE CENTRE.

HALO BUSINESS ANGEL NETWORK

Studio 27, The Tower, Trinity Technology & Innovation Campus, Pearse Street, Dublin D02 N768 T: (01) 474 8216 E: info@hban.org W: www.hban.org

Funding

Halo Business Angel Network is an all-island umbrella group responsible for the development of business angel syndicates on the island of Ireland. HBAN actively works to increase the number of angel investors investing in early stage technology, med-tech, agri-tech and food companies. It matches private investors with pre-screened investment opportunities in start-up, early stage and developing businesses and manages regional business angel networks and syndicate groups.

HANNA MOORE & CURLEY

Garryard House, 25/26 Earlsfort Terrace, Dublin 2, D02 PX51 T: (01) 661 3930
E: mail@hmc-ip.com W: www.hmc-ip.com

IP & Legal

Hanna Moore & Curley helps clients protect and use their intellectual property to
establish and maintain commercial advantage.

HARTNETT ENTERPRISE ACCELERATION CENTRE

Limerick Institute of Technology, Moylish Park, Limerick V94 E8YF T: (061)
293151 E: HartnettCentre@lit.ie W: www.hartnettcentre.ie

Incubation & Work space; Training & Mentoring

The Hartnett Enterprise Acceleration Centre is part of LIMERICK INSTITUTE OF
TECHNOLOGY's Enterprise Ladder, which includes enterprise programmes and
enterprise centres. It is LIT's on-campus incubator for innovation and growth-
driven business start-ups.

HEALTH & SAFETY AUTHORITY

The Metropolitan Building, James Joyce Street, Dublin D01 K0Y8 T: (01) 614
2000 E: wcu@hsa.ie W: www.hsa.ie

Information; Regulation & Standards; Training & Mentoring

The HSA has overall responsibility for the administration and enforcement of
health and safety at work in Ireland. It provides training through HSALEARNING.ie,
and a free safety management and risk assessment tool at BeSMART.ie.

HEALTH & SAFETY EXECUTIVE FOR NORTHERN IRELAND

83 Ladas Drive, Belfast BT6 9FR T: (0800) 0320 121 E: mail@hseni.gov.uk W:
www.hseni.gov.uk

Information; Regulation & Standards

HSENI is the lead body responsible for the promotion and enforcement of health
and safety at work standards in Northern Ireland.

HM REVENUE & CUSTOMS

Custom House, Custom House Square, Belfast BT1 3ET T: (03000) 599001

Information; Regulation & Standards

HMRC is responsible for collection, payment, administration and enforcement of
taxes in the UK and Northern Ireland.

HORIZON 2020

W: https://ec.europa.eu/programmes/horizon2020/en/what-horizon-2020

Funding; Innovation & R&D

Horizon 2020 is an €80bn EU research and innovation programme. It is the
financial instrument implementing the Innovation Union, a Europe 2020 flagship
initiative aimed at securing Europe's global competitiveness. Two year work
programmes announce the specific areas that will be funded by Horizon 2020; note
that many calls require a team of at least three partners.

HOUR KITCHEN

9 Churchtown Business Park, Beaumont Avenue, Churchtown, Dublin 14 T: (01) 298 0839 E: info@hourkitchen.ie W: www.hourkitchen.ie

Incubation & Work space

Hour Kitchen is a shared use commercial kitchen rental facility, providing food entrepreneurs with the means to prepare and process their food product for the consumer market.

HSALEARNING.IE

W: www.hsalearning.ie

Training & Mentoring

An online portal for free courses from the HEALTH & SAFETY AUTHORITY.

IADT MEDIA CUBE

Institute of Art, Design & Technology, Kill Avenue, Dún Laoire, Co. Dublin T: (01) 239 4625 E: annmarie.phelan@iadt.ie W: www.mediacube.ie

Incubation & Work space; Training & Mentoring

Located on the INSTITUTE OF ART, DESIGN & TECHNOLOGY's campus, the IADT Media Cube offers early stage digital ventures state-of-the-art facilities and a vibrant environment designed to help businesses grow.

IBEC

Confederation House, 84/86 Lower Baggot Street, Dublin 2 T: (01) 605 1500 E: info@ibec.ie W: www.ibec.ie

Policy

Ibec is Ireland's largest lobby group, representing Irish business both domestically and internationally. Its membership employs over 70% of the private sector workforce in Ireland. Ibec and its sector groups lobby government, policy-makers and other key stakeholders nationally and internationally to shape business conditions and drive economic growth.

IDA IRELAND

Wilton Park House, Wilton Place, Dublin 2 T: (01) 603 4000 E: idaireland@ida.ie W: www.idaireland.com

Inwards Investment

The IDA is Ireland's inward investment promotion agency, promoting Foreign Direct Investment into Ireland through a wide range of services.

IE DOMAIN REGISTRY CLG

2 Harbour Square – 4th Floor, Crofton Road, Dún Laoire, Co. Dublin A96 D6RO T: (01) 236 5400 E: customerrelations@iedr.ie W: www.iedr.ie

Regulation & Standards

IEDR manages the .ie namespace in the interest of the Irish and global e-business communities. It is the Irish national Internet registry.

INISHOWEN DEVELOPMENT PARTNERSHIP

St Mary's Road, Buncrana, Co. Donegal T: (074) 936 2218 E: admin@inishowen.ie
W: www.inishowen.ie

Community & Rural Development; Funding; Training & Mentoring

Inishowen Partnership Board is supported under LEADER and the Social Inclusion
& Community Activation Programme and is a member of the IRISH LOCAL
DEVELOPMENT NETWORK. It supports entrepreneurs seeking to set up a business.

INNER CITY ENTERPRISE

Unit F4, Spade Enterprise Centre, North King Street, Dublin 7 T: (01) 617 4852
E: innercityenter@gmail.com W: innercityenterprise.com

Funding; Social Enterprise

ICE is a not-for-profit charity that helps unemployed people in Dublin's inner city
to start their own business or social enterprise. ICE provides individual business
advice and supports, as well as access to micro-finance loans, through its own
revolving loan fund (funded through the LOCAL ENTERPRISE OFFICE DUBLIN CITY
and the SOCIAL FINANCE FOUNDATION) and through MICROFINANCE IRELAND.

INNOVATE UK

Polaris House, North Star Avenue, Swindon, Wiltshire SN2 1FL T: (0300) 321
4357 E: support@innovateuk.ukri.org W:
www.gov.uk/government/organisations/innovate-uk

Funding; Innovation & R&D

Innovate UK is the UK's innovation agency, and is part of UK Research &
Innovation. The R&D team at INVESTNI can help with funding applications.

INNOVATE-NI

Holywell DiverseCity, 10-14 Bishop Street, Londonderry BT48 6PW T: (07980)
444319 E: info@innovate-ni.com W: www.innovate-ni.com

Funding; Incubation & Work space; Training & Mentoring

Formerly NORIBIC, Innovate-NI is the BUSINESS INNOVATION CENTRE in Derry,
providing support services for those seeking to start their own businesses or to
develop existing businesses into sustainable, well-managed innovative businesses.

INNOVATION CENTRE

IT Sligo, Ash Lane, Sligo F91 YW50 T: (071) 930 5288 E: innovation@itsligo.ie W:
www. https://www.itsligo.ie/innovation/about-the-innovation-centre/

*Incubation & Work space; Innovation & R&D; Networking; Training &
Mentoring*

The Innovation Centre provides enterprise training, incubation space, mentoring
and networking opportunities and access to the INSTITUTE OF TECHNOLOGY
SLIGO's research expertise.

INNOVATION ULSTER LTD

Ulster University, Shore Road, Newtownabbey, Co. Antrim BT37 0QB T: (028) 9036 6702 E: t.brundle@ulster.ac.uk W: www.ulster.ac.uk/research/innovation/innovation-ulster-ltd/

Funding; Innovation & R&D

Innovation Ulster is a wholly-owned knowledge and technology venturing company of ULSTER UNIVERSITY and offers funding programmes to support innovation and the technology readiness development process.

INSPIRE BUSINESS CENTRE

Inspire Business Park, Carrowreagh Road, Dundonald, Belfast BT16 1QT T: (028) 9055 7557 E: enquiries@inspirebusinesscentre.co.uk W: www.inspirebusinesscentre.co.uk

Funding; Incubation & Workspace; Innovation & R&D; Training & Mentoring

Inspire Business Centre is a member of ENTERPRISE NORTHERN IRELAND and offers business support and business development services to local businesses.

INSTITUTE FOR MINORITY ENTREPRENEURSHIP

Dublin Institute of Technology, Aungier Street, Dublin 2 T: (087) 637 1066 E: info@ime.ie W: www.ime.ie/index.htm

Community & Rural Development; Training & Mentoring

The Institute for Minority Entrepreneurship was established to offer minority groups in Ireland equal opportunity through entrepreneurship education and training. The Institute aims to act as a hub in the gathering and dissemination of information relevant to minority entrepreneurship in Ireland.

INSTITUTE OF ART, DESIGN & TECHNOLOGY

Kill Avenue, Dún Laoire, Co. Dublin A96 KH79 T: (01) 239 4000 E: info@iadt.ie W: www.iadt.ie

Incubation & Work space; Training & Mentoring

IADT supports entrepreneurs through its IADT MEDIA CUBE incubation centre.

INSTITUTE OF CERTIFIED PUBLIC ACCOUNTANTS IN IRELAND

17 Harcourt Street, Dublin 2 T: (01) 425 1000 E: info@cpaireland.ie W: www.cpaireland.ie

Accounting & Business Planning

ICPAI is one of the accountancy bodies whose members are permitted to audit company accounts in Ireland. It has 5,000 members and students. If you're looking for an accountant, ICPAI can direct you to one of its members.

INSTITUTE OF DIRECTORS IN IRELAND

Europa House, Harcourt Street, Dublin 2 T: (01) 411 0010 E: info@iodireland.ie
W: www.iodireland.ie

Networking; Training & Mentoring

The Institute of Directors in Ireland focuses on the personal and professional
development of its 2,800 members *via* online resources, workshops, specialist
courses and events.

INSTITUTE OF MANAGEMENT CONSULTANTS & ADVISERS

51/52 Fitzwilliam Square West, Dublin 2 T: (01) 634 9636 E: info@imca.ie W:
www.imca.ie

Consulting; Information

IMCA is the professional body for management consultants and business advisers
in Ireland. IMCA's website gives guidelines on how to choose and use consultants,
as well as a listing of registered practices.

INSTITUTE OF PUBLIC ADMINISTRATION

57/61 Lansdowne Road, Dublin 4 T: (01) 240 3600 E: information@ipa.ie W:
www.ipa.ie

Information

Publisher of *Ireland – A Directory*, a reference database of 9,000+ entries about
Ireland and a useful research resource for any business.

INSTITUTE OF TECHNOLOGY BLANCHARDSTOWN

Blanchardstown Road North, Blanchardstown, Dublin D15 YV78 T: (01) 885
1000 E: info@itb.ie W: www.itb.ie

*Enterprise Support; Incubation & Work space; Innovation & R&D; Training &
Mentoring*

IT Blanchardstown's Learning & Innovation Centre (THE LINC) provides on-
campus R&D, as well as incubation facilities and business development training.

INSTITUTE OF TECHNOLOGY CARLOW

Kilkenny Road, Carlow T: (059) 917 5000 E: info@itcarlow.ie W: www.itcarlow.ie

*Enterprise Support; Incubation & Work space; Innovation & R&D; Training &
Mentoring*

IT Carlow's ENTERPRISE & RESEARCH INCUBATION CAMPUS provides services to
local industry, including research, training and consultancy.

INSTITUTE OF TECHNOLOGY SLIGO

Ash Lane, Sligo F91 YW50 T: (071) 931 8510 E: info@itsligo.ie W: www.itsligo.ie

Incubation & Work space; Innovation & R&D; Training & Mentoring

IT Sligo fosters entrepreneurs and innovation through its INNOVATION CENTRE.

INSTITUTE OF TECHNOLOGY TRALEE

Clash, Tralee, Co. Kerry T: (066) 714 5600 E: info@ittralee.ie W: www.ittralee.ie
Incubation & Work space; Innovation & R&D; Training & Mentoring
The TOM CREAN BUSINESS CENTRE at the Institute of Technology Tralee assists
entrepreneurs in taking their ideas from proof-of-concept to commercial success.

INSTITUTES OF TECHNOLOGY

There are Institutes of Technology in:

o   Athlone: ATHLONE INSTITUTE OF TECHNOLOGY.

o   Blanchardstown, Dublin: INSTITUTE OF TECHNOLOGY BLANCHARDSTOWN.

o   Carlow: INSTITUTE OF TECHNOLOGY CARLOW.

o   Cork: CORK INSTITUTE OF TECHNOLOGY.

o   Dún Laoire: INSTITUTE OF ART, DESIGN & TECHNOLOGY.

o   Dundalk: DUNDALK INSTITUTE OF TECHNOLOGY.

o   Galway / Mayo: GALWAY-MAYO INSTITUTE OF TECHNOLOGY.

o   Letterkenny: LETTERKENNY INSTITUTE OF TECHNOLOGY.

o   Limerick: LIMERICK INSTITUTE OF TECHNOLOGY.

o   Sligo: INSTITUTE OF TECHNOLOGY SLIGO.

o   Tallaght, Dublin: ITT DUBLIN.

o   Tralee: INSTITUTE OF TECHNOLOGY TRALEE.

o   Waterford: WATERFORD INSTITUTE OF TECHNOLOGY.

as well as the NATIONAL COLLEGE OF IRELAND, which provide a range of
services to entrepreneurs and industry.

INTELLECTUAL PROPERTY OFFICE

Concept House, Cardiff Road, Newport, South Wales NP10 8QQ T: (01633)
814000 E: feedback@ipo.gov.uk W: www.ipo.gov.uk
IP & Legal; Regulation & Standards
The Intellectual Property Office (formerly the Patent Office) is the official UK
government body responsible for intellectual property rights, including patents,
designs, trade marks and copyright.

INTERTRADEIRELAND

The Old Gasworks Business Park, Kilmorey Street, Newry, Co. Down BT34 2DE
T: (028) 3083 4100 E: info@intertradeireland.com W: www.intertradeireland.com
Cross-Border; Funding; Information; Innovation & R&D; Policy
InterTradeIreland's remit is to accelerate trade and business development across the
whole island of Ireland. It runs EquityNetwork, the Acumen and Fusion
programmes, and the annual Seedcorn Business Plan competition.

INVESTNI

Bedford Square, Bedford Street, Belfast, BT2 7ES T: (028) 9069 8000 E: info@investni.com W: www.investni.com

Funding; Information; Innovation & R&D; Inwards Investment

InvestNI is Northern Ireland's regional economic development agency. It supports business development, helps to increase productivity and export levels, attracts high quality inward investment, and stimulates a culture of entrepreneurship and innovation through financial support, tailored guidance and information.

INVEST-TECH

27 Ardmeen Park, Blackrock, Co. Dublin T: (01) 283 4083 E: info@planware.org W: www.planware.org

Accounting & Business Planning

Invest-Tech offers freeware, shareware and software for writing a business plan, making financial forecasts and strategic planning.

IRD DUHALLOW LTD

James O'Keeffe Institute, Newmarket, Co. Cork T: (029) 60633 E: duhallow@eircom.net W: www.irdduhallow.com

Community & Rural Development; Funding; Training & Mentoring

IRD Duhallow is a community-based rural development company, supported under LEADER and the Social Inclusion & Community Activation Programme and is a member of the IRISH LOCAL DEVELOPMENT NETWORK.

IRD KILTIMAGH

Enterprise House, Aiden Street, Kiltimagh, Co. Mayo T: (094) 938 1494 E: reception@ird-kiltimagh.ie W: www.ird-kiltimagh.ie

Community & Rural Development; Incubation & Work space; Training & Mentoring

IRD Kiltimagh promotes local socio-economic development, by offering hotdesks and work space for rent, as well business advice and mentoring. It is a member of the NATIONAL ASSOCIATION OF COMMUNITY ENTERPRISE CENTRES.

IRISH CO-OPERATIVE SOCIETY LTD

Plunkett House, 84 Merrion Square, Dublin D02 T882 T: (01) 676 4783 E: info@icos.ie W: www.icos.ie

Social Enterprise

ICOS supports the creation and development of commercially-viable co-operatives that are focused on the economic drivers promoted through co-operative principles.

IRISH COUNTRYWOMEN'S ASSOCIATION

58 Merrion Road, Dublin 4 T: (01) 668 0002 E: office@ica.ie W: www.ica.ie

Networking; Training & Mentoring

The ICA is the largest women's organisation in Ireland. Its members are involved in a wide range of activities within the ICA and in the community, including the residential adult education college at An Grianán.

IRISH EXPORTERS ASSOCIATION

28 Merrion Square North, Dublin 2 T: (01) 661 2182 E: iea@irishexporters.ie W: www.irishexporters.ie

Networking; Training & Mentoring

The IEA supports Irish exporters to conduct business in specialist markets through educational and networking events.

IRISH FRANCHISE ASSOCIATION

Kandoy House, 2 Fairview Strand, Dublin 3 T: (01) 813 4555 E: info@irishfranchiseassociation.com W: www.irishfranchiseassociation.com

Franchises

The Irish Franchise Association's mission is "to develop and promote best practice franchising in Ireland and create an environment within which ethical franchise businesses can grow".

IRISH INSTITUTE OF TRAINING & DEVELOPMENT

4 Sycamore House, Millennium Business Park, Naas, Co. Kildare W91 TF95 T: (045) 881166 E: info@iitd.com W: www.iitd.ie

Networking; Training & Mentoring

IITD is the professional body for human resource, training and development professionals in Ireland. It conducts courses nationwide in training and development, leading to Certificate or Diploma level qualifications, and supports continuing professional development through events and updates.

IRISH INTERNET ASSOCIATION

The Digital Hub, 157 Thomas Street, Dublin 8 T: (01) 542 4154 E: info@iia.ie W: www.iia.ie

Networking

The IIA supports those conducting business *via* the Internet in Ireland.

IRISH LEAGUE OF CREDIT UNIONS

33/41 Lower Mount Street, Dublin 2 T: (01) 614 6700 E: info@creditunion.ie W: www.creditunion.ie

Funding; Social Enterprise

Members of credit unions or businesses structured as co-operatives may qualify for a credit union loan. Each application is treated in the utmost confidence and will be considered on the member's record of saving and repayments, as well as ability to repay. ILCU's website offers a database of credit unions in Ireland.

IRISH LOCAL DEVELOPMENT NETWORK

Unit 24, Tait Business Centre, Dominic Street, Limerick T: (061) 404923 E: info@ildn.ie W: www.ildn.ie

Community & Rural Development

ILDN's members are Local Development Companies across Ireland, forming the largest non-governmental provider of local development supports and services in the State. Members include:

o   BALLYFERMOT CHAPELIZOD PARTNERSHIP COMPANY LTD.

o   BALLYHOURA DEVELOPMENT CLG.

o   BRAY AREA PARTNERSHIP.

o   BREFFNI INTEGRATED CLG.

o   CARLOW COUNTY DEVELOPMENT PARTNERSHIP CLG.

o   CLARE LOCAL DEVELOPMENT COMPANY LTD.

o   COMHAR NA NOILEÁN CTR.

o   CORK CITY PARTNERSHIP CLG.

o   COUNTY KILDARE LEADER PARTNERSHIP.

o   COUNTY SLIGO LEADER PARTNERSHIP COMPANY LTD.

o   COUNTY WICKLOW PARTNERSHIP.

o   DONEGAL LOCAL DEVELOPMENT COMPANY CLG.

o   DUBLIN CITY COMMUNITY CO-OP.

o   DUBLIN SOUTH CITY PARTNERSHIP.

o   EMPOWER.

o   FINGAL LEADER PARTNERSHIP.

o   FORUM CONNEMARA CLG.

o   GALWAY CITY PARTNERSHIP.

o   GALWAY RURAL DEVELOPMENT COMPANY.

o   INISHOWEN DEVELOPMENT PARTNERSHIP.

o   IRD DUHALLOW LTD.

o   KILKENNY LEADER PARTNERSHIP LTD.

o   LAOIS PARTNERSHIP COMPANY.

o   LEITRIM INTEGRATED DEVELOPMENT COMPANY LTD.

o   LONGFORD COMMUNITY RESOURCES LTD.

o   LOUTH LEADER PARTNERSHIP.

o   MAYO NORTH EAST LEADER PARTNERSHIP.

o   MEATH PARTNERSHIP.

o   MONAGHAN INTEGRATED DEVELOPMENT LTD.

o   NORTH TIPPERARY LEADER PARTNERSHIP.

o   NORTH, EAST & WEST KERRY DEVELOPMENT.

o   NORTHSIDE PARTNERSHIP.

o   OFFALY INTEGRATED LOCAL DEVELOPMENT CLG.

o   PAUL PARTNERSHIP LIMERICK.

- ○ ROSCOMMON LEADER PARTNERSHIP.
- ○ SOUTH & EAST CORK AREA DEVELOPMENT LTD.
- ○ SOUTH DUBLIN COUNTY PARTNERSHIP.
- ○ SOUTH KERRY DEVELOPMENT PARTNERSHIP.
- ○ SOUTH TIPPERARY DEVELOPMENT CLG.
- ○ SOUTH WEST MAYO DEVELOPMENT COMPANY CLG.
- ○ SOUTHSIDE PARTNERSHIP DLR LTD.
- ○ WATERFORD AREA PARTNERSHIP.
- ○ WATERFORD LEADER PARTNERSHIP CLG.
- ○ WEST LIMERICK RESOURCES LTD.
- ○ WESTMEATH COMMUNITY DEVELOPMENT LTD.
- ○ WEXFORD LOCAL DEVELOPMENT.

IRISH MANAGEMENT INSTITUTE

Sandyford Road, Dublin 16 T: (01) 207 8400 E: programmeadvisors@imi.ie W: www.imi.ie

Networking; Training & Mentoring

Ireland's centre for management development (now part of UNIVERSITY COLLEGE CORK), the IMI is a member organisation providing a forum for practising managers to exchange leading-edge experience, and facilitating access to Irish and international management experts. It offers full- and part-time courses, on-line support services and research resources.

IRISH NATURALISATION & IMMIGRATION SERVICE

Department of Justice & Equality, 13-14 Burgh Quay, Dublin D02 XK70 E: investmentandstartup@justice.ie W: www.inis.gov.ie

Inwards Investment; Regulation & Standards

INIS manages all immigration and visa requests, including the Investors & Entrepreneurs Scheme (**www.inis.gov.ie/en/INIS/Pages/New%20Programmes %20for%20Investors%20and%20Entrepreneurs**).

IRISH ORGANIC ASSOCIATION

Unit 13, Inish Carraig, Golden Island, Athlone, Co. Westmeath N37 N1W4 T: (090) 643 3680 E: info@irishoa.ie W: www.irishorganicassociation.ie

Regulation & Standards

The Irish Organic Association provides organic certification for famers, growers, processors and retailers, as well as working to promote organic food and farming.

IRISH RURAL LINK LTD

Moate Business Park, Moate, Co. Westmeath T: (090) 648 2744 W: info@irishrurallink.ie W: www.irishrurallink.ie

Community & Rural Development

A non-profit organisation, Irish Rural Link is a national network of organisations and individuals campaigning for sustainable rural development in Ireland / Europe.

IRISH SINGLE POINT OF CONTACT

W: www.pointofsinglecontact.ie

Information

The Irish Point of Single Contact provides general information on the procedures required for Irish and EU businesses that intend operating in Ireland. It is part of the European Commission EUGO Network of Points of Single Contact established in each EU country.

IRISH SMALL & MEDIUM ENTERPRISES ASSOCIATION

17 Kildare Street, Dublin 2 T: (01) 662 2755 E: info@isme.ie W: www.isme.ie

Networking; Policy; Training & Mentoring

ISME supports SME owner-managers by lobbying on their behalf, providing advice and information, offering discounts on products and services through an affinity programme, and offering training.

IRISH SOCIAL ENTERPRISE NETWORK

Bea Orpen Building, NorDubCo, DCU, Glasnevin, Dublin 9 T: (087) 270 0369 E: info@socent.ie W: www.socent.ie

Social Enterprise

A knowledge network for social enterprises in Ireland.

IRISH VENTURE CAPITAL ASSOCIATION

3 Rectory Slopes, Bray, Co. Wicklow A98 FR68 T: (01) 276 4647 W: www.ivca.ie

Funding

The IVCA represents the venture capital industry in Ireland. Its website has a list of members and associates.

ISLAND PATENTS

Island House, Oulart, Gorey, Co. Wexford T: (053) 30892 E: post@islandpatents.com W: www.islandpatents.com

IP & Legal

Island Patents provides intellectual property services covering all aspects of patents, designs and trade marks.

ITT DUBLIN

Tallaght, Dublin 24 T: (01) 404 2000 E: info@ittdublin.ie W: www.ittdublin.ie

Incubation & Work space; Innovation & R&D; Training & Mentoring

ITT Dublin supports entrepreneurs through the SYNERGY CENTRE and SYNERGY GLOBAL, as well as access to its research facilities.

JOE GILMORE ENTERPRISE CENTRE

Brickens, Claremorris, Co. Mayo T: (094) 938 0910 E: lohanpark@eircom.net
Incubation & Work space

The Joe Gilmore Enterprise Centre offers supports and resources for local entrepreneurs planning to start small local businesses. It is a member of the NATIONAL ASSOCIATION OF COMMUNITY ENTERPRISE CENTRES.

KELLS ENTERPRISE & TECHNOLOGY CENTRE

Kells Business Park, Virginia Road, Kells, Co. Meath T: (046) 907 3753 W: www.kellsenterprisecentre.com
Incubation & Work space; Training & Mentoring

Kells ETC provides high tech workspace to start-ups and SMEs. It is a member of the NATIONAL ASSOCIATION OF COMMUNITY ENTERPRISE CENTRES.

KERNEL CAPITAL PARTNERS

Rubicon Centre, Rossa Avenue, Bishopstown, Cork T: (021) 492 8974 W: www.kernelcapital.ie
Funding

Kernel's venture capital portfolio invests in companies across all sectors and targets opportunities in the €250k to €5m range.

KERRY LOCAL ENTERPRISE OFFICE

County Buildings, Rathass, Tralee, Co. Kerry T: (066) 718 3522 E: leo@kerrycoco.ie W: www.localenterprise.ie/kerry
Funding; Information; Training & Mentoring; Young Enterprise

Kerry Local Enterprise Office provides both direct supports (feasibility, priming or business expansion grants) and indirect supports (mentoring, management development, or other capacity building programmes).

KICKSTARTER

W: www.kickstarter.com
Funding

Kickstarter helps artists, musicians, filmmakers, designers, and other creators find the resources needed to make their ideas a reality. It is now open to Irish projects.

KILKENNY LEADER PARTNERSHIP LTD

8 Patrick's Court, Patrick Street, Kilkenny City, Co. Kilkenny T: (056) 775 2111 E: info@cklp.ie W: www.cklp.ie
Community & Rural Development; Enterprise Support; Funding

County Kilkenny Leader Partnership is supported under the Social Inclusion & Community Activation Programme and LEADER and is a member of the IRISH LOCAL DEVELOPMENT NETWORK. It supports start-ups locally.

KILKENNY RESEARCH & INNOVATION CENTRE

St. Kieran's College Campus, College Road, Kilkenny

Innovation & R&D

The Kilkenny Research and Innovation Centre aims to be at the forefront of next-generation internet development. It is a joint venture between the INSTITUTE OF TECHNOLOGY CARLOW, WATERFORD INSTITUTE OF TECHNOLOGY and the Invest Kilkenny campaign.

KILLARNEY TECHNOLOGY INNOVATION LTD

KTI Centre, Killarney, Co. Kerry T: (064) 663 7034 E: george@killarney-innovation.com W: www.killarney-innovation.com

Consulting; Incubation & Work space

KTI offers enterprise suites and desk spaces for knowledge-intensive enterprises. KTI also provides enterprise-related project development, project management and research services to public and private organisations. It is a member of the NATIONAL ASSOCIATION OF COMMUNITY ENTERPRISE CENTRES.

KNOWLEDGE TRANSFER IRELAND

Enterprise Ireland, East Point Business Park, The Plaza, Dublin D03 E5R6 T: (01) 727 2000 E: KTI@knowledgetransferireland.com W: www.knowledgetransferireland.ie

Information

Knowledge Transfer Ireland promotes the sharing of knowledge, skills and technologies between public research and enterprises for collective benefit. Its R&D funding tool helps find the supports and incentives available when engaging with public research in Ireland.

LABOUR RELATIONS AGENCY

2-16 Gordon Street, Belfast BT1 2LG T: (028) 9032 1442 *E:* info@lra.org.uk W: www.lra.org.uk

IP & Legal

The Labour Relations Agency is responsible for promoting the improvement of employment relations in Northern Ireland. It provides advice on good employment practices and assists with the development and implementation of employment policies and procedures. The Agency also helps to resolve disputes through its conciliation, mediation and arbitration services.

LAGAN RURAL PARTNERSHIP

Economic Development Unit, Lisburn City Council, Island Civic Centre, The Island, Lisburn BT27 4RL T: (028) 9250 9489 E: padraic.murphy@lisburncastlereagh.gov.uk W: https://www.lisburncastlereagh.gov.uk/resident/rural-development

Community & Rural Development; Funding

Lagan Rural Partnership is the delivery agent for LEADER / Priority 6 of the Northern Ireland Rural Development Programme 2014-2020.

LANTRA

The Business Centre, 80/82 Rainey Street, Magherafelt, Co. Londonderry BT45 5AJ T: (028) 7963 9290 E: ni@lantra.co.uk W: www.lantra.co.uk

Training & Mentoring

A UK-recognised awarding organisation, Lantra supports individuals and companies to achieve growth through training and qualifications.

LAOIS PARTNERSHIP COMPANY

Block 2, Aras an Chontae, James Fintan Lalor Avenue, Portlaoise, Co. Laois T: (057) 866 1900 E: info@laoispartnership.ie W: www.laoispartnership.ie

Community & Rural Development; Funding

Laois Partnership is supported under LEADER and the Social Inclusion & Community Activation Programme and is a member of the IRISH LOCAL DEVELOPMENT NETWORK. It also provides one-to-one supports to unemployed people who are interested in becoming self-employed.

LARKIN UNEMPLOYED CENTRE

57/58 North Strand Road, North Strand, Dublin 3 T: (01) 836 5544 E: info@larkinctr.com W: www.larkinctr.com

Training & Mentoring

The Larkin Unemployed Centre was established in 1986 and offers, among other services, information and support on self-employment.

LAW SOCIETY OF IRELAND

Blackhall Place, Dublin D07 VY24 T: (01) 672 4800 E: general@lawsociety.ie W: www.lawsociety.ie

IP & Legal

The Law Society is the educational, representative and regulatory body of the solicitors' profession in Ireland. If you're looking for a lawyer, the Law Society's website can direct you to one of its members.

LAW SOCIETY OF NORTHERN IRELAND

96 Victoria Street, Belfast BT1 3GN T: (028) 9023 1614 E: info@lawsoc-ni.org W: www.lawsoc-ni.org

IP & Legal

The Law Society regulates the solicitors' profession in Northern Ireland with the aim of protecting the public. If you're looking for a lawyer, its website can direct you to one of its members.

LEADER

W: www.drcd.gov.ie/about/rural/rural-development/leader/

Community & Rural Development; Funding

The LEADER programme is operated by Local Action Groups. See entries for:

- AVONDHU BLACKWATER PARTNERSHIP CLG.
- BALLYHOURA DEVELOPMENT CLG.
- BREFFNI INTEGRATED CLG.
- CARLOW COUNTY DEVELOPMENT PARTNERSHIP CLG.
- CLARE LOCAL DEVELOPMENT COMPANY LTD.
- COMHAR NA NOILEÁN CTR.
- COUNTY KILDARE LEADER PARTNERSHIP.
- COUNTY SLIGO LEADER PARTNERSHIP COMPANY LTD.
- COUNTY WICKLOW PARTNERSHIP.
- DONEGAL LOCAL DEVELOPMENT COMPANY CLG.
- FINGAL LEADER PARTNERSHIP.
- FORUM CONNEMARA CLG.
- GALWAY RURAL DEVELOPMENT COMPANY.
- INISHOWEN DEVELOPMENT PARTNERSHIP.
- IRD DUHALLOW LTD.
- KILKENNY LEADER PARTNERSHIP LTD.
- LAOIS PARTNERSHIP COMPANY.
- LEITRIM INTEGRATED DEVELOPMENT COMPANY LTD.
- LONGFORD COMMUNITY RESOURCES LTD.
- LOUTH LEADER PARTNERSHIP.
- MAYO NORTH EAST LEADER PARTNERSHIP.
- MEATH PARTNERSHIP.
- MONAGHAN INTEGRATED DEVELOPMENT LTD.
- MOY VALLEY RESOURCES IRD.
- NORTH TIPPERARY LEADER PARTNERSHIP.
- NORTH, EAST & WEST KERRY DEVLOPMENT.
- OFFALY INTEGRATED LOCAL DEVELOPMENT CLG.
- ROSCOMMON LEADER PARTNERSHIP.
- SOUTH & EAST CORK AREA DEVELOPMENT LTD.
- SOUTH KERRY DEVELOPMENT PARTNERSHIP.
- SOUTH TIPPERARY DEVELOPMENT CLG.
- SOUTH WEST MAYO DEVELOPMENT COMPANY CLG.
- ÚDARÁS NA GAELTACHTA.
- WATERFORD LEADER PARTNERSHIP CLG.
- WEST LIMERICK RESOURCES LTD.
- WESTMEATH COMMUNITY DEVELOPMENT LTD.
- WEXFORD LOCAL DEVELOPMENT.

LEADER NORTHERN IRELAND

W: www.daera-ni.gov.uk/articles/about-leader
Community & Rural Development; Funding
The LEADER programme in Northern Ireland is operated by Local Action Groups.
See individual entries for:

- ARDS & NORTH DOWN RURAL AREA PARTNERSHIP.
- CAUSEWAY COAST & GLENS LOCAL ACTION GROUP.
- DERRY & STRABANE RURAL PARTNERSHIP.
- FERMANAGH & OMAGH LOCAL ACTION GROUP.
- GROW SOUTH ANTRIM.
- LAGAN RURAL PARTNERSHIP.
- MID & EAST ANTRIM LOCAL ACTION GROUP.
- MID ULSTER RURAL DEVELOPMENT PARTNERSHIP.
- MOURNE, GULLION & LECALE RURAL DEVELOPMENT PARTNERSHIP.
- SOAR (ABC).

LEGAL-ISLAND

5 Steeple Road, Antrim BT41 1DN T: (028) 9446 3888 E: legal@legal-island.com
W: www.legal-island.com
Cross-Border; Information; IP & Legal; Training & Mentoring
Legal-Island is a multi-award-winning workplace compliance company working
across both Northern Ireland and the Republic of Ireland, helping HR
professionals understand employment law and how it applies to their workplace.

LEITRIM INTEGRATED DEVELOPMENT COMPANY LTD

Church Street, Drumshambo, Co. Leitrim T: (071) 964 1770 E: info@ldco.ie W:
www.ldco.ie
Community & Rural Development; Funding; Training & Mentoring
Leitrim Development Company is a community-led Local Development Company
that delivers a range of rural, social and economic programmes. It is supported
under LEADER and the Social Inclusion & Community Activation Programme and
is a member of the IRISH LOCAL DEVELOPMENT NETWORK and of the
NATIONAL ASSOCIATION OF COMMUNITY ENTERPRISE CENTRES.

LEITRIM LOCAL ENTERPRISE OFFICE

Aras an Chontae, Carrick-on-Shannon, Co. Leitrim T: (071) 965 0420 E:
info@leo.leitrimcoco.ie W: www.localenterprise.ie/leitrim
Funding; Information; Training & Mentoring; Young Enterprise
Leitrim Local Enterprise Office provides both direct supports (feasibility, priming
or business expansion grants) and indirect supports (mentoring, management
development, or other capacity building programmes).

LETTERKENNY INSTITUTE OF TECHNOLOGY

Port Road, Ballyraine, Letterkenny, Co. Donegal F92 FC93 T: (074) 918 6000 E: reception@lyit.ie W: www.lyit.ie

Incubation & Work space; Innovation & R&D; Training & Mentoring

Letterkenny IT supports entrepreneurs through its campus-based incubation centre, COLAB LYIT.

LIBRARIES NI BUSINESS INFORMATION SERVICE

E: business@librariesni.org.uk W: www.librariesni.org.uk/Services/Information/Pages/Business.aspx

Information

The Libraries NI Business Information Service provides free access to reliable and up-to-date information. It is helpful for those already in business, as well as those who are starting their own enterprise.

LICENCES.IE

W: www.licences.ie

Regulation & Standards

Licences.ie is a one-stop-shop for all Government and local authority licences, permits, certificates and registrations.

LIFFEY TRUST

117/126 Upper Sheriff Street, Dublin 1 T: (01) 836 4645 E: info@liffeytrust.ie W: www.liffeytrust.ie

Accounting & Business Planning; Consulting; Incubation & Work space; Marketing; Training & Mentoring

Founded in 1984 and financed entirely without Government assistance, the Liffey Trust helps to prepare business plans, feasibility studies and grant applications, free of charge; advises on raising finance; provides guidance on how to set up accountancy and control systems; provides free management and marketing consultancy; takes care of bureaucratic procedures; and rents incubator units at reduced rents until enterprises are established. Its Food Hub has 10 purpose-built kitchens, while in The Hive budding technology firms can start up faster.

LIMERICK ENTERPRISE DEVELOPMENT PARTNERSHIP

Roxboro Road, Limerick T: (061) 469060 E: info@ledp.ie W: www.ledp.ie

Community & Rural Development; Incubation & Work space

LEDP operates an Enterprise Centre on the site of the former Krupps factory and works closely with other regeneration agencies in Limerick. It is a member of the NATIONAL ASSOCIATION OF COMMUNITY ENTERPRISE CENTRES.

LIMERICK INSTITUTE OF TECHNOLOGY

Moylish Park, Limerick T: (061) 293000 E: information@lit.ie W: www.lit.ie

Incubation & Work space; Innovation & R&D; Training & Mentoring

Limerick Institute of Technology is a centre for research and development in the Mid-West region. It operates the CROOM COMMUNITY ENTERPRISE CENTRE, the NATIONAL FRANCHISE CENTRE, the Red Door Business Incubation Centre (Newcastlewest), the HARTNETT ENTERPRISE ACCELERATION CENTRE (on campus), the QUESTUM ACCELERATION CENTRE (Clonmel) and the Thurles Chamber Enterprise Centre. It is a member of the NATIONAL ASSOCIATION OF COMMUNITY ENTERPRISE CENTRES.

LINKEDFINANCE

43/45 Middle Abbey Street, Dublin D01 X8R2 T: (01) 906 0300
E: help@linkedfinance.com W: www.linkedfinance.com

Funding

LinkedFinance is Ireland's largest peer-to-peer business lending platform, connecting credit-worthy local companies with an online lending community.

LISBURN ENTERPRISE ORGANISATION LTD

6 Enterprise Crescent, Ballinderry Road, Lisburn, Co. Antrim BT28 2BP T: (028) 9266 1160 E: centre@lisburn-enterprise.co.uk W: www.lisburn-enterprise.co.uk

Funding; Incubation & Work space; Innovation & R&D; Training & Mentoring

Lisburn Enterprise Organisation is a member of ENTERPRISE NORTHERN IRELAND. LEO is an independent, not-for-profit organisation offering support in the form of guidance and advice, premises, conference facilities, administrative support and virtual office services.

LIVEPLAN.COM

W: www.liveplan.com

Accounting & Business Planning

LivePlan is online software that simplifies business planning, budgeting, forecasting, and performance tracking for small businesses and start-ups.

LOCAL ENTERPRISE DEVLOPMENT COMPANY LTD.

LEDCOM Industrial Estate, Bank Road, Larne, Co. Antrim BT40 3AW T: (028) 2826 9973 E: info@ledcom.org W: www.ledcom.org

Community & Rural Development; Consulting; Funding; Incubation & Work space; Innovation & R&D; Social Enterprise; Training & Mentoring

LEDCOM is a member of ENTERPRISE NORTHERN IRELAND and provides managed workspace, business incubation / innovation support, business skills training, business and economic development consultancy, community economic development, information and advice, international business match-making / trade missions and social enterprise development.

LOCAL ENTERPRISE OFFICE CARLOW

Enterprise House, O'Brien Road, Carlow T: (059) 912 9783 E: enterprise@carlowcoco.ie W: www.localenterprise.ie/carlow

Funding; Information; Training & Mentoring; Young Enterprise

Local Enterprise Office Carlow provides both direct supports (feasibility, priming or business expansion grants) and indirect supports (mentoring, management development, or other capacity building programmes).

LOCAL ENTERPRISE OFFICE CAVAN

Cavan Innovation & Technology Centre, Dublin Road, Cavan T: (049) 437 7200 E: localenterprise@cavancoco.ie W: www.localenterprise.ie/cavan

Funding; Information; Training & Mentoring; Young Enterprise

Local Enterprise Office Cavan provides both direct supports (feasibility, priming or business expansion grants) and indirect supports (mentoring, management development, or other capacity building programmes).

LOCAL ENTERPRISE OFFICE CLARE

Aras an Chontae, New Road, Ennis, Co. Clare V95 DXP2 T: (065) 682 1616 E: localenterprise@clarecoco.ie W: www.localenterprise.ie/clare

Funding; Information; Training & Mentoring; Young Enterprise

Local Enterprise Office Clare provides both direct supports (feasibility, priming or business expansion grants) and indirect supports (mentoring, management development, or other capacity building programmes).

LOCAL ENTERPRISE OFFICE CORK CITY

Cork City Council, City Hall, Cork T: (021) 496 1828 E: info@leo.corkcity.ie W: www.localenterprise.ie/corkcity

Funding; Information; Training & Mentoring; Young Enterprise

Local Enterprise Office Cork City provides both direct supports (feasibility, priming or business expansion grants) and indirect supports (mentoring, management development, or other capacity building programmes).

LOCAL ENTERPRISE OFFICE CORK NORTH & WEST

8 Kent Street, Clonakilty, Co. Cork P85 PH39 T: (023) 883 4700 / Blackwater House – Ground Floor, Mallow Business Park, Gouldshill, Mallow, Co. Cork P51 K3CX E: westcork@leo.corkcoco.ie W: www.localenterprise.ie/corknorthandwest

Funding; Information; Training & Mentoring; Young Enterprise

Local Enterprise Office Cork North & West provides both direct supports (feasibility, priming or business expansion grants) and indirect supports (mentoring, management development, or other capacity building programmes).

LOCAL ENTERPRISE OFFICE DUBLIN CITY

Civic Offices, Block 4, Floor 1, Wood Quay, Dublin 8 T: (01) 222 5611 E: info@leo.dublincoco.ie W: www.localenterprise.ie/dublincity

Funding; Information; Training & Mentoring; Young Enterprise

Local Enterprise Office Dublin City provides both direct supports (feasibility, priming or business expansion grants) and indirect supports (mentoring, management development, or other capacity building programmes).

LOCAL ENTERPRISE OFFICE DUN LAOGHAIRE-RATHDOWN

County Hall, Marine Road, Dun Laoghaire, Co. Dublin T: (01) 204 7083 E: contact@leo.dlrcoco.ie W: www.localenterprise.ie/DLR

Funding; Information; Training & Mentoring; Young Enterprise

Local Enterprise Office Dun Laoghaire-Rathdown provides both direct supports (feasibility, priming or business expansion grants) and indirect supports (mentoring, management development, or other capacity building programmes).

LOCAL ENTERPRISE OFFICE FINGAL

County Hall – 1st Floor, Main Street, Swords, Co. Dublin K67 X8Y2 T: (01) 890 0800 E: info@leo.fingal.ie W: www.localenterprise.ie/fingal

Funding; Information; Training & Mentoring; Young Enterprise

Local Enterprise Office Fingal provides both direct supports (feasibility, priming or business expansion grants) and indirect supports (mentoring, management development, or other capacity building programmes).

LOCAL ENTERPRISE OFFICE GALWAY

County Buildings – 1st Floor, Prospect Hill, Galway H91 H6XX T: (091) 509090 E: info@leo.galwaycoco.ie W: www.localenterprise.ie/galway

Funding; Information; Training & Mentoring; Young Enterprise

Local Enterprise Office Galway provides both direct supports (feasibility, priming or business expansion grants) and indirect supports (mentoring, management development, or other capacity building programmes).

LOCAL ENTERPRISE OFFICE KILDARE

Aras Chill Dara, Devoy Park, Naas, Co. Kildare W91 X77F T: (045) 980838 E: localenterprise@kildarecoco.ie W: www.localenterprise.ie/kildare

Funding; Information; Training & Mentoring; Young Enterprise

Local Enterprise Office Kildare provides both direct supports (feasibility, priming or business expansion grants) and indirect supports (mentoring, management development, or other capacity building programmes).

LOCAL ENTERPRISE OFFICE KILKENNY

42 Parliament Street, Kilkenny R95 TY2N T: (056) 775 2662 E: info@leo.kilkennycoco.ie W: www.localenterprise.ie/kilkenny

Funding; Information; Training & Mentoring; Young Enterprise

Local Enterprise Office Kilkenny provides both direct supports (feasibility, priming or business expansion grants) and indirect supports (mentoring, management development, or other capacity building programmes).

LOCAL ENTERPRISE OFFICE LAOIS

Business Support Unit, County Hall, Portlaoise, Co. Laois R32 EHP9 T: (057) 866 1800 E: localenterprise@laoiscoco.ie W: www.localenterprise.ie/laois

Funding; Information; Training & Mentoring; Young Enterprise

Local Enterprise Office Laois provides both direct supports (feasibility, priming or business expansion grants) and indirect supports (mentoring, management development, or other capacity building programmes).

LOCAL ENTERPRISE OFFICE LIMERICK

7/8 Patrick Street, Limerick T: (061) 557499 E: localenterprise@limerick.ie W: www.localenterprise.ie/limerick

Funding; Information; Training & Mentoring; Young Enterprise

Local Enterprise Office Limerick provides both direct supports (feasibility, priming or business expansion grants) and indirect supports (mentoring, management development, or other capacity building programmes).

LOCAL ENTERPRISE OFFICE LOUTH

Town Hall, Crowe Street, Dundalk, Co. Louth T: (1890) 202303 E: info@leo.louthcoco.ie W: www.localenterprise.ie/louth

Funding; Information; Training & Mentoring; Young Enterprise

Local Enterprise Office Louth provides both direct supports (feasibility, priming or business expansion grants) and indirect supports (mentoring, management development, or other capacity building programmes).

LOCAL ENTERPRISE OFFICE MAYO

Cedar House – 2nd Floor, Moneen, Castlebar, Co Mayo F23 WP71 T: (094) 904 7555 E: info@leo.mayococo.ie W: www.localenterprise.ie/mayo

Funding; Information; Training & Mentoring; Young Enterprise

Local Enterprise Office Mayo provides both direct supports (feasibility, priming or business expansion grants) and indirect supports (mentoring, management development, or other capacity building programmes).

LOCAL ENTERPRISE OFFICE MONAGHAN

Unit 9, M:TEK Building, Knockaconny, Monaghan T: (047) 71818 E: info@leo.monaghancoco.ie W: www.localenterprise.ie/monaghan

Funding; Information; Training & Mentoring; Young Enterprise

Local Enterprise Office Monaghan provides both direct supports (feasibility, priming or business expansion grants) and indirect supports (mentoring, management development, or other capacity building programmes).

LOCAL ENTERPRISE OFFICE OFFALY

Aras an Chontae, Charleville Road, Tullamore, Co. Offaly T: (057) 935 7480 E: info@leo.offalycoco.ie W: www.localenterprise.ie/offaly

Funding; Information; Training & Mentoring; Young Enterprise

Local Enterprise Office Offaly provides both direct supports (feasibility, priming or business expansion grants) and indirect supports (mentoring, management development, or other capacity building programmes).

LOCAL ENTERPRISE OFFICE ROSCOMMON

Aras an Chontae, Ardnanagh, Co. Roscommon F42 VR98 T: (090) 662 6263 E: localenterprise@roscommoncoco.ie W: www.localenterprise.ie/roscommon

Funding; Information; Training & Mentoring; Young Enterprise

Local Enterprise Office Roscommon provides both direct supports (feasibility, priming or business expansion grants) and indirect supports (mentoring, management development, or other capacity building programmes).

LOCAL ENTERPRISE OFFICE SLIGO

City Hall, Quay Street, Sligo T: (071) 911 4408 / (071) 911 4417 E: localenterprise@sligococo.ie W: www.localenterprise.ie/sligo

Funding; Information; Training & Mentoring; Young Enterprise

Local Enterprise Office Sligo provides both direct supports (feasibility, priming or business expansion grants) and indirect supports (mentoring, management development, or other capacity building programmes).

LOCAL ENTERPRISE OFFICE SOUTH CORK

Business Growth Hub, Cork County Council, Carrigrohane, Cork T: (021) 428 5200 E: southcork@leo.corkcoco.ie W: www.localenterprise.ie/southcork

Funding; Information; Training & Mentoring; Young Enterprise

Local Enterprise Office South Cork provides both direct supports (feasibility, priming or business expansion grants) and indirect supports (mentoring, management development, or other capacity building programmes).

LOCAL ENTERPRISE OFFICE WESTMEATH

Aras an Chontae, Mount Street, Mullingar, Co. Westmeath T: (044) 933 8945 E: localenterprise@westmeathcoco.ie W: www.localenterprise.ie/westmeath

Funding; Information; Training & Mentoring; Young Enterprise

Local Enterprise Office Westmeath provides both direct supports (feasibility, priming or business expansion grants) and indirect supports (mentoring, management development, or other capacity building programmes).

LOCAL ENTERPRISE OFFICE WICKLOW

Wicklow County Campus, Clermont House, Rathnew, Co. Wicklow T: (0404) 30800 E: enterprise@wicklowcoco.ie W: www.localenterprise.ie/wicklow

Funding; Information; Training & Mentoring; Young Enterprise

Local Enterprise Office Wicklow provides both direct supports (feasibility, priming or business expansion grants) and indirect supports (mentoring, management development, or other capacity building programmes).

LOCAL ENTERPRISE OFFICES

W: www.localenterprise.ie

Funding; Information; Training & Mentoring; Young Enterprise

There are Local Enterprise Offices in each county in Ireland – some have more than one, to serve larger or more dispersed populations. Each provides broadly the same range of supports to start-ups and growing businesses – direct supports (feasibility, priming or business expansion grants) and indirect supports (mentoring, management development, or other capacity building programmes) – with some variations for local needs. See individual entries for:

o   Carlow: LOCAL ENTERPRISE OFFICE CARLOW.
o   Cavan: LOCAL ENTERPRISE OFFICE CAVAN.
o   Clare: LOCAL ENTERPRISE OFFICE CLARE.
o   Cork City: LOCAL ENTERPRISE OFFICE CORK CITY.
o   Cork North & West: LOCAL ENTERPRISE OFFICE CORK NORTH & WEST.
o   Cork South: LOCAL ENTERPRISE OFFICE SOUTH CORK.
o   Donegal: DONEGAL LOCAL ENTERPRISE OFFICE.
o   Dublin City: LOCAL ENTERPRISE OFFICE DUBLIN CITY.
o   Dublin South: DUBLIN SOUTH LOCAL ENTERPRISE OFFICE.
o   Dun Laoghaire-Rathdown: LOCAL ENTERPRISE OFFICE DUN LAOGHAIRE-RATHDOWN.
o   Fingal: LOCAL ENTERPRISE OFFICE FINGAL.
o   Galway: LOCAL ENTERPRISE OFFICE GALWAY.
o   Kerry: KERRY LOCAL ENTERPRISE OFFICE.
o   Kildare: LOCAL ENTERPRISE OFFICE KILDARE.
o   Kilkenny: LOCAL ENTERPRISE OFFICE KILKENNY.
o   Laois: LOCAL ENTERPRISE OFFICE LAOIS.
o   Leitrim: LEITRIM LOCAL ENTERPRISE OFFICE.

- o   Limerick: LOCAL ENTERPRISE OFFICE LIMERICK.
- o   Longford: LONGFORD LOCAL ENTERPRISE OFFICE.
- o   Louth: LOCAL ENTERPRISE OFFICE LOUTH.
- o   Mayo: LOCAL ENTERPRISE OFFICE MAYO.
- o   Meath: MEATH LOCAL ENTERPRISE OFFICE.
- o   Monaghan: LOCAL ENTERPRISE OFFICE MONAGHAN.
- o   Offaly: LOCAL ENTERPRISE OFFICE OFFALY.
- o   Roscommon: LOCAL ENTERPRISE OFFICE ROSCOMMON.
- o   Sligo: LOCAL ENTERPRISE OFFICE SLIGO.
- o   Tipperary: TIPPERARY LOCAL ENTERPRISE OFFICE.
- o   Waterford: WATERFORD LOCAL ENTERPRISE OFFICE.
- o   Westmeath: LOCAL ENTERPRISE OFFICE WESTMEATH.
- o   Wexford: WEXFORD LOCAL ENTERPRISE OFFICE.
- o   Wicklow: LOCAL ENTERPRISE OFFICE WICKLOW.

LOMBARD

Ulster Bank Group Centre, Georges Quay, Dublin 2 T: (1850) 215 000 W:
www.lombard.ie

Funding

Part of ULSTER BANK, Lombard provides asset finance, financing commonly-used
assets such as vehicles through to agricultural and construction equipment.

LONGFORD COMMUNITY RESOURCES LTD

Longford Community Enterprise Centre, Business & Technology Park, Ballinalee
Road, Longford N39 T9Y1 T: (043) 334 5555 E: enquiries@lcrl.ie W:
www.lcrl.ie

Community & Rural Development; Funding

Longford Community Resources is supported under LEADER and the Social
Inclusion & Community Activation Programme and is a member of the IRISH
LOCAL DEVELOPMENT NETWORK. It provides supports to local start-ups and
businesses.

LONGFORD LOCAL ENTERPRISE OFFICE

Longford County Council, Great Water Street, Longford T: (043) 334 3346 E:
info@leo.longfordcoco.ie W: www.localenterprise.ie/longford

Funding; Information; Training & Mentoring; Young Enterprise

Longford Local Enterprise Office provides both direct supports (feasibility, priming
or business expansion grants) and indirect supports (mentoring, management
development, or other capacity building programmes).

LOUGH SHORE INVESTMENTS

47A Botanic Avenue, Belfast BT7 1JL T: (028) 9043 8510 W: www.loughshore.co

Funding

Lough Shore Investments invests in established and promising next generation start-ups operating in the web, mobile and enterprise space.

LOUTH CRAFTMARK

Highlanes Gallery, St. Laurence Street, Drogheda, Co. Louth T: (041) 980 3283 E: shop@louthcraftmark.com W: www.louthcraftmark.com

Funding; Marketing; Networking

Louth Craftmark showcases the work of local artists and craftspeople. A membership organisation, it promotes and supports its members through accessing funding, networking and collaborative projects.

LOUTH LEADER PARTNERSHIP

Partnership Court, Park Street, Dundalk, Co. Louth A91 V2KF T: (042) 933 0288 E: reception@louthleaderpartnership.ie W: www.louthleaderpartnership.ie

Community & Rural Development; Funding

Louth LEADER Partnership is supported under LEADER and the Social Inclusion & Community Activation Programme and is a member of the IRISH LOCAL DEVELOPMENT NETWORK. It provides supports to local start-ups and businesses.

LUDGATE HUB

The Old Bakery, Townshend Street, Skibbereen, Co. Cork P81 T324 T: (087) 190 4174 E: info@ludgate.ie W: www.ludgate.ie

Incubation & Work space; Networking

The Ludgate Hub offers co-working and work space, for long-term or casual users.

MACLACHLAN & DONALDSON

2b Clonskeagh Square, Clonskeagh Road, Dublin D14 V0N2 T: (01) 676 3465 E: mail@maclachlan.ie W: www.maclachlan.ie

IP & Legal

MacLachlan & Donaldson are European patent and Community trade mark attorneys. The firm also trades as Dermot P Cummins & Co.

MACROOM E BUSINESS CENTRE

Macroom Environmental Industrial Park, Bowl Road, Macroom, Co. Cork T: (026) 20520 E: info@macroom-e.com W: www.macroom-e.com

Incubation & Work space; Training & Mentoring

Macroom E is a community enterprise centre that helps start-up and growing businesses in the Lee Valley region. It offers a wide choice of office space, ranging from hot-desks and small offices to industrial units, as well as other supports.

MALLUSK ENTERPRISE PARK

2 Mallusk Drive, Newtownabbey BT36 4GN T: (028) 9083 8860 E: business@mallusk.org W: www.mallusk.org

Funding; Incubation & Work space; Innovation & R&D; Training & Mentoring

Mallusk Enterprise Park provides work space and business support programmes to start-ups and SMEs. It is a member of ENTERPRISE NORTHERN IRELAND.

MARINE INSTITUTE

Rinville, Oranmore, Co. Galway H91 R673 T: (091) 387200 E: institute.mail@marine.ie W: www.marine.ie

Innovation & R&D; Policy

The Marine Institute is the State agency responsible for marine research, technology development and innovation in Ireland. It provides scientific and technical advice to Government to help inform policy and to support the sustainable development of Ireland's marine resource.

MARKETING INSTITUTE OF IRELAND

Marketing House, South County Business Park, Leopardstown, Dublin 18 T: (01) 295 2355 E: hello@mii.ie W: www.mii.ie

Marketing; Training & Mentoring

The Marketing Institute is the professional representative body for marketing people in Ireland. Through the provision of insights and expert content, it aims to enhance the professional effectiveness of its members.

MAYNOOTHWORKS

Eolas Building – 2nd Floor, North Campus, Maynooth University, Maynooth, Co. Kildare E: maynoothworks@mu.ie W: www.maynoothuniversity.ie/maynoothworks

Incubation & Work space; Networking; Training & Mentoring

MaynoothWorks is NATIONAL UNIVERSITY OF IRELAND MAYNOOTH's business incubator for technology companies. It offers networking and mentoring.

MAYO NORTH EAST LEADER PARTNERSHIP

Lower Main Street, Foxford, Co. Mayo T: (094) 925 6745 E: info@mayonortheast.com W: www.mayonortheast.com

Community & Rural Development; Funding; Training & Mentoring

Mayo North East LEADER Partnership is supported under the Social Inclusion & Community Activation Programme and LEADER, and is a member of the IRISH LOCAL DEVELOPMENT NETWORK. It supports local businesses and start-ups.

MEATH ENTERPRISE

Meath Enterprise Centre, Trim Road, Navan, Co. Meath T: (046) 907 3753 E: info@meathenterprise.ie W: www.meathenterprise.ie

Incubation & Work space; Innovation & R&D; Training & Mentoring

Meath Enterprise offers enterprise space along with services and supports required to help business succeed. It also operates the Boyne Valley Food Innovation District, the Kells Tech Hub and the Digital Hub Navan. It is a member of the NATIONAL ASSOCIATION OF COMMUNITY ENTERPRISE CENTRES.

MEATH LOCAL ENTERPRISE OFFICE

Buvinda House, Dublin Road, Navan, Co. Meath C15 Y291 T: (046) 909 7000 E: localenterprise@meathcoco.ie W: www.localenterprise.ie/meath

Funding; Information; Training & Mentoring; Young Enterprise

Meath Local Enterprise Office provides direct supports (feasibility, priming or business expansion grants) and indirect supports (mentoring, management development or other capacity building programmes).

MEATH PARTNERSHIP

Unit 7, Kells Business Park, Cavan Road, Kells, Co. Meath T: (046) 928 0790 E: info@meathpartnership.ie W: www.meathpartnership.ie

Community & Rural Development; Funding; Training & Mentoring

Meath Partnership is supported under the Social Inclusion & Community Activation Programme and LEADER, and is a member of the IRISH LOCAL DEVELOPMENT NETWORK. It supports individuals and community groups through capital grant aid, technical assistance, guidance and mentoring, information and support, training opportunities and development initiatives.

MICHELIN DEVELOPMENT

W: www.michelindevelopment.co.uk

Community & Rural Development; Funding; Training & Mentoring

Michelin Development in the UK aims to contribute to the economic regeneration and long term prosperity of the areas in which Michelin's sites are located. It supports new start-ups or existing SMEs from the manufacturing and B2B service sectors located in and around Ballymena or relocating to the area.

MICROFINANCE IRELAND

13 Richview Office Park, Clonskeagh Road, Dublin D14 Y867 T: (01) 260 1007 E: info@microfinanceireland.ie W: www.microfinanceireland.ie

Funding; Training & Mentoring

Microfinance Ireland provides loans less than €25,000 to businesses with less than 10 employees and turnover under €2 million that are creating at least one new job. Borrowers also receive free mentoring.

MID & EAST ANTRIM LOCAL ACTION GROUP

Ecos Centre, Kernohan's Lane, Ballymena BT43 7QA T: (028) 2563 3266 E: RDP@midandeastantrim.gov.uk W: www.meardp.com

Community & Rural Development; Funding

Mid & East Antrim Local Action Group manages the delivery of grant funding from the Northern Ireland Rural Development Programme (2014-2020) / LEADER. It encourages and supports the creation and development of micro and small enterprises, including on-farm diversification and private tourism provision.

MID ULSTER RURAL DEVELOPMENT PARTNERSHIP

Gortalowry House, 94 Church Street, Cookstown BT80 8HX T: (028) 8676 4714 E: rdp@midulstercouncil.org W: www.midulsterrdp.org

Community & Rural Development; Funding

Mid Ulster Rural Development Partnership is the LEADER Local Action Group for Mid Ulster and manages the delivery of a Local Development Strategy for rural areas of Mid Ulster District Council.

MIDLANDS INNOVATION & RESEARCH CENTRE

Athlone Institute of Technology, Dublin Road, Athlone, Co. Westmeath T: (0906) 471882 E: mirc@ait.ie W: www.mirc.ie

Enterprise Support; Incubation & Work space; Training & Mentoring

The Midlands Innovation & Research Centre at ATHLONE INSTITUTE OF TECHNOLOGY – working in partnership with ENTERPRISE IRELAND – provides incubation and business support for innovative start-ups, delivers the NEW FRONTIERS entrepreneur development programme in collaboration with NATIONAL UNIVERSITY OF IRELAND MAYNOOTH, and makes available the resources and expertise of AIT to support enterprise in the region.

MML GROWTH CAPITAL PARTNERS

Huguenot House, 35/38 St. Stephen's Green, Dublin 2 T: (01) 619 0000 W: www.mmlcapital.ie

Funding

MML Growth Capital Partners invests between €2m and €15m in private Irish businesses for expansion, acquisition, recapitalisations and shareholder reorganisations.

MOHILL ENTERPRISE CENTRE

Knockalongford, Mohill, Co. Leitrim T: (071) 963 2024 E: info@mct.ie W: www.mct.ie

Incubation & Work space; Training & Mentoring

Mohill Enterprise Centre is run by the Mohill Community Development Association Ltd, a voluntary community organisation that promotes economic activity in the area and trains people to compete effectively in an evolving jobs market, particularly in ICT. It is a member of the NATIONAL ASSOCIATION OF COMMUNITY ENTERPRISE CENTRES.

MONAGHAN INTEGRATED DEVELOPMENT LTD

Monaghan Road, Castleblayney, Co. Monaghan T: (042) 974 9500 E: info@monaghanintegrateddevelopment.ie / LEADER@midl.ie W: www.midl.ie

Community & Rural Development; Funding

Monaghan Integrated Development is supported under LEADER and the Social Inclusion & Community Activation Programme and is a member of the IRISH LOCAL DEVELOPMENT NETWORK. It provides a range of supports to local start-ups and businesses.

MOUNTMELLICK DEVELOPMENT ASSOCIATION

Irishtown, Mountmellick, Co. Laois T: (057) 862 4525 E: info@mountmellickdevelopment.com W: www.mountmellickdevelopment.com

Community & Rural Development; Incubation & Work space

Mountmellick Development Association works to improve the social, cultural and economic development of the town of Mountmellick and its surrounding area. It offers conference facilities and commercial kitchens for rent. It is a member of the NATIONAL ASSOCIATION OF COMMUNITY ENTERPRISE CENTRES.

MOURNE, GULLION & LECALE RURAL DEVELOPMENT PARTNERSHIP

Newry, Mourne & Down District Council, Downshire Civic Centre, Downshire Estate, Ardglass Road, Downpatrick BT30 6GQ T: (0300) 013 2233 ext 2506 E: info@mournegullionlecale.com W: mournegullionlecale.com

Community & Rural Development; Funding

The Mourne, Gullion & Lecale Rural Development Partnership is responsible for delivering LEADER / Priority 6 of the Northern Ireland Rural Development Programme 2014-2020 in its area.

MOY VALLEY RESOURCES IRD

Greenhills Enterprise Centre, Bunree Road, Ballina, Co. Mayo T: (096) 70905 E: info@moyvalley.ie W: www.moyvalley.ie

Accounting & Business Planning; Community & Rural Development; Funding; Incubation & Work space; Social Enterprise; Training & Mentoring

Officially IRD North Mayo West Sligo Ltd, Moy Valley Resources aims to facilitate the economic and social development of the Moy Valley Region in Mayo and Sligo. It offers start-ups advice, mentoring and assistance with business plans, as well incubation and work space. It is a member of the NATIONAL ASSOCIATION OF COMMUNITY ENTERPRISE CENTRES and is supported by LEADER.

MULLINGAR EMPLOYMENT ACTION GROUP

The Enterprise Centre, Bishopsgate Street, Mullingar, Co. Westmeath T: (044) 934 3444 W: www.meag.ie

Incubation & Work space; Training & Mentoring

MEAG operates the Mullingar Enterprise Centre in Mullingar and the Mullingar Technology & Innovation Centre in Clonmore. It is a member of the NATIONAL ASSOCIATION OF COMMUNITY ENTERPRISE CENTRES.

MURGITROYD

Unit 1 Block 8, Blanchardstown Corporate Park, Cruiserath Road, Blanchardstown, Dublin 15 T: (01) 882 9400 E: joanne.lecky@murgitroyd.com W: www.murgitroyd.com

IP & Legal

Murgitroyd is a global firm of European patent attorneys and trade mark attorneys, with an office in Dublin.

NATIONAL ASSOCIATION OF COMMUNITY ENTERPRISE CENTRES

E: info@enterprisecentres.ie W: www.enterprisecentres.ie

Incubation & Work space

The National Association of Community Enterprise Centres is a network of community enterprise centres in the Republic of Ireland, many of which were developed with the support of ENTERPRISE IRELAND, County Enterprise Boards (now LOCAL ENTERPRISE OFFICES), Local Development Groups and other local community organisations. Members include:

- ACE ENTERPRISE PARK.
- ARDEE COMMUNITY DEVELOPMENT COMPANY LTD.
- ARKLOW BUSINESS ENTERPRISE CENTRE.
- ATHY COMMUNITY ENTERPRISE COMPANY LTD.
- BALBRIGGAN ENTERPRISE & TRAINING CENTRE.
- BALLINASLOE AREA COMMUNITY DEVELOPMENT LTD.
- BALLYHAUNIS ENTERPRISE CENTRE.
- BASE ENTERPRISE CENTRE CLG.
- BOLTON TRUST.
- BOYLE ENTERPRISE & MORE.
- CARLOW COMMUNITY ENTERPRISE CENTRES LTD.
- CARRICK BUSINESS CENTRE.
- CASTLEBLAYNEY ENTERPRISE CENTRE.
- CASTLECOMER ENTERPRISE GROUP LTD.
- CAVAN COUNTY ENTERPRISE FUND.
- CAVAN INNOVATION & TECHNOLOGY CENTRE.
- CLANE PROJECT CENTRE.
- CONNEMARA WEST.

- COOLOCK DEVELOPMENT COUNCIL.
- CREATIVE SPARK CLG.
- DRINAN ENTERPRISE CENTRE.
- DÚN LAOIRE ENTERPRISE CENTRE.
- DUNGARVAN ENTERPRISE CENTRE.
- DUNHILL ECOPARK.
- ENNISCORTHY ENTERPRISE & TECHNOLOGY CENTRE.
- ENNISTYMON ENTERPRISE CENTRE LTD.
- ENTERPRISE YOUGHAL.
- ENTERPRISING MONAGHAN.
- EWRNE ENTERPRISE DEVELOPMENT COMPANY LTD.
- FERBANE BUSINESS & TECHNOLOGY PARK.
- FIONTARLANN TEO.
- FOOD HUB.
- GALWAY TECHNOLOGY CENTRE.
- IRD KILTIMAGH.
- JOE GILMORE ENTERPRISE CENTRE.
- KELLS ENTERPRISE & TECHNOLOGY CENTRE.
- KILLARNEY TECHNOLOGY INNOVATION LTD.
- LEITRIM INTEGRATED DEVELOPMENT COMPANY LTD.
- LIMERICK ENTERPRISE DEVELOPMENT PARTNERSHIP.
- LIMERICK INSTITUTE OF TECHNOLOGY.
- MEATH ENTERPRISE.
- MOHILL ENTERPRISE CENTRE.
- MOUNTMELLICK DEVELOPMENT ASSOCIATION.
- MOY VALLEY RESOURCES IRD.
- MULLINGAR EMPLOYMENT ACTION GROUP.
- NUTGROVE ENTERPRISE PARK.
- PARTAS.
- PILTOWN COMMUNITY ENTERPRISE.
- PORTARLINGTON ENTERPRISE CENTRE.
- PORTLAOISE ENTERPRISE CENTRE.
- PREMIER SERVICES.
- SCCUL ENTERPRISE CENTRE.
- SLIGO ENTERPRISE & TECHNOLOGY CENTRE.
- SPADE ENTERPRISE CENTRE.
- TERENURE ENTERPRISE CENTRE.
- THE BASE ENTERPRISE CENTRE.
- THE HIVE.
- WEXFORD ENTERPRISE CENTRE.
- WICKLOW ENTERPRISE CENTRE.

NATIONAL COLLEGE OF IRELAND

Mayor Street, IFSC, Dublin D01 Y300 T: 1850 221 721 E: info@ncirl.ie W: www.ncirl.ie

Incubation & Work space; Training & Mentoring

Through its campus in the IFSC, its network of 40 off-campus centres, on-site educational hubs within industry and online programmes, NCI provides Business, Management, Financial Services, Informatics, Humanities programmes. It also operates a BUSINESS INCUBATION CENTRE at its IFSC site.

NATIONAL FRANCHISE CENTRE

LIT O'Connell Street Campus, Bank House, 106/108 O'Connell Street, Limerick T: (061) 293550 E: nfc@lit.ie W: www.nationalfranchisecentre.ie

Franchises; Incubation & Work space; Training & Mentoring

The National Franchise Centre is part of LIMERICK INSTITUTE OF TECHNOLOGY's Enterprise Ladder, which includes enterprise programmes and enterprise centres. It is a franchise development and research centre.

NATIONAL GUILD OF MASTER CRAFTSMEN

3 Greenmount Lane, Harolds Cross, Dublin 12 T: (01) 473 2543 E: info@nationalguild.ie W: www.nationalguild.ie

Networking; Regulation & Standards

NGMC is dedicated to achieving the highest standards of quality and workmanship in all trades and disciplines. It operates a referral system for members.

NATIONAL RURAL NETWORK

Moate Business Park, Clara Road, Moate, Co. Westmeath N37 W9R0 T: (090) 648 2744 W: www.nationalruralnetwork.ie

Community & Rural Development

The NRN is a component of the Rural Development Programme 2014-2020 led by IRISH RURAL LINK in partnership with The Wheel, NATIONAL UNIVERSITY OF IRELAND GALWAY and Philip Farrelly & Co. Its aim is to build and sustain a membership-based network that maximises the beneficial outcomes of the Rural Development Programme.

NATIONAL STANDARDS AUTHORITY OF IRELAND

1 Swift Square, Northwood, Santry, Dublin D09 A0E4 T: (01) 807 3800 E: info@nsai.ie W: www.nsai.ie

Information; Regulation & Standards

NSAI develops and publishes standards to meet international demands for quality, design, performance, safety and environmental impact of products and services.

NATIONAL UNIVERSITY OF IRELAND GALWAY

University Road, Galway H91 TK33 T: (091) 524411 W: www.nuigalway.ie

Enterprise Support; Incubation & Work space; Innovation & R&D; Training & Mentoring

NUIG supports entrepreneurs through its on-campus incubator, the BUSINESS INNOVATION CENTRE NUI GALWAY.

NATIONAL UNIVERSITY OF IRELAND MAYNOOTH

Maynooth, Co. Kildare T: (01) 708 6000 W: www.maynoothuniversity.ie

Enterprise Support; Incubation & Work space; Innovation & R&D; Training & Mentoring

NUI MAYNOOTH supports entrepreneurs through its on-campus business incubator, MAYNOOTHWORKS and the EDEN CENTRE FOR ENTREPRENEURSHIP, DESIGN & INNOVATION.

NDRC

Digital Exchange, Crane Street, Dublin D08 HKR9 T: (01) 480 6252 E: info@ndrc.ie W: www.ndrc.ie

Funding; Training & Mentoring

NDRC is an accelerator that also invests up to €500,000 (typically in the range €20,000 to €100,000) in ICT / digital tech-connected businesses.

NETWORK FOR ENTERPRISING WOMEN

Marketing Solutions, 16a Main Street, Belleek, Co. Fermanagh BT93 3FX T: (0796) 240 9131 E: think6@gmail.com W: www.networkforenterprisingwomen.net

Networking

NEW is a networking group for women in Fermanagh and Tyrone, who run their own business, support a partner in business, aspire to be in business, work in the corporate, voluntary or community sectors, or work for an organisation that supports enterprise development.

NETWORK IRELAND

W: www.networkireland.ie

Networking; Training & Mentoring

Network is a national organisation for women in business, management, the professions and the arts. It facilitates women in the promotion and development of their careers through regular meetings and educational seminars.

NEW FRONTIERS

W: www.newfrontiers.ie

Funding; Training & Mentoring

New Frontiers is a national programme providing an integrated and comprehensive set of business development supports (including funding) to participants, delivered at 16 locations around the country *via* the INSTITUTES OF TECHNOLOGY and funded by ENTERPRISE IRELAND.

NEWMARKET KITCHEN

Unit 3, Atlas Court, IDA Business Park, Southern Cross Road, Bray, Co. Wicklow A98 Y977 E: hello@newmarketkitchen.com W: www.newmarketkitchen.com

Incubation & Work space; Training & Mentoring

Newmarket Kitchen provides kitchen space for food producers to co-exist, create and prosper. It also provides training.

NEWRY & MOURNE ENTERPRISE AGENCY

Enterprise House, WIN Business Park, Canal Quay, Newry, Co. Down BT35 6PH T: (028) 3026 7011 E: info@nmea.net W: www.nmea.net

Funding; Incubation & Work space; Social Enterprise; Training & Mentoring

Newry & Mourne Enterprise Agency is a member of ENTERPRISE NORTHERN IRELAND, and the first Local Enterprise Agency on the island of Ireland. It supports start-ups and existing businesses, including social enterprises.

NEXUS INNOVATION CENTRE

Tierney Building, University of Limerick, Plassey, Limerick T: (061) 518376 E: nexusinnovation@ul.ie W: www.nexusinnovation.ie

Incubation & Work space; Training & Mentoring

Nexus is a purpose-built innovation centre at the UNIVERSITY OF LIMERICK, with a growing community of entrepreneurs.

NIBUSINESSINFO.co.uk

Bedford Square, Bedford Street, Belfast BT2 7ES T: 0800 181 4422 W: www.nibusinessinfo.co.uk

Information

An online business advice and guidance service provided by INVESTNI, including a business support finder tool.

NORTH CITY BUSINESS CENTRE LTD

2 Duncairn Gardens, Belfast BT15 2GG T: (028) 9074 7470 E: mailbox@north-city.co.uk W: www.north-city.co.uk

Funding; Incubation & Work space; Training & Mentoring

North City Business Centre is a member of ENTERPRISE NORTHERN IRELAND and is the Local Enterprise Agency for North Belfast. It provides support for the small business sector and those interested in starting up a business.

NORTH DOWN DEVELOPMENT ORGANISATION LTD

Enterprise House, 2-4 Balloo Avenue, Balloo Industrial Estate, Bangor, Co. Down BT19 7QT T: (028) 9127 1525 E: mail@nddo.co.uk W: www.nddo.co.uk

Funding; Incubation & Work space; Training & Mentoring

NDDO is a member of ENTERPRISE NORTHERN IRELAND. It provides advice, training, support and mentoring for small businesses.

NORTH TIPPERARY FOODWORKS

Rearcross, Newport, Co. Tipperary T: (067) 33086 E: northtippfoodworks@gmail.com

Incubation & Work space

North Tipperary Foodworks offers a fully-equipped timeshare kitchen and three production units for rent.

NORTH TIPPERARY LEADER PARTNERSHIP

Friars Court – 2nd Floor, Nenagh South, Nenagh, Co. Tipperary T: (067) 56676 E: info@ntlp.ie W: www.ntlp.ie

Community & Rural Development; Funding; Training & Mentoring

North Tipperary LEADER Partnership is supported under LEADER and the Social Inclusion & Community Activation Programme, and is a member of the IRISH LOCAL DEVELOPMENT NETWORK. It supports local businesses and start-ups through grants, training and mentoring.

NORTH, EAST & WEST KERRY DEVELOPMENT

Aras an Phobail, Croílár na Mistéalach, Tralee, Co. Kerry T: (066) 718 0190 E: seamusohara@nekd.ie W: www.nekd.net

Community & Rural Development; Funding; Training & Development

North, East & West Kerry Development is supported under LEADER and the Social Inclusion & Community Activation Programme, and is a member of the IRISH LOCAL DEVELOPMENT NETWORK. It supports local businesses and start-ups and runs the Rural Food Skillnet.

NORTHERN & WESTERN REGIONAL ASSEMBLY

The Square, Ballaghaderreen, Co. Roscommon T: (094) 986 2970 E: info@nwra.ie W: www.nwra.ie

Policy

The Northern and Western Regional Assembly is crafting a vibrant, connected, natural, inclusive and smart vision for the region with three objectives: working to create better places by adopting best practice in international spatial and economic development, Achieving competitiveness by optimising EU and exchequer funding and harnessing the strengths of our 'place', through collaboration.

NORTHERN IRELAND CHAMBER OF COMMERCE & INDUSTRY

4/5 Donegall Square South, Belfast BT1 5JA T: (028) 9024 4113 E: mail@northernirelandchamber.com W: www.northernirelandchamber.com

Networking

NICCI represents 1,200 member businesses, representing over 100,000 employees, across Northern Ireland. It provides members with a range of services and events.

NORTHERN IRELAND FOOD & DRINK ASSOCIATION

Belfast Mills, 71/75 Percy Street, Belfast BT13 2HW T: (028) 9024 1010 E: info@nifda.co.uk W: www.nifda.co.uk

Marketing; Networking; Training & Mentoring

NIFDA helps Northern Ireland food and beverage companies compete successfully by promoting, informing, educating and developing member businesses.

NORTHERN IRELAND RURAL WOMEN'S NETWORK

Unit 13A, Ballysaggart Business Complex, 8 Beechvalley Way, Dungannon, Co. Tyrone BT70 1BS T: 028 8775 3389 E: info@nirwn.org W: www.nirwn.org

Networking

NIRWN is a membership-based organisation, promoting and supporting rural women in rural Northern Ireland.

NORTHERN IRELAND SCREEN

Alfred House – 3rd Floor, 21 Alfred Street, Belfast BT2 8ED T: (028) 9023 2444 E: info@northernirelandscreen.co.uk W: www.northernirelandscreen.com

Funding; Incubation & Work space; Training & Mentoring

Northern Ireland Screen supports the development of a diverse range of projects, through script, project and slate development grants. It also operates the Pixel Mill, which offers incubation, coaching and a community hub.

NORTHERN IRELAND SMALL BUSINESS LOAN FUND

PO Box 40, Limavady, Co. Londonderry BT49 4AJ T: (0800) 988 2879 E: enquiry@nisblf.com W: www.nisblf.com

Funding

The NI Small Business Loan Fund provides unsecured loans to individuals, private companies and social enterprises in the SME and micro enterprise size range, in the start-up and growth phases of development. It is managed by Ulster Community Investment PLC, a subsidiary of ULSTER COMMUNITY INVESTMENT TRUST.

NORTHERN IRELAND STATISTICS & RESEARCH AGENCY

Colby House, Stranmillis Court, Belfast BT9 5RR T: (028) 9038 8400 E: info@nisra.gov.uk W: www.nisra.gov.uk

Information

NISRA is an Agency of the DEPARTMENT FOR THE ECONOMY and the principal source of official statistics and social research on Northern Ireland.

NORTHERN IRELAND TECHNOLOGY CENTRE

Queen's University Belfast, University Road Belfast, BT7 1NN T: (208)

Innovation & R&D

The Northern Ireland Technology Centre is a technology and innovation centre specialising in design, knowledge engineering and manufacturing, bridging the gap between academic research and commercial production to meet industry needs.

NORTHSIDE ENTERPRISE CENTRE

Bunratty Drive, Coolock, Dublin 17 T: (01) 867 5200 E: W: www.nec.ie

Incubation & Work space

Established by the COOLOCK DEVELOPMENT COUNCIL, the Northside Enterprise Centre provides business units for entrepreneurs.

NORTHSIDE PARTNERSHIP

Coolock Development Centre, Bunratty Drive, Coolock, Dublin 17 T: (01) 848 5630 E: info@northsidepartnership.ie W: www.northsidepartnership.ie

Community & Rural Development; Social Enterprise; Training & Mentoring

The Northside Partnership provides a start-up support service to unemployed local people. It is supported under the Social Inclusion & Community Activation Programme and is a member of the IRISH LOCAL DEVELOPMENT NETWORK.

NOVAUCD

Belfield Innovation Park, University College Dublin, Belfield, Dublin 4 T: (01) 716 3700 E: innovation@ucd.ie W: www.ucd.ie/innovation/

Incubation & Work space; Innovation & R&D

NovaUCD is an innovation and technology transfer centre on the UNIVERSITY COLLEGE DUBLIN campus, supporting entrepreneurs and campus companies.

NSC CAMPUS

Mahon, Cork T12 XY2N T: (021) 230 7000 E: info@nsc-campus.com W: www.nsc-campus.com

Incubation & Work space

The NSC offers premium office space with high-tech support.

NUTGROVE ENTERPRISE PARK

Nutgrove Way, Rathfarnham, Dublin 14 T: (01) 494 8400 E: contact@nutgrove-enterprisepark.ie W: www.nutgrove-enterprisepark.ie

Incubation & Work space

Nutgrove Enterprise Park offers incubation and work space. It is a member of the NATIONAL ASSOCIATION OF COMMUNITY ENTERPRISE CENTRES.

O'BRIEN (JOHN A.) & ASSOCIATES

Unit 4, The Courtyard Business Centre, Orchard Lane, Blackrock, Co. Dublin A94 NV07 T: (01) 288 3877 E: mail@obrienja.ie

IP & Legal

A firm of patent agents and trade mark attorneys.

O'CONNOR INTELLECTUAL PROPERTY

Suite 207, Q House, Furze Road, Sandyford, Dublin 18 T: (01) 293 2922 E: post@oconnorIP.ie W: www.oconnorip.com

IP & Legal

O'Connor Intellectual Property offers a full range of Irish, European and international patent, trade mark, design and copyright services.

OAK TREE PRESS

33 Rochestown Rise, Rochestown, Cork T12 EVT0 T: (086) 244 1633 E: brian.okane@oaktreepress.com W: www.oaktreepress.com / www.SuccessStore.com

Information; Training & Mentoring

Oak Tree Press develops and delivers information, advice and resources for entrepreneurs and managers. It is Ireland's leading business book publisher, with an unrivalled reputation for quality titles across business, management, HR, law, marketing and enterprise topics. In addition, Oak Tree Press occupies a unique position in start-up and small business support in Ireland through its standard-setting titles, as well training courses, mentoring and advisory services.

OFFALY INTEGRATED LOCAL DEVELOPMENT CLG

Millennium House, Main Street, Tullamore, Co. Offaly T: (057) 935 2467 / 932 2850 E: info@offalyldc.ie W: www.offalyldc.ie

Community & Rural Development; Funding; Training & Mentoring

Offaly Integrated Local Development is supported under LEADER and the Social Inclusion & Community Activation Programme, and is a member of the IRISH LOCAL DEVELOPMENT NETWORK. It supports local businesses and start-ups through funding, training and mentoring.

OFFICE OF THE DIRECTOR OF CORPORATE ENFORCEMENT

16 Parnell Square, Dublin 1 T: (01) 858 5800 E: info@odce.ie W: www.odce.ie

Information; IP & Legal; Regulation & Standards

The ODCE's mission is to improve the compliance environment for corporate activity in the Irish economy by encouraging adherence to the requirements of the *Companies Acts*, and bringing to account those who disregard the law. It publishes guidance documents for entrepreneurs on their company law responsibilities.

OMAGH ENTERPRISE COMPANY LTD

Great Northern Road, Omagh, Co. Tyrone BT78 5LU T: (028) 8224 9494 E: info@omaghenterprise.co.uk W: www.omaghenterprise.co.uk

Funding; Incubation & Work space; Training & Mentoring

Omagh Enterprise Company is a member of ENTERPRISE NORTHERN IRELAND. It offers a range of services to support start-ups and existing businesses.

OPTIMUM RESULTS LTD

The Business Centre, Blackthorn Business Park, Dundalk, Co. Louth T: (042) 933 3033 E: info@optimumresults.ie W: www.optimumresults.ie

Consulting; Training & Mentoring

Optimum Results provides consulting and training for SMEs.

ORGANIC COLLEGE

Dromcollogher, Co. Limerick T: (063) 83604 W: www.organiccollege.com

Training & Mentoring

The Organic College offers courses in organic horticulture and sustainability.

ORIGIN8

National College of Art & Design, 100 Thomas Street, Dublin 8 T: (01) 636 4272 E: mcgarryd@ncad.ie W: www.ncad.ie/research-and-innovation/origin8/

Incubation & Work space; Innovation & R&D

Origin8 is the industry gateway and innovation hub of the National College for Art & Design (part of UNIVERSITY COLLEGE DUBLIN), where campus spin-outs work to establish their business and design researchers collaborate with companies.

ORMEAU BUSINESS PARK

8 Cromac Avenue, Belfast BT7 2JA T: (028) 9033 9906 E: info@ormeaubusinesspark.com W: www.ormeaubusinesspark.com

Funding; Incubation & Work space; Innovation & R&D; Training & Mentoring

Ormeau Business Park is a member of ENTERPRISE NORTHERN IRELAND and is a key provider of business support in South Belfast, providing rented workspace, training facilities and enterprise training and mentoring.

ORTUS GROUP

Filor Building, Twin Spires Complex, 155 Northumberland Street, Belfast BT13 2JF T: (028) 9031 1002 E: sheila@ortus.org W: www.ortus.org

Funding; Incubation & Work space; Innovation & R&D; Social Enterprise; Training & Mentoring

The Ortus Group (West Belfast Enterprise Board t/a Ortus Group) is a member of ENTERPRISE NORTHERN IRELAND. It provides business support programmes and affordable commercial property, as well as complementary services to start-ups and established enterprises across all business sectors.

OYSTER CAPITAL PARTNERS

Oyster Point, Temple Road, Blackrock, Dublin, A94 E3P9 T: (01) 279 9580

Funding

Oyster Capital Partners is a business creation company founded by entrepreneur Bill McCabe.

PARTAS

Bolbrook Enterprise Centre, Avonmore Road, Tallaght, Dublin D24 K07Y T: (01) 414 5700 W: www.partas.ie

Community & Rural Development; Incubation & Work space; Social Enterprise; Training & Mentoring

With four enterprise centres in Tallaght, Bolbrook, Brookfield and Killinarden, Partas offers training in personal and business development, computer skills, mentoring programmes and microfinancing. It is a member of the NATIONAL ASSOCIATION OF COMMUNITY ENTERPRISE CENTRES.

PATENTS OFFICE

Government Buildings, Hebron Road, Kilkenny R95 H4XC T: (056) 772 0111 E: patlib@patentsoffice.ie W: www.patentsoffice.ie

Information; IP & Legal; Regulation & Standards

The principal statutory functions of the Patents Office are: the granting of patents; the registration of industrial designs and trade marks; providing information in relation to patents, designs and trade marks; and certain limited functions under the *Copyright Act* in relation to copyright disputes.

PAUL PARTNERSHIP LIMERICK

Unit 25a, The Tait Centre, Dominic Street, Limerick T: (061) 419388 E: info@paulpartnership.ie W: www.paulpartnership.ie

Community & Rural Development; Social Enterprise; Training & Mentoring

Paul Partnership Limerick is supported under the Social Inclusion & Community Activation Programme, and is a member of the IRISH LOCAL DEVELOPMENT NETWORK. It supports local businesses and social enterprises through training, advice and mentoring.

PERMANENT TSB

56-59 St. Stephen's Green, Dublin 2 T: (01) 212 4101 W: www.permanenttsb.ie

Funding

Though geared primarily towards the personal banking market, Permanent TSB offers current account facilities, overdrafts and loans to business customers.

PILTOWN COMMUNITY ENTERPRISE

Ardclone, Piltown, Co. Kilkenny T: (051) 643152 E: mail@piltown.ie W:
www.piltown.ie

Incubation & Work space

Piltown Community Enterprise operates the Old Creamery Enterprise Centre and
offers training and other supports to local businesses. It is a member of the
NATIONAL ASSOCIATION OF COMMUNITY ENTERPRISE CENTRES.

PLATO DUBLIN

Guinness Enterprise Centre, Taylor's Lane, Dublin 8 T: (086) 823 4309 E:
dublin@plato.ie W: www.platodublin.ie

Training & Mentoring

Plato Dublin is an 18-month business development programme for owner-
managers of SMEs, funded by the LOCAL ENTERPRISE OFFICES in the Dublin
region, which provides practical training, business counselling and support.

PLUS 10

2A Drinan Street, Sullivans Quay, Cork T12 CY28 T: (086) 250 0841 E:
info@plus10.org W: www.plus10.org

Incubation & Work space

Plus10.org is a membership-based coworking community of start-ups, micro-
enterprises, freelancers and digital nomads in Cork city.

POBAL

Holbrook House, Holles Street, Dublin 2 T: (01) 511 7000 E: enquiries@pobal.ie
W: www.pobal.ie

Enterprise Support

Pobal administers and manages Government and EU funding to address
disadvantage and to support social inclusion.

POLARIS PARTNERS

CHQ Building, Custom House Quay, Dublin 1 T: (01) 901 0336 W:
www.polarispartners.com

Funding

A US-based VC firm with an office in Dublin, Polaris invests in exceptional
technology and healthcare companies.

PORTARLINGTON ENTERPRISE CENTRE

Canal Road, Portarlington, Co. Laois T (057) 864 5405 E: info@pec.ie W:
www.pec.ie

Incubation & Work space; Training & Mentoring

A member of the NATIONAL ASSOCIATION OF COMMUNITY ENTERPRISE
CENTRES, PEC offers incubation and work space, and a FabLab / Maker Space.

PORTLAOISE ENTERPRISE CENTRE

Clonminam Business Park, Portlaoise, Co. Laois, R32 DW97 T: (057) 868 8714 E: enquiries@enterprisecentre.ie W: www.enterprisecentre.ie

Incubation & Work space

Portlaoise Enterprise Centre offers office space and training rooms. It is a member of the NATIONAL ASSOCIATION OF COMMUNITY ENTERPRISE CENTRES.

POWERSCOURT CAPITAL PARTNERS

46 Upper Mount Street, Dublin 2 T: (01) 247 4050 E: info@powerscourtcapital.ie W: www.powerscourtcapital.ie

Funding

Powerscourt Capital Partners invests in high potential early-stage companies, leveraging its industry experience, contacts and strategic partnerships.

PREMIER BUSINESS CENTRES

12 Lower Hatch Street, Dublin D02 R682 T: (01) 639 2939 E: info@premierbusinesscentres.com W: www.premierbusinesscentres.com

Incubation & Work space

Premier Business Centres provide serviced and virtual offices in Dublin and Kildare.

PREMIER SERVICES

Enterprise House, The Diamond, Milford, Co. Donegal F92 P8YD T: (074) 9153736 E: terence@premierservices.ie W: www.thisismilford.com

Community & Rural Development

Premier Services is the trading name of Milford & District Resource Ltd (previously IRD Milford Ltd). It is an agent for change in the Milford area and a member of the NATIONAL ASSOCIATION OF COMMUNITY ENTERPRISE CENTRES.

PRINCE'S TRUST NORTHERN IRELAND

Unit 8, Weavers Court, Belfast BT12 5GH T: (028) 9089 5083 E: webinfoni@princes-trust.org.uk W: www.princes-trust.org.uk

Funding; Training & Mentoring; Young Enterprise

The Prince's Trust Northern Ireland works with 18 to 30-year-olds to turn big ideas into a business reality through its Enterprise programme, which offers training and mentoring support as well as funding and other resources.

PUBLIC RELATIONS CONSULTANTS ASSOCIATION OF IRELAND

84 Merrion Square, Dublin 2 T: (01) 661 8004 E: info@prca.ie W: www.prca.ie

Marketing

The Public Relations Consultants Association of Ireland represents most of the PR consultancy businesses in Ireland. Its website advises on choosing a consultancy.

PUBLIC RELATIONS INSTITUTE OF IRELAND

84 Merrion Square, Dublin 2 T: (01) 661 8004 E: info@prii.ie W: www.prii.ie

Marketing

The Public Relations Institute of Ireland is the professional body for public relations practitioners (individuals) in Ireland.

PURDYLUCEY

6/7 Harcourt Terrace, Dublin D02 P210 T: (01) 676 0792 E: info@purdylucey.com W: www.purdylucey.com

IP & Legal

PurdyLucey is a European intellectual property firm that provides professional services in the areas of patents, trade marks, designs and copyright.

QUBIS LTD

Queen's University Belfast, 63 University Road, Belfast BT7 1 NF T: (028) 9068 2321 E: info@qubis.co.uk W: www.qubis.co.uk

Funding; Innovation & R&D

Qubis commercialises the research and development activities of QUEEN'S UNIVERSITY BELFAST through the formation of 'spin-out' businesses.

QUEEN'S UNIVERSITY BELFAST

University Road, Belfast BT7 1NN T: (028) 9024 5133 W: www.qub.ac.uk

Funding; Incubation & Work space; Innovation & R&D

Queen's University has a long-established reputation for research. The Research & Regional Services department handles all consultancy enquiries from business. The NORTHERN IRELAND TECHNOLOGY CENTRE, built on the QUB campus, operates as a self-financing practical experience centre dedicated to technology transfer. QUBIS manages the university's equity investments in campus companies.

QUESTUM ACCELERATION CENTRE

Ballingarrane Science & Technology Park, Clonmel, Co. Tipperary E91 V239 T: (0504) 28027 E: derek.blackweir@lit.ie W: www.questum.ie

Incubation & Work space

The QUESTUM Acceleration Centre is part of LIMERICK INSTITUTE OF TECHNOLOGY's Enterprise Ladder, which includes enterprise programmes and enterprise centres.

RDJSTARTUPS.IE

Ronan Daly Jermyn, 2 Park Place, Citygate Park, Mahon Point, Cork T: (021) 480 2700 W: www.rdjstartups.ie

IP & Legal

Free legal guidance online for start-ups and early stage companies.

REGIONAL DEVELOPMENT CENTRE

Dundalk Institute of Technology, Dublin Road, Dundalk T: (042) 937 0400 E: info@rdc.ie W: www.rdc.ie

Incubation & Work space; Training & Mentoring

The Regional Development Centre provides business support, advice, training and incubation space to entrepreneurs.

REPUBLIC OF WORK

12 South Mall, Cork T: (021) 239 8110 E: ask@republicofwork.com W: www.republicofwork.com

Incubation & Work space; Networking

In its own words, Republic of Work "provides space for work to happen".

REVENUE COMMISSIONERS

Dublin Castle, Dublin 2 W: www.revenue.ie

Information; Regulation & Standards

Revenue's mission is to serve the community by fairly and efficiently collecting taxes and duties and implementing import and export controls. You can now submit returns online to the Revenue Commissioners using the Revenue Online Service (ROS) – see the Revenue website.

ROE VALLEY ENTERPRISES LTD

Aghanloo Industrial Estate, Aghanloo Road, Limavady, Co. Londonderry BT49 0HE T: (028) 7776 2323 E: info@roevalleyenterprises.co.uk W: www.roevalleyenterprises.com

Funding; Incubation & Work space; Training & Mentoring

Roe Valley Enterprises is a member of ENTERPRISE NORTHERN IRELAND. It encourages new business start-up and growth within the SME sector by offering an extensive range of business support services.

ROSCOMMON LEADER PARTNERSHIP

Unit 12, Tower B, Roscommon West Business Park, Golf Links Road, Roscommon Town, Co. Roscommon T: (090) 663 0252 E: reception@rldc.ie W: www.rldc.ie

Community & Rural Development; Funding; Training & Mentoring

Roscommon LEADER Partnership (also known as Roscommon Integrated Development Company) is supported under LEADER and the Social Inclusion & Community Activation Programme, and is a member of the IRISH LOCAL DEVELOPMENT NETWORK. It supports local businesses and start-ups.

RUBICON CENTRE

CIT Campus, Bishopstown, Cork T: (021) 492 8900 E:
paul.healy@rubiconcentre.ie W: www.rubiconcentre.ie

Enterprise Support; Incubation & Work space; Training & Mentoring

Based on the CORK INSTITUTE OF TECHNOLOGY campus, the Rubicon Centre
provides access to a range of supports for entrepreneurs who want to start, grow
and expand their business. The Rubicon Cube offers coworking space.

RURAL COMMUNITY NETWORK

38A Oldtown Street, Cookstown, Co. Tyrone BT80 8EF T: (028) 8676 6670 W:
www.ruralcommunitynetwork.org

Community & Rural Development; Networking

RCN identifies and provides a voice on issues of concern to rural communities in
relation to poverty, disadvantage and community development.

RURAL DEVELOPMENT COUNCIL

17 Loy Street, Cookstown, Co. Tyrone BT80 8PZ T: (028) 8676 6980 E:
info@rdc.org.uk W: www.rdc.org.uk

Community & Rural Development; Training & Mentoring

The RDC supports and encourages integrated rural development by providing
development, support, training and delivery services for individuals, farmers, farm
families, groups, communities, public and private sector organisations.

RURAL NETWORK NI

Network Support Unit, 17 Loy Street, Cookstown, Co. Tyrone BT80 8PZ T: (028)
8676 6980 E: info@ruralnetworkni.org.uk W: www.ruralnetworkni.org.uk

Community & Rural Development; Networking

The Rural Network for Northern Ireland aims to enhance networking amongst
farmers, rural dwellers and businesses, researchers, environmentalists and other
rural bodies and organisations.

RURAL PARTNERS ARDS & NORTH DOWN

Ards & North Down Borough Council, Signal Centre, 2 Innotec Drive, Balloo
Road, Bangor BT19 7PD T: (028) 9147 3788 E: info@ruralpartnersand.co.uk W:
www.ruralpartnersand.co.uk

Community Development; Funding

Rural Partners Ards & North Down delivers the LEADER elements of the Northern
Ireland Rural Development Programme 2014-2020 through funding schemes.

RURAL SUPPORT

Estate Building, Loughry College, Cookstown, Co. Tyrone BT80 9AA T: (028)
8676 0040 E: info@ruralsupport.org.uk W: www.ruralsupport.org.uk

Community & Rural Development; Social Enterprise

Rural Support offers a listening and signposting service for farmers and rural
families, including on-farm business support and advice on social farming.

SAGE IRELAND

1 Central Park, Dublin 18 T: (1890) 882020 W: www.sage.ie

Accounting & Business Planning

A leading supplier of accounting, payroll, CRM and business management software and services for small and medium-sized businesses.

SALES INSTITUTE OF IRELAND

30 Upper Fitzwilliam Street, Dublin 2 T: (01) 662 6904 E: enquiries@salesinstitute.ie W: www.salesinstitute.ie

Marketing; Networking

A network for sales directors from progressive companies, helping them learn from and network with other sales directors.

SCCUL ENTERPRISE CENTRE

Castlepark Road, Ballybane, Galway T: (091) 386004 E: admin@scculenterprises.ie W: scculenterprises.ie

Incubation & Work space

SCCUL Enterprises CLG, is a registered charity founded in 2002 by St. Columba's Credit Union Ltd. It runs the SCCUL Enterprise Centre, Ballybane, which offers affordable enterprise space to enterprises and community groups. It is a member of the NATIONAL ASSOCIATION OF COMMUNITY ENTERPRISE CENTRES.

SCHOOL OF FOOD

Dublin Road, Thomastown, Co. Kilkenny T: (056) 775 4397 E: info@schooloffood.ie W: www.schooloffood.ie

Community & Rural Development; Incubation & Work space; Training & Mentoring

The School of Food is a community-led initiative, based in a custom-developed food education and incubation centre, that promotes Kilkenny as a food destination and supports the production and promotion of local, quality food ingredients, as well as developing an educational food hub.

SCREEN IRELAND

Queensgate, 23 Dock Road, Galway H91 CR33 T: (091) 561398 E: info@screenireland.ie W: www.screenireland.ie

Funding

Formerly the Irish Film Board, Screen Ireland is the national development agency for the Irish film, television and animation industry, supporting and developing talent, creativity and enterprise. It provides loans and equity to independent Irish film-makers to assist in the development and production of Irish films.

SEA-FISHERIES PROTECTION AUTHORITY

Park Road, Clogheen, Clonakilty, Co. Cork T: (023) 885 9300 E: sfpa_info@sfpa.ie W: www.sfpa.ie

Regulation & Standards

The SFPA is Ireland's competent authority for seafood safety and sea-fisheries protection. It supports a sustainable and profitable commercial fishing sector, while protecting and conserving fisheries resources for long-term exploitation.

SEEDUPS.IE

Unit1, Devlin's Complex, Bridgend, Co. Donegal E: info@seedups.com W: www.seedups.ie

Funding

SeedUps.ie offers equity crowdfunding for technology start-ups.

SENIOR ENTERPRISE

Mid East Regional Authority, County Buildings, Wicklow Town, Co. Wicklow T: (0404) 66058 E: info@seniorenterprise.ie W: www.seniorenterprise.ie

Information

Senior Enterprise, an EU-supported initiative through INTERREG IVB NWE, encourages a greater involvement with enterprise by those aged over 50, through starting a business, acquiring or investing in a business, advising an entrepreneur or supporting innovation within a business owned by another.

SEROBA LIFE SCIENCES LTD

6 Northbrook Road, Ranelagh, Dublin D06 PH32 T: (01) 633 4028 W: www.seroba-lifesciences.com

Funding

Seroba Life Sciences invests (up to €7m) in breakthrough medical technologies that promise to improve lives and transform healthcare.

SHANNON COMMERCIAL PROPERTIES

Universal House, Shannon Free Zone, Shannon, Co. Clare T: (061) 710000 W: www.shannonproperties.ie

Incubation & Work space

Shannon Commercial Properties (SCP) is a subsidiary of SHANNON GROUP PLC, and owns and manages one of Ireland's largest property portfolios, incorporating eight business and technology parks, over 2.4 million sq. ft of building space across 300 buildings, and spanning over 40 locations across counties Clare, Limerick, Tipperary, Offaly and Kerry.

SHANNON GROUP PLC

Shannon Airport, Shannon, Co. Clare V14 EE06 T: (061) 712000 E: info@shannongroup.ie W: www.shannongroup.ie

Incubation & Work space

Shannon Group plc is a commercial semi-state company, comprising four strategic businesses focused on delivering economic benefits for the West of Ireland and the wider national economy: Shannon Airport, Shannon Heritage, the International Aviation Services Centre (IASC) and Shannon Commercial Enterprises DAC, trading as SHANNON COMMERCIAL PROPERTIES.

SHELL LIVEWIRE UK

Adamson House – 2nd Floor, 65 Westgate Road, Newcastle Upon Tyne NE1 1SG T: (0191) 691 4900 E: enquiries@shell-livewire.org W: www.shell-livewire.org

Funding; Innovation & R&D; Training & Mentoring; Young Enterprise

The Shell LiveWIRE programme supports innovative young UK entrepreneurs whose ideas meet the energy and resource needs of a fast-growing population.

SILICONREPUBLIC.com

Digital Exchange, Crane Street, Dublin D08 HKR9 T: (01) 625 1444 E: info@siliconrepublic.com W: www.siliconrepublic.com

Information

Siliconrepublic.com is Ireland's No. 1 resource for technology news.

SLIGO ENTERPRISE & TECHNOLOGY CENTRE

Sligo Airport Business Park, Strandhill, Co. Sligo T: (071) 916 8477 E: info@sligoenterprise.com W: www.sligoenterprise.com

Incubation & Work space

Sligo Enterprise & Technology Centre was established by the Sligo County Enterprise Fund Company and provides office and work spaces. It is a member of the NATIONAL ASSOCIATION OF COMMUNITY ENTERPRISE CENTRES.

SMALL BUSINESS ADVICE

Unit H, Northside Business Campus, North Ring Road, Cork T: (021) 421 1433 E: applications@smallbusinessadvice.ie W: www.smallbusinessadvice.ie

Training & Mentoring

Small Business Advice is a free and confidential advice service offered by Ireland's business community to help small businesses grow. It matches the knowledge, skills, insights and entrepreneurial capability of experienced business practitioners and advisors with your business. It is sponsored by Ervia and PLATO DUBLIN and supported by CHAMBERS OF COMMERCE nationwide.

SMALL FIRMS ASSOCIATION

Confederation House, 84/86 Lower Baggot Street, Dublin 2 T: (01) 605 1500 E: info@sfa.ie W: www.sfa.ie

IP & Legal; Networking; Policy; Training & Mentoring

The Small Firms Association is the national organisation exclusively representing the needs of small enterprises in Ireland, and provides economic, commercial, employee relations and social affairs advice and assistance to over 8,000 member companies, as well as seminar programmes and member networking evenings. In addition, its website provides information and services on-line to members.

SMILE

Mullingar Enterprise Centre, Bishopsgate Street, Mullingar, Co. Westmeath N91 Y099 E: info@smilebrewing.com W: www.smilebrewing.com

Training & Mentoring

SMILE (Sustainable Microbrewers Learning across Europe) is developing training for entrepreneurs and new entrants into the brewery business in Europe.

SOAR (ABC)

The Civic Centre, Lakeview Road, Craigavon BT64 1AL T: (028) 3831 2573 E: info@soarni.org W: www.soarni.org

Community & Rural Development; Funding

SOAR (ABC) is the LEADER Local Action Group that delivers Priority 6 of the NI Rural Development Programme 2014-2020 on behalf of the DEPARTMENT FOR AGRICULTURE, ENVIRONMENT & RURAL AFFAIRS. It supports local entrepreneurs and start-ups.

SOCIAL ENTERPRISE DEVELOPMENT COMPANY LTD

35 Exchequer Street, Dublin 2 / Ballyfermot Community Civic Centre, Ballyfermot, Dublin 10 T: (01) 620 7193 E: info@sedco.ie W: sedco.ie

Social Enterprise

SEDCo's mission is to transform Ireland into a country in which social enterprise is achieving its potential, by empowering a community of people and organisations who are committed to using entrepreneurship as a means of overcoming our biggest challenges. It welcomes and supports anybody interested in social enterprise and offers support to existing entrepreneurs and formal incubation programmes for those wanting to start new initiatives.

SOCIAL ENTERPRISE NI

171 York Road – 1st Floor, Belfast BT15 3HB T: (028) 9046 1810 E: info@socialenterpriseni.org W: www.socialenterpriseni.org

Social Enterprise

Social Enterprise NI is the representative body for social enterprises and social entrepreneurs across Northern Ireland, connecting, supporting, developing and sustaining vibrant businesses to create social change.

SOCIAL ENTREPRENEURS IRELAND

11/12 Warrington Place – Lower Ground Floor, Dublin 2 T: (01) 685 3191 E: info@socialentrepreneurs.ie W: www.socialentrepreneurs.ie

Funding; Social Enterprise

Social Entrepreneurs Ireland is an Irish not-for-profit organisation that supports people with new solutions to Ireland's biggest social problems. SEI helps these individuals to increase their impact by providing significant funding alongside in-depth technical and practical support.

SOCIAL INNOVATION FUND IRELAND

Unit 16, Trinity Technology & Enterprise Campus, Pearse Street, Dublin D02 YN67 E: hello@socialinnovation.ie W: www.socialinnovation.ie

Funding; Social Enterprise

Created by Government to fill the gap in funding innovation in the non-profit sector, the Social Innovation Fund finds and backs innovative solutions to critical social issues in Ireland by supporting non-profits, charities and social enterprises.

SOLAS

Castleforbes House, Castleforbes Road, Dublin 1 T: (01) 533 2500 E: info@solas.ie W: www.solas.ie

Training & Mentoring

Solas is the State body responsible for funding, planning and co-ordinating further education and training in Ireland. It manages the National Apprenticeship Scheme, eCollege, Safepass and the Construction Skills Certification Scheme.

SOS VENTURES

Republic of Work, 12 South Mall, Cork T12 RD43 W: www.sosv.com

Funding

SOSV runs multiple world-class vertical accelerator programmes, and provides seed, venture and growth stage follow-on investment of between $30,000 and $2m. It has funded over 700 start-ups to date.

SOUTH & EAST CORK AREA DEVELOPMENT LTD

Midleton Community Enterprise Centre, Owennacurra Business Park, Knockgriffin, Midleton, Co. Cork T: (021) 461 3432 E: info@secad.ie W: www.secad.ie

Community & Rural Development; Funding; Training & Development

SECAD is supported under LEADER and the Social Inclusion & Community Activation Programme, and is a member of the IRISH LOCAL DEVELOPMENT NETWORK. SECAD provides supports for entrepreneurs and self–employed people.

SOUTH DUBLIN COUNTY PARTNERSHIP

Unit D1, Nangor Road Business Park, Nangor Road, Dublin 12 T: (01) 464 9300
E: info@sdcpartnership.ie W: www.sdcpartnership.ie

Community & Rural Development; Social Enterprise

South Dublin County Partnership is funded under the Social Inclusion &
Community Activation Programme and is a member of the IRISH LOCAL
DEVELOPMENT NETWORK. It supports local entrepreneurs and start-ups.

SOUTH EAST BUSINESS INNOVATION CENTRE

Unit 1B, Industrial Park, Cork Road, Waterford X91 DT38 T: (051) 356300 E:
info@southeastbic.ie W: www.southeastbic.ie

Consulting; Incubation & Work space; Training & Mentoring

South East Business Innovation Centre supports the development of new innovative
enterprises by providing tailored consultancy services and active incubation.

SOUTH KERRY DEVELOPMENT PARTNERSHIP

West Main Street, Cahersiveen, Co. Kerry T: (066) 947 2724 E: info@skdp.net W:
www.southkerry.ie

Community & Rural Development; Funding

South Kerry Development Partnership is supported under LEADER and is a member
of the IRISH LOCAL DEVELOPMENT NETWORK. It fosters the development of new
and existing enterprises.

SOUTH TIPPERARY DEVELOPMENT CLG

Unit 2C, Carrigeen Commercial Park, Clogheen Road, Cahir, Co. Tipperary T:
(052) 744 2652 E: info@stdc.ie W: www.stdc.ie

Community & Rural Development; Funding

South Tipperary Development is supported under LEADER and the Social Inclusion
& Community Activation Programme and is a member of the IRISH LOCAL
DEVELOPMENT NETWORK. It provides a range of support for the development of
new and existing enterprises.

SOUTH WEST MAYO DEVELOPMENT COMPANY CLG

Carey Walsh Building, Georges Street, Newport, Co. Mayo F28 X329 T: (098)
41950 E: info@southmayo.com W: www.southmayo.com

Community & Rural Development; Funding

South West Mayo Development is supported under LEADER and the Social
Inclusion & Community Activation Programme, and is a member of the IRISH
LOCAL DEVELOPMENT NETWORK. It supports local businesses and start-ups.

SOUTHERN REGIONAL ASSEMBLY

Assembly House, O'Connell Street, Waterford X91 F8PC T: (051) 860700 E:
info@southernassembly.ie W: www.southernassembly.ie

Policy

The Southern Regional Assembly manages and monitors EU programmes of
assistance; co-ordinates, promotes and supports strategic planning and sustainable
development of the region; promotes effective local government and public services
in the region; and prepares and oversees the implementation of Regional Spatial
and Economic Strategies.

SOUTHSIDE PARTNERSHIP DLR LTD

The Old Post Office, 7 Rock Hill, Main Street, Blackrock, Co. Dublin T: (01) 706
0100 F: (01) 275 5729 E: info@sspship.ie W: www.southsidepartnership.ie

Community & Rural Development; Social Enterprise; Training & Mentoring

Southside Partnership is supported under the Social Inclusion & Community
Activation Programme and is a member of the IRISH LOCAL DEVELOPMENT
NETWORK. It provides supports for self-employment and social enterprise.

SPADE ENTERPRISE CENTRE

North King Street, Dublin 7 T: (01) 617 4800 W: www.spade.ie

Incubation & Work space

SPADE Enterprise Centre is community-based and offers incubator and work space
(including food units) for small businesses. It is a member of the NATIONAL
ASSOCIATION OF COMMUNITY ENTERPRISE CENTRES.

SPARK CROWDFUNDING

27 South William Street, Dublin 2 T: (01) 443 3944
E: info@sparkcrowdfunding.com W: www.sparkcrowdfunding.com

Funding

Spark is an Irish-based equity crowdfunding platform that connects companies
looking to raise funds with investors seeking new investment opportunities.

START UP EUROPE CLUB

W: www.startupeuropeclub.eu

Information; Networking

Start Up Europe is an initiative of the European Commission. Its objectives are to:
connect start-ups, investors, accelerators, corporate networks and universities;
connect local start-up ecosystems; help start-ups soft-land in other markets; and
celebrate entrepreneurs' success. Startup Lighthouse, offered by DCU RYAN
ACADEMY, aims to connect Irish start-ups with others across Europe.

START UP LOANS COMPANY

71-75 Shelton Street, Covent Garden, London WC2H 9JQ W:
www.startuploans.co.uk

Funding

The Start Up Loans Company is a subsidiary of the British Business Bank and
delivers the Government's Start Up Loans programme, providing finance and
support for businesses that struggle to access other forms of finance. The Start Up
Loans Company's Delivery Partner for Northern Ireland is ENTERPRISE
NORTHERN IRELAND and its Local Enterprise Agencies.

START-UP REFUNDS FOR ENTREPRENEURS

W: www.sure.gov.ie

Funding

Entrepreneurs who start a new business may be entitled to an income tax refund of
up to 41% of the capital they invest, based on PAYE paid in the six years before
start-up. **www.sure.gov.ie** is an online tool that helps you calculate what might be
due and is a joint initiative of the DEPARTMENT OF BUSINESS, ENTERPRISE &
INNOVATION and the REVENUE COMMISSIONERS.

STARTUPS.ie

E: info@startups.ie W: www.startups.ie

Information

An online resource for anyone starting and growing a business.

STRABANE ENTERPRISE AGENCY

Orchard Road Industrial Estate, Orchard Road, Strabane, Co. Tyrone BT82 9FR
T: (028) 7138 2518 E: info@seagency.co.uk W: www.seagency.co.uk

Funding; Incubation & Workspace; Training & Mentoring

Strabane Enterprise Agency provides a range of services for individuals considering
starting their own business and for businesses looking to grow and develop. It is a
member of ENTERPRISE NORTHERN IRELAND.

STRATEGIC BANKING CORPORATION OF IRELAND

Treasury Building, Grand Canal Street, Dublin D02 XN96 T: (01) 238 4000 E:
infoSBCI@ntma.ie W: www.sbci.gov.ie

Funding

SBCI is a strategic SME funding company that delivers lower cost, long-term and
accessible funding *via* flexible products – including a Brexit loan – offered through
its lending partners. SBCI is not a bank and does not lend direct to SMEs.

SUIR VALLEY VENTURES

Dogpatch Labs, The CHQ Building, Custom House Quay, Dublin 1 E: suirvalley@shardcapital.com W: www.suirvalleyventures.com

Funding

An entrepreneur-led venture capital fund that invests in early stage software companies, working in partnership with Shard Capital, a London-based specialist broker and asset manager.

SUPPORTINGSMES.IE

W: www.supportingsmes.ie

Information

An online guide, part of the Irish Government's Supporting SMEs campaign, to increase awareness of the range of Government supports for start-ups and small businesses. Answer eight questions to find out which supports (of the 170+ currently available) would suit your business.

SUSTAINABLE ENERGY AUTHORITY OF IRELAND

Wilton Park House, Wilton Place, Dublin D02 T228 T: (01) 808 2100 E: info@seai.ie W: www.seai.ie

Training & Mentoring

SEAI is Ireland's national sustainable energy authority. It leads the transition to smarter and more sustainable energy activities and supports the development of clean energy technologies that cause less harm to the environment.

SYNERGY CENTRE

ITT Dublin, Tallaght, Dublin 24 T: (01) 404 2026 E: innovate@synergycentre.ie W: www.synergycentre.ie

Incubation & Work space; Training & Mentoring

The Synergy Centre at ITT DUBLIN is the innovation centre for South Dublin County, providing office space and business supports to early-stage high-technology and knowledge-intensive enterprises.

SYNERGY GLOBAL

3015 Lake Drive, Citywest Business Campus, Dublin 24 T: (01) 403 8403 E: reception@synergyglobal.ie

Incubation & Work space

Synergy Global is a modern incubation facility acquired by ITT DUBLIN in 2011.

TALENT GARDEN DUBLIN

DCU Alpha Innovation Campus, Old Finglas Road, Glasnevin, Dublin 11 T: (01) E: dublin@talentgarden.ie W: wwtalentgarden.org/ie/campus/dublin/

Incubation & Work space; Networking; Training & Mentoring

Founded in Brescia, Italy, in 2011, Talent Garden is an innovation platform and coworking network for digital innovation with 23 campuses in 8 countries. Its Innovation School trains students, professionals and companies in digital skills.

TALLOW ENTERPRISE CENTRE

Nora Herlihy House, West Street, Tallow, Co. Waterford T: (058) 56445 E: info@tallowenterprise.ie W: www.tallowenterprise.ie

Community & Rural Development; Incubation & Work space; Training & Mentoring

Established by the Tallow Enterprise Group Ltd, Tallow Enterprise Centre aims to promote community development, as well as offering work space and training for local businesses.

TEAGASC

Oak Park, Carlow R93 XE12 T: (059) 917 0200 E: info@hq.teagasc.ie W: www.teagasc.ie

Consulting; Innovation & R&D; Training & Mentoring

Teagasc – the Agriculture & Food Development Authority – is the national body providing integrated research, advisory and training services to the agriculture and food industry and rural communities. It runs the Ashtown Food Centre in Dublin, Animal & Grassland Research Centres in Athenry, Grange, Co. Meath and Moorepark, Co. Cork, the Moorepark Food Research Centre and Dairy Products Research Centre, and the Crops Research Centre in Carlow.

TECHNOLOGY IRELAND

Confederation House, 84/86 Lower Baggot Street, Dublin 2 T: (01) 605 1550 E: info@technology-ireland.ie W: www.technology-ireland.ie

Innovation & R&D; Networking

Technology Ireland represents Ireland's tech sector and provides a united voice for the digital and software technology sector.

TECHNOLOGY IRELAND INNOVATION FORUM

Confederation House, 84/86 Lower Baggot Street, Dublin 2 T: (01) 605 1550 E: dave.feenan@ibec.ie W: www.isin.ie

Innovation & R&D; Networking

Technology Ireland Innovation Forum (formerly ISIN) is the innovation forum of TECHNOLOGY IRELAND and drives transformational, innovative, and impactful collaboration throughout the digital technology cluster by supporting organisations to scale. It provides up-to-date information on funding, R&D tax credits, IP licensing and enterprise / incubation centres.

TECHSTARTNI

21 Talbot Street – 3rd Floor, Belfast BT1 2LD T: 028 9032 5506 E: info@techstartni.com W: www.techstartni.com

Funding; Training & Mentoring

TechStartNI helps entrepreneurs build successful technology businesses from the ground up, through the provision of advice, grants and seed investment.

TERENURE ENTERPRISE CENTRE

17 Rathfarnham Road, Terenure, Dublin 6W T: (01) 490 3237 E:
mhannon@terenure-enterprise.ie W: www.terenure-enterprise.ie

*Community & Rural Development; Incubation & Work space; Information;
Training & Mentoring*

Terenure Enterprise Centre (officially Community Enterprise Society Ltd, a charity)
provides business incubator units (including food units), business advice and
assistance with business plans, funding applications, etc. for small start-up projects
unable to secure such support from other sources. It is a member of the NATIONAL
ASSOCIATION OF COMMUNITY ENTERPRISE CENTRES.

THE BASE ENTERPRISE CENTRE

Railway Road, Stranorlar, Co. Donegal T: (074) 919 0909 E:
info@thebaseenterprise.ie W: www.thebaseenterprise.ie

Incubation & Work space

Ballybofey & Stranorlar Integrated Community Company runs The Base Enterprise
Centre and is a member of the NATIONAL ASSOCIATION OF COMMUNITY
ENTERPRISE CENTRES.

THE HIVE

Dublin Road, Carrick-on-Shannon, Co. Leitrim N41 FD83 T: (071) 961 6275 W:
www.the-hive.ie

Incubation & Work space

The Hive is Leitrim's Technology Enterprise Centre and offers fully-serviced office
spaces, hot desk work areas and meeting rooms. It is a member of the NATIONAL
ASSOCIATION OF COMMUNITY ENTERPRISE CENTRES.

THE LINC

Institute of Technology Blanchardstown, Blanchardstown Road North, Dublin 15
T: (01) 885 1502 E: claire.macnamee@itb.ie W:
www.itb.ie/IndustryInnovation/thelinc.html

Enterprise Support; Incubation & Work space; Training & Mentoring

The LINC Centre at the INSTITUTE OF TECHNOLOGY BLANCHARDSTOWN
provides support for start-ups through office space, business support, training,
access to college resources and applied / collaborative research.

THINKBUSINESS.IE

W: www.thinkbusiness.ie

Information

ThinkBusiness.ie, powered by BANK OF IRELAND, provides practical, actionable
information and guidance on starting, growing and running a business. It offers
guides, tools, templates, checklists and other content tailored to meet the needs of
Irish business owners and managers.

TIPPERARY LOCAL ENTERPRISE OFFICE

Ballingarrane House, Cahir Road, Clonmel, Co. Tipperary T: (076) 106 6200 / Civic Office, Limerick Road, Nenagh, Co. Tipperary T: (076) 106 5000 E: leo@tipperarycoco.ie W: www.localenterprise.ie/tipperary

Funding; Information; Training & Mentoring; Young Enterprise

Tipperary Local Enterprise Office provides both direct supports (feasibility, priming or business expansion grants) and indirect supports (mentoring, management development, or other capacity building programmes).

TOM CREAN BUSINESS CENTRE

Kerry Technology Park, Tralee, Co. Kerry T: (066) 714 4229 E: info@creancentre.com W: www.creancentre.com

Incubation & Work space: Training & Mentoring

The Tom Crean Centre at the INSTITUTE OF TECHNOLOGY TRALEE provides technology and knowledge-intensive start-ups with office space and business support services to help entrepreneurs to build and scale an international business.

TOMKINS

5 Dartmouth Road, Dublin D06 F9C7 T: (01) 202 6700 E: post@tomkins.com W: www.tomkins.com

IP & Legal

Tomkins are European intellectual property experts. Established in 1930 by Arthur Bellamy Tomkins, the firm is one of Europe's longest established IP law specialists.

TOURISM NORTHERN IRELAND

Linum Chambers – Floors 10-12, Bedford Square, Bedford Street, Belfast BT2 7ES T: (028) 9023 1221 E: info@tourismni.com W: www.tourismni.com

Community & Rural Development; Funding; Marketing; Regulation & Standards

Tourism NI is responsible for the development of tourism and the marketing of Northern Ireland as a tourist destination. It provides advice and funding for tourist businesses, as well as regulating them.

TOWNSEND BUSINESS PARK

28 Townsend Street, Belfast BT3 2ES T: (028) 9043 5778 E: admin@townsend.co.uk W: www.townsend.co.uk

Incubation & Work space

Townsend Enterprise Park offers industrial units and office units for rent.

TRINITY COLLEGE DUBLIN

College Green, Dublin 2 T: (01) 896 1000 W: www.tcd.ie

Enterprise Support; Incubation & Work space; Innovation & R&D; Training & Mentoring

TCD supports entrepreneurs through its innovation and incubation centre, TRINITY TECHNOLOGY & ENTERPRISE CAMPUS.

TRINITY TECHNOLOGY & ENTERPRISE CAMPUS

The Tower, Trinity Technology & Enterprise Campus, Pearse Street Dublin 2 T: (01) 677 5655 E: paoshea@tcd.ie W: www.trinityenterprisenetwork.ie

Incubation & Work space

The Trinity Technology & Enterprise Campus supports the development of knowledge-based enterprises by providing incubation space and meeting rooms.

TYNDALL NATIONAL INSTITUTE

Lee Maltings Complex, Dyke Parade, Cork T12 R5CP T: (021) 234 6177 E: info@tyndall.ie W: www.tyndall.ie

Innovation & R&D

Tyndall National Institute is a leading European research centre in integrated ICT hardware and systems.

ÚDARÁS NA GAELTACHTA

Na Forbacha, Gaillimh T: (091) 503100 E: eolas@udaras.ie W: www.udaras.ie

Community & Rural Development; Funding; Incubation & Work space

Údarás na Gaeltachta is the regional authority responsible for the economic, social and cultural development of the Gaeltacht region. It offers grant schemes and incentives to help small and medium-sized enterprises in the Gaeltacht areas, broadly in line with those available nationally from ENTERPRISE IRELAND. Some of its activities are funded under the LEADER programme.

ULSTER BANK

George's Quay, Dublin D02 VR98 W: www.ulsterbank.ie

Franchises; Funding

Ulster Bank, a member of the RBS-NatWest Group, offers overdrafts, loans, leasing and invoice discounting, as well as Internet banking and e-commerce facilities. It has experience in supporting franchises.

ULSTER COMMUNITY INVESTMENT TRUST LTD

13/19 Linenhall Street, Belfast BT2 8AA T: (028) 9031 5003 T: (041) 685 8637 E: info@ucitltd.com W: www.ucitltd.com

Community & Rural Development; Cross-Border; Funding; Social Enterprise; Training & Mentoring

Ulster Community Investment Trust Ltd is a provider of social finance, free advice, business support and mentoring to the social economy sector in Northern Ireland and the Republic of Ireland (through COMMUNITY FINANCE (IRELAND)).

ULSTER UNIVERSITY

Jordanstown Campus, Shore Road, Newtownabbey BT37 0QB T: (028) 7012 3456 E: enquiry@ulster.ac.uk W: www.ulster.ac.uk

Funding; Innovation & R&D

INNOVATION ULSTER is Ulster University's knowledge and technology venturing company, providing access to its research portfolio and supporting commercialisation of in-house research.

UNIVERSITIES

There are 7 universities in Ireland and 2 in Northern Ireland:

o   DUBLIN CITY UNIVERSITY.

o   NATIONAL UNIVERSITY OF IRELAND GALWAY.

o   NATIONAL UNIVERSITY OF IRELAND MAYNOOTH.

o   QUEEN'S UNIVERSITY BELFAST.

o   TRINITY COLLEGE DUBLIN.

o   ULSTER UNIVERSITY.

o   UNIVERSITY COLLEGE CORK.

o   UNIVERSITY COLLEGE DUBLIN.

o   UNIVERSITY OF LIMERICK.

All support entrepreneurs, usually through on-campus incubation centres, as well as technology transfer offices that provide access to research.

UNIVERSITY COLLEGE CORK

College Road, Cork T: (021) 490 3000 W: www.ucc.ie

Enterprise Support; Incubation & Work space; Innovation & R&D; Training & Mentoring

UCC supports entrepreneurs through its innovation and incubation centre, GATEWAY UCC.

UNIVERSITY COLLEGE DUBLIN

Belfield, Dublin 4 T: (01) 716 7777 W: www.ucd.ie

Enterprise Support; Incubation & Work space; Innovation & R&D; Training & Mentoring

UCD supports entrepreneurs through its innovation and incubation centre, NOVAUCD.

UNIVERSITY OF LIMERICK

Plassey, Limerick V94 T9PX T: (061) 202700 W: www.ul.ie

Enterprise Support; Incubation & Work space; Innovation & R&D; Training & Mentoring

UL supports entrepreneurs through its on-campus innovation and incubation centre, the NEXUS INNOVATION CENTRE.

UNLTD

123 Whitecross Street, Islington, London EC1Y 8JJ T: (0207) 566 1100 W: www.unltd.org.uk

Funding; Social Enterprise; Training & Mentoring

UnLtd finds, funds, and supports social entrepreneurs to bring their ideas to life and build sustainable social ventures.

WATERFORD AREA PARTNERSHIP

Unit 4, Westgate Business Centre, Tramore Road, Waterford T: (051) 841740 E: info@wap.ie W: www.wap.ie

Community & Rural Development

Waterford Area Partnership is a Local Development Company, funded under the Social Inclusion & Community Activation Programme, and is a member of the IRISH LOCAL DEVELOPMENT NETWORK.

WATERFORD INSTITUTE OF TECHNOLOGY

Cork Road, Waterford T: (051) 302000 E: info@wit.ie W: www.wit.ie

Incubation & Work space; Innovation & R&D; Training & Mentoring

WIT supports and develops innovation activity through its ARCLABS incubation centre and research facilities.

WATERFORD LEADER PARTNERSHIP CLG

Lismore Business Park, Lismore, Co. Waterford T: (058) 54646 E: info@wlp.ie W: www.wlp.ie

Community & Rural Development; Funding

WLP is supported under LEADER and is a member of the IRISH LOCAL DEVELOPMENT NETWORK. It supports local businesses and start-ups.

WATERFORD LOCAL ENTERPRISE OFFICE

35 The Mall, Waterford X91 DN23 / Civic Offices, Dungarvan, Co. Waterford X35 Y326 T: (076) 110 2905 E: info@leo.waterfordcouncil.ie W: www.localenterprise.ie/waterford

Funding; Information; Training & Mentoring; Young Enterprise

Waterford Local Enterprise Office provides direct supports (feasibility, priming or business expansion grants) and indirect supports (mentoring, management development, or other capacity building programmes).

WELDON (MICHAEL) & CO.

Shannon Lodge, Bandon, Co. Cork T: (023) 52144 E: mweldon@indigo.ie

IP & Legal

A firm of patent agents and trade mark attorneys.

WEST CORK DEVELOPMENT PARTNERSHIP LTD

West Cork Technology Park, Clonakilty, Co. Cork T: (023) 883 4035 W: www.wcdp.ie

Community & Rural Development

WCDP is a member of the IRISH LOCAL DEVELOPMENT NETWORK.

WEST LIMERICK RESOURCES LTD

St Mary's Road, Newcastlewest, Co. Limerick T: (069) 62222 E: info@wlr.ie W: www.wlr.ie

Community & Rural Development; Funding

West Limerick Resources is supported under LEADER and the Social Inclusion & Community Activation Programme and is a member of the IRISH LOCAL DEVELOPMENT NETWORK. It supports local people towards self-employment.

WESTBIC

Galway Technology Centre, Mervue Business Park, Galway T: (091) 730 850 E: info@westbic.ie W: www.westbic.ie

Accounting & Business Planning; Incubation & Work space; Marketing; Networking; Training & Mentoring

WestBIC supports and champions the practical needs of start-ups with tailored assistance through market validation, business modelling, sourcing capital, incubation and networking.

WESTERN DEVELOPMENT COMMISSION

Dillon House, Ballaghaderreen, Co. Roscommon T: (094) 986 1441 E: info@wdc.ie W: www.wdc.ie

Community & Rural Development; Funding; Policy

The Western Development Commission is a statutory body promoting economic and social development in counties Donegal, Leitrim, Sligo, Mayo, Roscommon, Galway and Clare. It manages the Western Investment Fund, which invests between €100,000 and €1m across all sectors.

WESTERN MANAGEMENT CENTRE

Galway Business Park, Dangan, Galway T: (091) 528777 W: www.wmcgalway.com

Training & Mentoring

The Western Management Centre offers training and development programmes geared towards the needs of business owners and entrepreneurs.

WESTMEATH COMMUNITY DEVELOPMENT LTD

Mullingar ETI Centre, Mullingar Business Park, Mullingar, Co. Westmeath N91 X012 T: (044) 934 8571 E: info@westcd.ie W: www.westcd.ie

Community & Rural Development; Funding; Incubation & Work space; Training & Mentoring

Westmeath Community Development is supported under LEADER and the Social Inclusion & Community Activation Programme. It is a member of the IRISH LOCAL DEVELOPMENT NETWORK and offers work space in the Business Development Centre in Athlone, as well as a Business Development Programme for people considering self-employment.

WEXFORD ENTERPRISE CENTRE

Strandfield Business Park, Rosslare Road, Kerlogue, Co. Wexford T: (053) 914 1711 E: enquiries@wec.ie W: www.wec.ie

Incubation & Work space; Social Enterprise

Wexford Enterprise Centre is a social enterprise division of Innovation Wexford, the registered trade name of Wexford Community Development Association Society Ltd. It offers co-working, incubation and work space and is a member of the NATIONAL ASSOCIATION OF COMMUNITY ENTERPRISE CENTRES.

WEXFORD LOCAL DEVELOPMENT

Block A, County Hall, Spawell Road, Townparks, Wexford T: (053) 915 5800 E: info@wld.ie / leader@wld.ie W: www.wld.ie

Community & Rural Development; Funding; Training & Mentoring

Wexford Local Development is supported under LEADER and the Social Inclusion & Community Activation Programme, and is a member of the IRISH LOCAL DEVELOPMENT NETWORK. It offers a variety of services to people who wish to develop or start a business within County Wexford.

WEXFORD LOCAL ENTERPRISE OFFICE

Wexford County Council, Carricklawn, Wexford T: (053) 919 6020 E: info@leo.wexfordcoco.ie W: www.localenterprise.ie/wexford

Funding; Information; Training & Mentoring; Young Enterprise

Wexford Local Enterprise Office provides direct supports (feasibility, priming or business expansion grants) and indirect supports (mentoring, management development, or other capacity building programmes).

WHITEROCK CAPITAL PARTNERS

City Exchange – 8th Floor, 11/13 Gloucester Street, Belfast BT1 4LS T: (028) 9500 1060 E: info@whiterockcp.co.uk W: www.whiterockcp.co.uk

Funding

WhiteRock provides loan finance to established SMEs based in Northern Ireland that can demonstrate growth potential in the manufacturing, engineering or export tradable services sectors.

WICKLOW ENTERPRISE CENTRE

The Murrough, Co. Wicklow T: (0404) 66433 E: info@wicklowenterprise.ie W: www.wicklowenterprise.ie

Incubation & Work space; Training & Mentoring

Wicklow Enterprise Centre provides a turn-key facility for new and developing businesses. It is a member of the NATIONAL ASSOCIATION OF COMMUNITY ENTERPRISE CENTRES.

WOMENMEANBUSINESS.com

T: (086) 235 1558 W: www.womenmeanbusiness.com

Information; Networking

The website **www.womenmeanbusiness.com** offers news, interviews, reviews, and advice specifically written for businesswomen and female entrepreneurs.

WORK WEST ENTERPRISE AGENCY

301 Glen Road, Belfast BT11 8BU T: (028) 9061 0826 E: info@workwest.co.uk W: www.workwest.co.uk

Funding; Incubation & Work space; Innovation & R&D; Social Enterprise; Training & Mentoring

Work West is a member of ENTERPRISE NORTHERN IRELAND and supports start-ups and existing businesses (both private and social) to start up and grow.

WORKPLACE INNOVATION TOOLKIT

W: www.witool.dbei.gov.ie

Innovation & R&D

The Workplace Innovation Toolkit – an initiative of the DEPARTMENT OF BUSINESS, ENTERPRISE & INNOVATION – provides an online questionnaire designed to facilitate self-evaluation of an organisation's capacity to be an innovative workplace, and also signposts resources and supports to enhance performance in employee engagement, training, innovation and productivity.

WORKPLACERELATIONS.ie

Department of Business, Enterprise & Innovation, O'Brien Road, Carlow R93 E920 W: www.workplacerelations.ie

Information; IP & Legal

WorkplaceRelations.ie provides information on industrial relations and rights and obligations under Irish employment and equality legislation.

WORKSPACE ENTERPRISES LTD

The Business Centre, 5/7 Tobermore Road, Draperstown, Co. Londonderry BT45 7AG T: (028) 7962 8113 E: info@theworkspacegroup.org W: www.workspace.org.uk

Community & Rural Development; Funding; Incubation & Workspace; Social Enterprise; Training & Mentoring; Young Enterprise

Workspace Enterprises provides a range of free supports to the local community through a variety of enterprise initiatives, including supporting people who are interested in starting their own business or social enterprise. It is a member of ENTERPRISE NORTHERN IRELAND.

YOUNG ENTERPRISE NORTHERN IRELAND

Grove House, 145/149 Donegall Pass, Belfast BT7 1DT T: (028) 9032 7003 E: info@yeni.co.uk W: www.yeni.co.uk

Young Enterprise

Young Enterprise Northern Ireland is a charity developing the entrepreneurial skills and aspirations of young people aged four to 25 to prepare them for the new economy and to ensure they leave education prepared for life and work. It is a member of Junior Achievement Worldwide.

YOUNG SOCIAL INNOVATORS

DCU Alpha, Old Finglas Road, Glasnevin, Dublin D11 KXN4 T: (01) 1 645 8030 E: admin@youngsocialinnovators.ie W: www.youngsocialinnovators.org

Innovation & R&D; Social Enterprise; Training & Mentoring; Young Enterprise

Young Social Innovators promotes education for social innovation through a range of social innovation programmes for young people as well as training, resources and professional development opportunities for educators.

YOUR EUROPE

W: https://europa.eu/youreurope/business/

Information

A practical online guide to doing business in Europe.

More than 20 years on, **STARTING YOUR OWN BUSINESS: A WORKBOOK** is still in publication and is the standard text on practical business planning for Irish entrepreneurs. This fourth edition has been updated and expanded to reflect changing trends in Irish small business. **STARTING YOUR OWN BUSINESS: A WORKBOOK** is designed to take a potential entrepreneur through the whole process of starting a business, from first thoughts about self-employment to the practicalities of start-up. Throughout it, you will find checklists, flowcharts and questionnaires designed to make you think about your proposed business.

This **revised and updated 2nd edition** of **MONEY FOR JAM** contains everything that someone who is new to the food business in Ireland, Northern Ireland and the UK will need to get started and to keep going. It will help bakers, jam and honey-makers, ice cream, yogurt and cheese-makers, egg producers, sausage roll, pie and pastie-bakers, chocolatiers, and dessert-makers. It covers the what, where, who and how for small food producers – including legislation and registration, labelling and packaging, suppliers and distributors – in an easy-to-read and easy-to-follow format.

RIGHT FROM THE START: ESSENTIAL HR FOR START-UPS & EARLY STAGE COMPANIES focuses on how to meet legal HR requirements cost-effectively, the classic pitfalls to avoid and how to build the right culture in your developing company. The idea for this eBook came about after the author **Zahra Khan** was repeatedly approached for advice from start-up companies from a HR perspective on the internal challenges a start-up business faces – from setting up the corporate culture, staffing issues, the roles and responsibilities of founders and employees, compensation structures, communication issues, etc.

Available from **www.SuccessStore.com.**

ABOUT THE AUTHOR

Brian O'Kane is the managing director of Oak Tree Press, Ireland's leading business book publisher. Trained as a chartered accountant, he has edited the professional membership magazines of two of the world's largest accountancy bodies.

Brian is the author (or co-author with Ron Immink) of a number of key Irish business planning texts, including: *Starting Your Own Business: A Workbook* (now in its 4th edition); *Could You Be Your Own Boss?*; *TENBizPlan: Dynamic Business Planning for Start-ups*; the *Steps to Entrepreneurship* series and *Growing Your Own Business: A Workbook*. He is the webmaster for **www.startingabusinessinireland.com**.

Brian holds a BComm degree from University College Dublin, and a Master's degree by research from Waterford IT. He is a Fellow of Chartered Accountants Ireland and the Institute of Management Consultants & Advisers, and a Member of the Marketing Institute of Ireland.

OAK TREE PRESS

Oak Tree Press develops and delivers information, advice and resources for entrepreneurs and managers. It is Ireland's leading business book publisher, with an unrivalled reputation for quality titles across business, management, human resources, law, marketing and enterprise topics.

In addition, Oak Tree Press occupies a unique position in start-up and small business support in Ireland through its standard-setting titles, as well as training courses, mentoring and advisory services.

Oak Tree Press is comfortable across a range of communication media – print, web and training, focusing always on the effective communication of business information.

OAK TREE PRESS
33 Rochestown Rise, Rochestown, Cork, Ireland.
T: + 353 86 244 1633 / + 353 86 330 7694
E: info@oaktreepress.com
W: www.oaktreepress.com / www.SuccessStore.com.